The Life of
Maynard Dixon

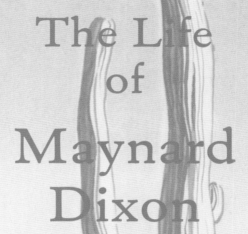

The Life
of
Maynard
Dixon

Donald J. Hagerty

GIBBS SMITH
TO ENRICH AND INSPIRE HUMANKIND

For My Wife, Rebecka Ann Hagerty.

First Edition
14 13 12 11 10   5 4 3 2 1

Published by
Gibbs Smith
P.O. Box 667
Layton, Utah 84041

1.800.835.4993 orders
www.gibbs-smith.com

Designed and produced by Kurt Wahlner
Printed and bound in China
Gibbs Smith books are printed on either recycled, 100% post-consumer
waste or on FSC-certified papers or on paper produced from a 100% certified
sustainable forest/controlled wood source.

Library of Congress Cataloging-in-Publication Data

Hagerty, Donald J.
  The life of Maynard Dixon / Donald J. Hagerty. — 1st ed.
      p. cm.
  Includes bibliographical references and index.
  ISBN-13: 978-1-4236-0379-5
  ISBN-10: 1-4236-0379-6
  1. Dixon, Maynard, 1875–1946. 2. Painters—United States—Biography.
  I. Dixon, Maynard, 1875–1946. II. Title.
  ND237.D5H353 2010
  759.13–dc22
  [B]
                          2009026446

Contents

Acknowledgments | 6

Introduction | 8

Chronology | 14

1 Picking Up the Trail, 1875–1893 | 19

2 *Fin-de-Siécle* Illustrator, 1893–1900 | 29

3 Going East to See the West, 1900–1907 | 51

4 The New York Years, 1907–1912 | 88

5 Turn of the Tide, 1912–1920 | 107

6 The City and the Desert, 1920–1931 | 136

7 From Chaos to Taos, 1931–1940 | 181

8 Back to the Home Corral, 1940–1946 | 222

Endnotes | 239

Bibliography | 243

Index | 249

Acknowledgments

Over sixteen years have passed since the first edition of this book appeared in 1993 and eleven years since a revised edition in 1998. During this time, numerous individuals have contributed their support and knowledge toward the understanding of Maynard Dixon and his legacy. I want to again recognize those who made these early editions so successful. The memory of Edith Hamlin, in particular, still graces these pages with her friendship, advice, and encouragement. Daniel (recently deceased) and John Dixon, the sons of Maynard Dixon and Dorothea Lange, have continued their efforts toward the understanding of the lives of both of their parents, as has Becky Jenkins, Dixon's granddaughter.

This third edition has profited from the work of numerous individuals. Drs. Mark and Kathleen Sublette as well as Jamie Gould at Medicine Man Gallery have never failed to respond to requests for images and information. Gerald Peters, Nicole Crawford, and Ana Archuleta at the Gerald Peters Gallery are key players in the development of a catalogue raisonné on Dixon's work that will flesh out his remarkable painting journey. Other dealers have offered their expertise and contacts with Dixon collectors, and have assisted me with the procurement of images. Among them are Jeffery Mitchell and Gillian Blitch, Mitchell Brown Fine Art; John and Joel Garzoli, Garzoli Gallery; William A. Karges, William A. Karges Fine Arts; Robert DeLapp, Nat Owings, Owings-Dewey Fine Arts; Patrick Jolly, Patrick Jolly Fine Arts; Ray Redfern, Redfern Gallery; Gary Fillmore, Blue Coyote Gallery; Abe Hays, Arizona West Galleries; and Thom Gianetto, Edenhurst Gallery.

Special thanks are offered to Ian and Annette Cumming, W. Donald Head, Dr. David Hunt, William Foxley, Bruce Paltenghi, Dr. Richard Paltenghi, Dr. Larry Krames, Michael and Patty Gold, Jon Stuart, Ginger K. Renner, Ed Mell, Gary Ernest Smith, Mark Richardson, Dan and Virginia Maridesh, Ulrike Kantor, David Picerne, Jesse Bravo, Jon Hoffman, Peter and Kirsten Bedford, Dr. Van Kirke Nelson, and others who wish to remain anonymous for their support.

When I undertook the research for the first edition, I had the immense good fortune to meet Gary F. Kurutz, Principal Librarian at the California State Library in Sacramento. Gary has had an equal passion for Maynard Dixon, and we have collaborated on many projects over the years. Gary's wide-ranging knowledge of Dixon, California history (particularly the California gold rush), and the visual arts of the state are unparalleled. I also wish to recognize other museum and library personnel, including Thomas B. Smith, Tucson Museum of Art; Denver Art Museum; Amy Scott, Autry Museum of the American West; Kim Walters, Braun Research Library, Southwest Museum of the American Indian; Michelle Kim, Southwest Museum of the American Indian; Bruce Dinges, Deborah Shelton, and Laraine Daly Jones, Arizona Historical Society; Natalie Russell, Huntington Library; Shane Culpepper, Gilcrease Museum; Charles Falhauber and Susan Snyder, Bancroft Library; Scott Shields and Allison Henley, Crocker Art Museum; Merideth Sutton, Blanton Museum of Art, The University of Texas at Austin; Dawn Physey and Emily Poulsen, Museum of Art, Brigham Young University; Jeff Donaldson, Booth Western Art Museum.

The auction houses have been supportive over the years, alerting me to Maynard Dixon works in upcoming sales. I particularly want to recognize Scot Levitt and Alissa Ford, Bonham and Butterfield's; Elizabeth Kervella, Christies, Los Angeles; and Mike Overby and Bob Drummond, Coeur d' Alene Art Auction.

I also want to recognize the role Gibbs Smith has played in the emergence of Maynard Dixon on the national stage. His passionate interest in Dixon's life and art has contributed immensely to the ever-increasing knowledge about the artist's role in American art. In addition, I want to express my gratitude to my editor, Linda Nimori, for her patient support and guidance.

Finally, I want to applaud the role my wife, Rebecka, has played over the years with her support for the various writing projects. She has guided me into the digital age, patiently explaining the intricacies and abilities of the computer, scanning, and other technical situations.

Introduction

On an early morning before the traffic arrives, take a walk on San Francisco's Montgomery Street where you will soon come to the 700 block of Montgomery. This block, once a vibrant colorful center of San Francisco's cultural life, is today overwhelmed by expensive antique shops, law firms, and aluminum, glass, and concrete high-rise office buildings. Stop at one address, 728 Montgomery Street. Now vacant and forlorn, this location offers no hint of the magic that occurred there. Located in what was once the city's heart of bohemia, a three-story brick building erected in 1854 occupies the space, surviving the 1906 earthquake, frequent remodeling, and the passage of time. Over the years, a succession of artists used the building for studios, living quarters, meeting places, and celebrations, among them Jules Tavernier, Amedee Joullin, Charles Dormon Robinson, Theodore Wores, Emil Carlsen, Arthur Mathews, Xavier Martinez, Gottardo Piazzoni, Ralph Stackpole, and Armin Hansen. The last tenant was attorney Melvin Belli, who refurbished the building for his law offices. In the years between World Wars I and II, writers, artists, and craftsmen burrowed into the narrow brick structure. In those days, there was nothing romantic about the ventilation, crumbling plaster, dank stairways, or ancient plumbing. In the 1920s and 1930s, 728 Montgomery Street could be entered through a tall green door; the peeling paint showing archaeological glimpses of its history. The door was never locked, night or day, and during the Depression years, jobless men sometimes slept in the hallway at the base of the stairs. On the wall, nameplates identified the tenants; some were handwritten, but most were represented with elaborate care in highly individual designs. Ornate or plain, each in its own way reflected the profession of the occupant. One pictured an Indian thunderbird captured in a circle. Maynard Dixon, it read.

Dixon's studio was on the top floor of 728 Montgomery Street, two long flights up, at the rear of the building. A single room, it measured twenty feet long and twenty feet wide with a north-facing skylight overhead. The studio walls were crowded with Indian artifacts and cowboy gear, with hundreds of drawings scattered about, testimony to the history of the American West, and a number of Dixon's sun-drenched, boldly designed paintings. Over the door, a bleached buffalo skull greeted visitors. Harold Von Schmidt, later to become a noted western illustrator, remembered the first time he met Dixon, just before World War I:

Maynard Dixon was one of the best painters in California at that time, and I heard he kept open house at his studio on Saturdays. I finally got up the courage to call on him; went up to the third floor and knocked on the door. The door had one of those pebbled glass windows that you can't see through and with the light coming from behind him as he came to the door, his silhouette got bigger and bigger. I thought, Christ, he must be eight feet tall! He opened the door and was only five-foot-eleven, very thin.[1]

Maynard Dixon would draw admiring comments as he strolled down one of San Francisco's streets on his way to the studio (fig. 1). Slender, almost angular, thin-faced with deep blue eyes, he had dark straight hair cascading toward one eye, a rakish mustache, a slightly hooked nose, and long, slim, facile hands. A tailored black suit made him seem taller. His wide-brimmed black Stetson hat and hand-tooled high-heeled Texas cowboy boots accentuated the effect. His step was light and careful— "walks like a deer," someone once said—each step answered by a faint ominous buzzing of the rattle still attached to his rattlesnake hatband. Often he clutched an ebony sword

1. *Maynard Dixon*, ca. 1929–1930, California History Section, California State Library

cane, tipped and headed with silver. Embedded into its handle was his professional signature—the same thunderbird that appeared on his nameplate. As Dixon neared his studio, a waiter at a nearby café might shout out a greeting, "Morning Mr. Dixon, cold fog"; Dixon might reply, "Cold as Christian Charity."[2] Dixon loathed hypocrisy and superstition, and his sarcasm was often mistaken for arrogance. He was mercilessly demanding of others and more so of himself. Those who encountered Dixon, even in the simplest of associations, never forgot him. He had a way of looking past people, particularly when he disliked them. But his squinting gaze also seemed to belong to someone used to looking across wide spaces, searching the glare of desert horizons with distant intensity.

Often, other people could be found in the studio, perhaps fellow artists—Gottardo Piazzoni, Otis Oldfield, Ralph Stackpole, or Edward Borein—exchanging ideas, opinions, and gossip. Von Schmidt recalled that sometimes in the late fall during the early 1920s, Dixon would go down to the train station, pick up Charles M. Russell, and bring him to the Montgomery Street studio. In the last several years before his death in 1926, Russell fled Montana's cold winters to his home in Pasadena. He and Dixon would spend all day and night talking about the West and things Western, go from one restaurant to another, ending at an all-night coffeehouse, then back to the studio for more talking. Finally, Dixon would put Russell on the morning train to Los Angeles.

Sometimes after school on a Friday afternoon, one of Dixon's sons might stop by the studio. "What kind of story do you want today?" his father would ask. Daniel Dixon remembers:

> "I don't know. Any kind. Cowboys?"
>
> "All right, cowboys," my father said. He went to the corner, lifted a booted foot, and toppled a cylinder of brown butcher paper. Another kick rolled it across the floor, leaving several feet of paper behind. My father took a box of colored crayons and got down on his hands and knees. I squatted beside him. He squinted at me over his glasses.
>
> "Injuns, too?" he asked.
>
> "Sure, Injuns!"
>
> Then my father would tell me one of his stories. Sometimes it was an Indian myth or legend. Sometimes it came out of the history books—a tale about Kit Carson or the Pony Express or the great warrior Geronimo. Sometimes it was an account of his own journeys into the far places of the Southwest—expeditions that could last for months, that had taken him on horseback from Montana into Mexico, and that had taught him to sing the songs of the Blackfoot and the Navajo.
>
> As he spoke, my father illustrated his narrative on the brown butcher paper. His thin left wrist turned, color jumped out of his fingers, and suddenly his words became living things. Cowpunchers, trappers in buckskins, Mexican vaqueros, Indians hooded in robes or naked in the sun. Dusty horned toads, lizards and rattlesnakes, soaring eagles, wolves and coyotes, grizzly bears, mustangs, and longhorns. Log cabins with flat sod roofs, tents and tepees, adobe ranchos and pueblos, false-fronted stores and saloons. And all of this set in one uninterrupted landscape—sky, sun, and shadow, clouds massed for thunderstorms, sagebrush and alkali dwindling into distance, red rimrock, junipers and poplars and cottonwoods, rivers and little streams in green valleys. Wherever the story led, there was no break in the horizon. Here flowed into there, now into then, event into memory, and all things were related.[3]

By the time Dixon finished the story, dinnertime had arrived. Then he would bring out teacups, a gallon jug of red wine, and a bottle of raw California brandy. Shortly, other people started arriving at the studio. Dorothea Lange, Dixon's second wife, usually arrived first from her portrait photography studio a half block away. Twenty years younger than Dixon, a small bright-eyed woman, she had a smooth face and a leg that had been twisted in childhood by polio. Heavy Navajo silver bracelets encircled her wrists, and her hands smelled faintly of chemicals used in the darkroom. Perry Dilley, a puppeteer, might come next. Confined to a wheelchair, he would be carried upstairs to Dixon's studio by friends. Other friends—writers, artists, poets, book dealers—from nearby rooms or studios drifted in singly or in small groups.

Dixon would telephone his favorite Chinese restaurant and order food, consulting no one about the menu; everyone shared the bill but not the choices. At the table, talk jumped from subject to subject—art, politics and neighborhood gossip. As the wine and brandy sank lower in the bottles, the conversation became clamorous, then bawdy. The hilarity lasted for a while, but then the mood turned quiet as Perry Dilley's sad, sweet tenor voice came floating out of the shadows. While Dixon and the others sat still or hummed harmonies, he sang brooding folk songs of being alone, of longing, of bottles almost empty. Around the studio, Dixon's paintings added to the setting, testaments to loneliness and lonely places, expansive uninterrupted skies, far horizons, "places where no one went," places beyond where the roads ended and only the Navajo or Hopi knew the names. Silence, space, clarity of air, an uninhabited exhilarating landscape seemed to surround the people, as if part of the West's earth and space had been gathered onto canvas and scattered around the studio. His friend Wilbur Hall saw it: "What he paints best is something so big that you have to live with it to get it. Mountains, deserts, with people of such places, are his subjects. I think I know my West some, but to realize how big and splendid and free and magnificent and God-made it really is, once in a while, I have to look on Maynard Dixon's pictures."[4]

By the early 1920s, Maynard Dixon had achieved considerable acclaim as one of the West's leading artists. His long productive life would become a work of art in its own right. From the beginning, Dixon was different, an authentic, iconoclastic, self-created individual. Born in Fresno, California, he had no formal academic art training except for three miserable months at San Francisco's Mark Hopkins Institute of Art in early 1893, and he did not make an obligatory pilgrimage to Paris for study as so many American artists would. He was an active, outspoken, if sometimes ambivalent, participant in California and the West's cultural life. Disdainful and bothered, yet intrigued and involved by the self-absorbed onslaught of modernism in the art world, he developed enduring themes by the 1920s: the timeless truth of the majestic western landscape, the religious mysticism of the Native American, and the people of the American West haunted by the Great Depression.

In reality, two Maynard Dixons seem to reside in his body of work. Part of his art lamented the "flickering out of old campfires," knowing the change was coming, an Old West departing and a New West arriving. Like many other American artists at that time, Dixon, contemptuous of fashion and convention, resisted the inroads made on the

West by the nation's rapid urbanization and industrial progress. One response to this loss was an art of "looking back," reflecting nostalgia, myth, and romantic commercialism. Like most artists, Dixon produced his share of "potboilers," uneven work, anecdotal or pseudo-historical, which sometimes moralized about Native Americans, for example, rather than portraying them in more appropriate cultural ways. Dixon resisted, but not always successfully, popular characterizations of the "noble Red Man" so prevalent in much of early twentieth-century painting. But he knew more about the depth of thought in Native American philosophy, art, and design than most observers could understand.

The other Dixon and his other art emerged in the early 1920s as a clear unequivocal product of the aloof reality of the American West's landscapes. Infused with Dixon's consistent philosophy of art and life and his search for meaningful goals in an increasingly technological era, these paintings were characterized by intense feeling for man's place in the grand natural scheme. Dixon's work is a reflection not only of his own inner nature and laborious craftsmanship but of a people and land with which he became allied. Ansel Adams once commented that for Dixon, "the West was uncrowded, unlittered, unorganized and free."[5] Adams might have added that Dixon would allow no fences to surround him, imaginary or real.

As Dixon discovered, there was a difference between the frontier and the West. The frontier, a historical concept concerned with certain American values, had faded into myth, while the West itself seemed timeless, impervious to change, even spiritual. Ultimately, he would conclude the West's landscapes held the answers to his searching, arguing that American painting could best work its influence on the lives and thoughts of people when painters based their work upon native material and their native reaction to it. Maynard Dixon was a regionalist long before the term arrived, with a confirmed belief in the vitality of regional America. For him, that region ultimately encompassed the arid terrain of Southern California, Nevada, Utah, Arizona, and New Mexico.

Dixon scorned the pursuit of art for its own sake. He was skeptical about the sanctity of the act of painting itself. Rather, he reached for a personal, even idiosyncratic, vision in his art through the visible world. His was a process of organic creation rather than one consciously organized by imported formula or rule. By the middle 1920s, Dixon had developed a flatter surface treatment and bolder composition in his painting, which included "space division," an increased concern for compositional and schematic arrangements, with striking light and dark earth-tone patterns. A distinctive vocabulary, an underlying geometric feeling, even cubist-realism suggesting formal abstraction emerged in his painting. He recast nature, stripping away superstructure in his canvases, searching for an underlying aesthetic reality, the essential rhythms, and structure. Though isolated from the mainstream of American art, Maynard Dixon is one of those vital connecting links between late nineteenth-century and twentieth-century contemporary American art.

From 1900 to his death in 1946, Maynard Dixon roamed the American West's plains, mesas, and deserts—by foot, horseback, buckboard, and, ultimately, the dreaded automobile—drawing, painting, and expressing his creative personality in poems, essays, and letters in a quest to uncover the region's spirit. These long, often solitary excursions into lands "where no one went" were prompted by intense personal and philosophic examinations. "Otherness" and "remoteness" are basic to ideas about the American West, and Maynard Dixon possessed this concept of a region as qualitatively, not just quantitatively, different. In obtaining this insight, Dixon moved through several transitions in his artistic life, never easily. From the middle 1890s until 1912, he became a noted magazine, newspaper, and book illustrator. But by 1912, he had concluded he could no longer portray the West in "false" terms. By then he had become one of America's foremost illustrators of western life, his art bound up with literary appeal for a departed and increasingly mythic Old West, in an era acknowledged as the Golden Age of Illustration. Hundreds of Dixon illustrations appeared in articles for leading newspapers like the *San Francisco Call*, the *Chronicle*, the *Examiner*; and magazines like *Sunset Magazine*, *Overland Monthly*, *Life*, *Scribner's*, *Collier's*, *Century Magazine*, *Pearson's*, *Hamptons*, *Short Stories*, and *McClure's*; or in books for authors such as Jack London, John Muir, Stewart Edward White, O. Henry, Mary Austin, Eugene Manlove Rhodes, Dane Coolidge, and Clarence Mulford's Hopalong Cassidy series. Between 1912 and 1921, he devoted increasing attention to easel and mural painting, experimenting with impressionism, postimpressionism, quasi-pointillism, and large-scale mural decoration while still pursuing a career in commercial art, particularly outdoor billboard design. The exacting demands of billboard design, with its simplified, sculpturally rendered images, served him well, for the draftsmanship gave strength to his later creative painting.

In 1921, supported and encouraged by his second wife, Dorothea Lange, who would achieve renown for her Depression-era photography, Dixon began to downplay his commercial art activities. With changes in the world introduced by World War I, Dixon entered a new phase in his development—modern thought and modern art. Searching for a new interpretation of the West's life and land, he painted numerous important murals in the 1920s and an acclaimed series of social-realist paintings in the 1930s, drawn from American cultural experience shaped by an American natural environment. His organized and structured painting technique celebrated the ancient and contemporary rhythms of the western landscape and indigenous lives. Dixon, keeping pace, never losing his individuality, learned to paint the present, not the past, for he discovered that in the vast and silent land that he re-created on canvas, time matters little. In the silence of the desert, that infinite space of sky and fauvist colored landscape, he found ways to state his vision. Those travels between the city and the desert and his struggle with the impact of modern art defined and shaped both him and his work.

Through long and sympathetic searching, he learned how the almost imperceptible contours of flat plains rise and fall as they flow toward the horizon and how the architecture of mesas and buttes marches rhythmically over the landscape, swelled with the freedom of a deep blue sky. Whether Dixon painted in the field or studio, he ultimately re-created the West in terms of its own colors, its own light, its own forms, with an instinctive feeling for landscape elements that met his demand for something beyond objectivity. Maynard Dixon had something to say, stating it in an art that has both vision and design. We can understand the riches of his experience through his art. Where many have looked, few have seen. Among them is Maynard Dixon.

Chronology of Events, Commissions, and Exhibitions in the Life of Maynard Dixon

1875 Born January 24 in Fresno, California. Originally named Henry St. John Dixon, but changed to Lafayette Maynard Dixon on September 8.

1881–1890 Begins drawing, senses influence of flat San Joaquin Valley, particularly on trips to Refuge, the family ranch.

1891–1892 Family moves to Coronado, near San Diego, because of father's illness. Dixon sketches the old mission at San Juan Capistrano and the local landscape. Sends a letter to Frederic Remington, who responds with encouragement and advice. Decides to become an illustrator.

1893 Dixon enrolls at the California School of Design in San Francisco (renamed Mark Hopkins Institute of Art in March). Withdraws from school after three months. Has first illustrations accepted for December *Overland Monthly.*

1894 Numerous illustrations in *Overland Monthly.* Goes on lengthy horseback trip through Yosemite National Park.

1895 Hired by the *San Francisco Morning Call* as an illustrator. Meets Charles F. Lummis in San Francisco. Dixon travels to Monterey and into the Big Sur. In November, the *San Francisco Examiner* carries an article on the trip, Dixon's first significant publicity. Does his first cover and first poster for *Overland Monthly* in November.

1896 Illustrations for *Overland Monthly* and the *San Francisco Call.* Starts writing poetry. First exhibit of drawings at Mark Hopkins Institute of Art.

1897 Becomes involved with *The Lark.* First book illustrations for Verner Z. Reed's *Tales of the Sun-Land* and *Lo-To-Kah.* Starts providing illustrations for *Land of Sunshine.* Begins working in oil and watercolor.

1898 First published poem, "Bronco New Year," appears in January *Overland Monthly.* Father dies on August 27.

1899 Hired by William Randolph Hearst as art director of the *San Francisco Examiner Sunday Magazine* in August. Illustrates Jack London's "Malamute Kid" stories in *Overland Monthly.*

1900 Resigns position at the *San Francisco Examiner* in May. Decides to "go East to see the West." Lengthy trip through Arizona and New Mexico, including Fort Mojave, Prescott, Phoenix, Tempe, Isleta, and Santa Fe. Jack London's first book, *Son of the Wolf,* published with frontispiece by Dixon.

1901 Accompanied by Edward Borein, Dixon goes on lengthy horseback trip through western Nevada, northeastern California, into eastern Oregon, ending at Boise, Idaho. *Harper's Weekly* includes several Dixon illustrations on its covers during March and April.

1902 Helps form California Society of Artists. Exhibits with them and at the Bohemian Club. Returns to the Southwest, staying at Hubbell's Trading Post in Ganado, Arizona. Meets John Lorenzo Hubbell, who becomes a close friend. Works in oil, watercolor, and drawings. Goes on to Gallup, New Mexico, then to Isleta and Laguna. Begins illustration work for *Sunset Magazine*.

1903 Joins Bohemian Club. Works in a studio at 604 Merchant Street. *Sunset Magazine* features Dixon painting, *Navajo Indian from Life*, on cover of February issue. Returns to Navajo country during spring. *Sunset Magazine* publishes two Dixon poems in November. Several of his paintings are included in an article he writes for the December issue of *Sunset Magazine*. Exhibits at Mark Hopkins Institute of Art, San Francisco Art Association, and the Newspaper Artists League.

1904 Moves to a new studio at 424 Pine Street. Meets artist Lillian West Tobey. Numerous illustrations for *Sunset Magazine* and the *San Francisco Chronicle*. Exhibits at Press Club, Bohemian Club, and San Francisco Art Association. Makes brief trip to the Navajo Reservation.

1905 Helps paint murals in Coppa's restaurant. Dixon and fellow artist Xavier Martinez go to Guadalajara, Mexico. When Dixon returns, he marries Lillian West Tobey in Los Angeles at Charles F. Lummis's home on May 7. Leaves almost immediately to do illustrations for *Cosmopolitan* magazine in Goldfield and Tonopah, Nevada. Dixon painting used as frontispiece for the novel *Ben Blair*, published by A. C. McClurg. Returns to Ganado for the month of November.

1906 San Francisco earthquake and fire destroys his studio on April 18. Dixon lives in Sausalito and Oakland for several weeks, then accepts position in Los Angeles with the *San Francisco Chronicle*. Returns to San Francisco and resumes freelance illustration work for *Sunset Magazine* and the *San Francisco Chronicle*.

1907 Starts to exhibit at Del Monte Art Gallery in Monterey. Paints his first murals for Southern Pacific's Tucson station: *Irrigation, The Apache, The Cattleman, The Prospector*. Does illustrations for *Western World*. Illustrates Idah Meacham Strobridge's book *The Loom of the Desert*. Leaves for New York and better possibilities in illustration work. Establishes studio at 1947 Broadway in New York. Begins close friendship with Sophie Treadwell before he leaves San Francisco.

1908 Becomes one of the most successful of illustrators working in western fiction books and magazines. Meets Charles M. Russell in New York. Becomes friends with Robert Henri and Ernest Blumenschein. Develops friendships with Eugene Manlove Rhodes and Dane Coolidge. Illustrates *Francisca Reina*, a book dedicated to the rebuilding of San Francisco.

1909 Moves to a new studio at 17 East 19th Street. Travels to Idaho and Montana in the spring, paints and sketches at Saint Ignatius, Montana, on Flathead Indian Reservation. Numerous illustrations for western fiction stories in leading magazines. Exhibits three paintings at the Del Monte Art Gallery. Illustrates Florence Kelly's *The Delafield Affair*.

1910 Moves to Nepperham, New York. Daughter Constance is born in October. Has illustrations in Idah Meacham Strobridge's final book, *The Land of Purple Shadows*, and in a Mary Austin serialized novelette. Illustrates Cyrus Townsend Brady's *The West Wind* and Edgar Beecher Bronson's *The Red-Blooded Heroes of the Frontier*. Paints five full-page color illustrations for Clarence Mulford's book *Hopalong Cassidy*. Does illustrations for Dane Coolidge's book *Hidden Water*.

1911 Moves to Royalton, Vermont, then to Winsted, Connecticut. Returns to New York in October, living at 57 West 22nd Street. Elected member of New York Society of Illustrators, Salmagundi Club, and the Architectural League. Illustrates *Bar-20 Days*, another Clarence Mulford book on Hopalong Cassidy. Provides illustrations for Dane Coolidge's book *The Texican*.

1912 Several paintings are accepted for inclusion in the National Academy of Design's annual exhibition. Returns to San Francisco and opens a studio at 728 Montgomery Street. *Sunset Magazine* immediately engages him as an illustrator. Exhibits three paintings at Bohemian Club in November. Anita Baldwin McClaughry commissions him to paint murals for the Indian Hall and the Jinks Room in her new home, Anoakia, near Pasadena.

1913 Returns to San Francisco in August, reopens the studio at 728 Montgomery Street. Illustrates Peter B. Kyne's book *The Three Godfathers*. Provides illustrations for another Clarence Mulford book, *The Coming of Cassidy*. Travels to eastern Oregon to paint and sketch in the desert.

1914 Completes murals for Anita Baldwin McClaughry's Jinks Room. Numerous exhibitions in San Francisco galleries.

1915 Enters three paintings at 1915 Panama-Pacific International Exposition in San Francisco, where one wins a bronze medal. Dixon, Tobey, and Constance travel through northern Arizona for several months. *International Studio* runs feature article on Dixon. First one-man exhibition at Bohemian Club during November. Painting shifts toward an impressionist style.

1916 Exhibits three paintings at Post-Exposition Exhibition at the Palace of Fine Arts. Starts work at Foster and Kleiser, a commercial art company, designing outdoor billboard and magazine advertisements. Frequent covers and illustrations for *Sunset Magazine*. Numerous exhibitions of his art at local galleries.

1917 Secures divorce from Tobey in April. Accompanied by daughter, Constance, travels to Glacier National Park in Montana on commission for the Great Northern Railway. Joined by artist Frank Hoffman. Visits Charles M. Russell at Lake McDonald. Lives with several Blackfeet Indian families at Cutbank and Browning, Montana. Returns to San Francisco in October. Painting style now moves toward postimpressionism.

1918 Continues working for Foster and Kleiser. Illustrates *The Grove Plays of the Bohemian Club*. Exhibits several paintings at the Museum of Fine Arts in Santa Fe, New Mexico. Suffers nervous breakdown. Starts teaching at the California School of Fine Arts.

1919 Forms Hammer and Tongs Club. Exhibits at a major exhibition, The California Group of Contemporary American Artists. Goes on painting trip to Inyo County, California. Meets portrait photographer Dorothea Lange at the Hill Tolerton Print Room.

1920 Marries Dorothea Lange on March 21. Moves into the "Little House" on Russian Hill. Painting style begins change to simplified realism. Major exhibit at S & G Gump of recent paintings. Resigns teaching position at California School of Fine Arts.

1921 Paints mural for passenger liner *Silver State*. Travels to family ranch, Refuge, in San Joaquin Valley during the spring, producing many paintings and sketches. Goes on trip with Lange and her family to the eastern Sierra Nevada, through the Owens Valley into the Panamint and Inyo mountains.

1922 At the invitation of John Wetherill, Dixon and Lange go to Kayenta, Arizona, on the Navajo Reservation. Dixon begins to focus on clouds as part of his compositions.

1923 Visits New York in attempt to penetrate the eastern art market. Important one-man exhibition at Macbeth Gallery. Exhibits two paintings at the National Academy of Design in New York. Dixon and Lange accompany Anita Baldwin to Walpi, Arizona, in late summer. Dixon stays until November. His *Poems and Seven Drawings* is published by Grabhorn Press, and G. P. Putnam publishes his *Injun Babies*. Paints two mural lunettes for dining room of steamship *Sierra*.

1924 Exhibits at the Biltmore Salon, Los Angeles. Joins the Painters of the West. Exhibits again at Macbeth Gallery. Paints mural, *Sunol Water Temple*, for foyer of Spring Valley Water Company. First paintings with evidence of cubist-realist influence.

1925 First son, Daniel Rhodes Dixon, is born. Paints two mural hangers for Barker Brothers Building in Los Angeles. Travels to Arizona in attempt to interest Southern Pacific Railroad in a tourist hotel on the Apache Trail. Exhibits at Painters of the West in Los Angeles. Helps form Club Beaux Arts and Galerie Beaux Arts in San Francisco to foster progressive, modernist art.

1926 In cooperation with fellow painter Frank Van Sloun, paints murals for the Room of the Dons at the Mark Hopkins Hotel in San Francisco.

1927 Paints murals for the auditorium of Oakland Technical High School. One of Dixon's paintings is used as the cover of a brochure on the Apache Trail issued by Southern Pacific Railroad. Rejected in an important mural competition for the Los Angeles Public Library. Embarks on a four-month journey through Nevada.

1928 Second son, John Eaglefeather, is born. Completes *Spirit of India* mural in foyer of West Coast Theatre in Oakland. Paints important mural, *Pageant of Tradition*, for third-floor reading room of California State Library in Sacramento. Charles F. Lummis dies November 25. Paints mural, *The Legend of Earth and Sun*, for Arizona Biltmore Hotel in Phoenix. Exhibits at Wichita Art Association, California State Fair, Pacific Southwest Exposition, Oakland Art League, University of California, and many other places.

1929 Starts to work on his illustrated version of Walt Whitman's *Leaves of Grass* but eventually abandons project. Paints murals for Guaranty Building and Loan Association in conjunction with Conrad Buff. Dixon, Lange, and their two sons travel to Inyo County. Stock market collapses in October, signaling onslaught of Great Depression.

1930 Explores the Tehachapi Mountains, painting some of his most important canvases. Paints *Shapes of Fear*. Resigns from Bohemian Club in protest over conservative policies regarding modern art. Exhibits at Honolulu Academy of Arts. Paints preliminary design view of Golden Gate Bridge for a bond issue. John Lorenzo Hubbell dies on November 1. *Touring Topics* commissions him to produce twelve magazine covers during 1930.

1931 *Shapes of Fear* wins Harold L. Mack Prize at San Francisco Art Association Annual Exhibition. Dixon, Lange, and two sons go to Taos, New Mexico, for six months. Exhibits at Museum of Fine Arts in Santa Fe during November.

1932 Returns to San Francisco in January. Enters painting, *Shapes of Fear*, in 1932 National Academy of Design annual exhibition. Wins Henry Ward Ranger Prize, and painting is placed in Brooklyn Institute of Arts and Sciences. Lange begins to photograph the unemployed and "forgotten man." Exhibits at Pennsylvania Academy of Arts. Depression forces Dixon and Lange to curtail their work.

1933 Family goes to Zion National Park in Utah. Paints mural, *The Arrival of Fremont in California*, for John C. Fremont High School in Los Angeles. Meets Everett Ruess.

1934 Goes to Boulder, Nevada, for Public Works of Art Project to document construction activities at Boulder Dam. Eugene Manlove Rhodes dies June 27. Lange begins working with Paul Schuster Taylor on migrant worker project. Inspired by San Francisco's maritime strike, Dixon starts painting "forgotten man" and "strike" series. Meets artist and muralist Edith Hamlin. Does last illustration for *Sunset Magazine*.

1935 Along with several other San Francisco artists, Dixon forms the Art Students League, a cooperative art school. Paints two murals for the Kit Carson Café. Dixon and Lange are divorced in October. Lange marries Paul Taylor in December. Dixon goes on extensive trip through southern Nevada and eastern California during the fall months. Exhibits at California-Pacific International Exposition in San Diego and at the Corcoran Gallery in Washington, D.C.

1936 Travels to the Wind River area of Wyoming. Exhibits at various locations in Utah.

1937 Sells over eighty paintings and drawings to Brigham Young University. Marries Edith Hamlin in Carson City, Nevada. Exhibits at the National Academy of Design.

1938 Stays at El Cajon near San Diego during spring and summer. Paints mural, *The Road to El Dorado*, for post office at Martinez, California. Decides to close Montgomery Street studio. Receives commission from the Bureau of Indian Affairs for two murals, *The Indian Yesterday* and *The Indian Today*, at the Department of the Interior headquarters in Washington, D.C.

1939 Bureau of Indian Affairs murals completed and installed. Exhibits three paintings at Golden Gate International Exposition on Treasure Island. Paints two large murals, *Grassland* and *Ploughed Land*, on building adjacent to the fair's Court of Pacifica. Stays at Desert Camp near the Salton Sea during the spring. Dixon and Hamlin go to Zion National Park, purchase land for a studio at Mount Carmel. Dixon closes Montgomery Street studio.

1940 IBM purchases painting for inclusion in their exhibit at the New York World's Fair. Dixon and Hamlin move to their house at Mount Carmel, Utah, and begin construction of a studio-home in Tucson.

1941 Alternates living at Mount Carmel during summer months and staying in Tucson during the winter, a pattern adhered to for the next several years.

1942 Paints mural, *Palomino Ponies*, for Canoga Park Post Office. Numerous painting trips through southern Arizona, around Zion National Park, and in the Arizona strip.

1943 Does his last book illustrations, this time for the Limited Editions Club's *Oregon Trail*. Paints at Bryce Canyon National Park and Capitol Reef National Monument in Utah.

1944 Increasingly crippled by emphysema but manages to continue painting.

1945 Major retrospective exhibition at Scripps College in Claremont, California, in November, and at the Los Angeles County Museum of Art thereafter. On oxygen nearly twenty-four hours a day as emphysema steadily worsens.

1946 Completes last mural, *Grand Canyon of the Colorado*, for Santa Fe Railway's Hill Street ticket office in Los Angeles. Dies November 13 at Tucson, Arizona.

ONE

Picking Up the Trail
1875–1893

MAYNARD DIXON could trace his ancestry back to Jamestown and the very beginnings of America. One of the members in his lineage was John Rolfe, who married a Powhatan Indian woman named Matoaka in April 1614. She, of course, has become known as Pocahontas. Another ancestor, John Dixon, emigrated from Durham, England, in 1745 to settle in James County, Virginia, where he helped start Williamsburg's *Virginia Gazette*, the first newspaper in that colony. When the Revolutionary War began, he gave up his editorial position and raised a regiment of cavalry, serving as a colonel under Generals George Washington and Light Horse Harry Lee. After the war, Henry St. John Dixon, John's only son, remained in Williamsburg. There his son and Maynard Dixon's grandfather, Richard Lawrence Dixon, was born in 1814.

Around 1830, young Richard Dixon left Williamsburg, moving across the Blue Ridge Mountains to homestead in the Shenandoah Valley. Drawn by stories of virgin land along the Yazoo River near Jackson, Mississippi, he again migrated in 1833, this time with his new bride, Julia Phillips, daughter of a U.S. District Judge for whom he had worked as a law clerk. Sometime later, they moved to a cotton plantation called "The Sycamores," located near Greenville, Mississippi. There Richard worked variously as a lawyer, a clerk of the state's Superior Court, a probate judge, and a successful planter. He was prosperous and influential in his community. Long after his grandfather's death in 1889, Dixon remembered:

He always dressed in a black broad-cloth "hued" shirt, black bow tie, wide black hat and square-toed high boots of very thin French calf and they fit his smallish feet like kid gloves. He was stern and quiet, humorous and kindly. His will was immovable and his word once given was sacred. No man who knew him cared to question it and the few who did got into trouble. "A gentleman's word," he would say, "is as good as his bond." At seventy-three he kicked such a one — a two-hundred-pounder of thirty years — out of his office and down two flights of stairs, for which act his associates presented him with a gold-headed cane inscribed with the date. He had a great

2. *Harry St. John Dixon, 1871,*
private collection

respect for knowledge and real intelligence, but detested smart-alecks and all shams. He knew the meaning of common sense and how to use it. He valued simple things and was a born conservative.[1]

Harry St. John Dixon (fig. 2), the eldest of Richard's six sons, was born on August 2, 1843, in Jackson, Mississippi, and lived with his parents at The Sycamores until he was seventeen. In the fall of 1860, he enrolled at the University of Virginia, intending to study law, but ominous signs of the coming Civil War forced him to leave. Harry entered military service at Richmond, Virginia, in November of 1861 with the Confederate Army's Eleventh Mississippi Infantry. He served as an aide to Brigadier General Samuel Gibbs French (who was also from Mississippi) during the campaigns in northern Virginia and eventually became his personal assistant. In May 1862, at the age of eighteen, Harry enlisted as a private in Company D, Twenty-Eighth Mississippi Volunteer Cavalry, serving with the Confederate Army of Tennessee in Mississippi, Georgia, Tennessee, and Alabama. In the next three years, Harry and his comrades fought at Lost Mountain, Dallas, Mount Carmel, Powder Springs, New Hope Church, Ezra Church—from Atlanta to Jonesboro, Georgia, and from Fayetteville, Arkansas, to Greenville, Mississippi. The men of Company D were, for the most part, planters' sons who had been raised on horseback with guns in their hands. The regiment earned its nickname, the "Bloody Twenty-Eighth," from the results of many a fierce charge. The broken remnant of this gallant regiment—Harry among them—surrendered to federal forces at Gainesville, Alabama, on May 8, 1865. Upon returning to Mississippi, he discovered his family destitute, Sycamores burned to the ground, and the region's plantation economy wrecked. Harry studied some law with his father, returned to the University of Virginia to finish a law degree in 1867, and afterwards passed the Mississippi bar examination.

When the Civil War started in 1861, Richard Dixon had remained a strict constitutionalist, refusing to join the Confederacy or take any active part against the Union. Nevertheless, Greenville was overrun by Union forces after Vicksburg's fall in the summer of 1863, and Richard was forced to flee into Demopolis, Alabama, abandoning his home and estate. After the war ended, he and his family found that postwar changes in the "reconstructed" South continued to devastate the lifestyle and economic foundation he had nurtured. Three years after Lee's surrender at Appomattox, Harry St. John Dixon, along with younger brother, James Phillip, joined an exodus of disaffected southerners to California's southern San Joaquin Valley. They traveled by ship from New York to Panama, crossed the isthmus on foot, sailed on another vessel to San Francisco, took a steamboat

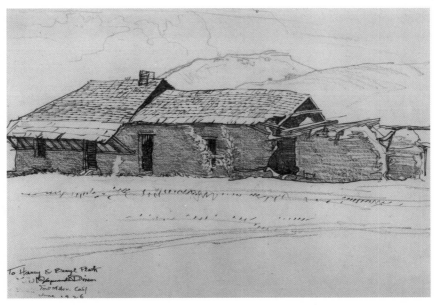

3. *Fort Miller*, 1926, pencil on paper, 10¹/₂ x 15 inches, private collection

down to Stockton, and finished the journey by wagon from Stockton to Fort Miller (fig. 3), settling near Millerton, where the San Joaquin River leaves the Sierra Nevada foothills and enters the valley floor. The town site and the remnants of the fort disappeared under the waters of Lake Millerton when Friant Dam was completed in 1944. In 1871, Richard Dixon sold the Mississippi plantation and joined his two sons with the remainder of the family—his wife, four other sons, and a daughter—in California in an area called the "Alabama Colony," north of the present city of Fresno.

The early pioneers of the Alabama settlement, mostly displaced Southerners who had served in the Confederate Army, enjoyed affluence in the prewar South but came to the San Joaquin Valley destitute. They were enthusiastic, envisioning the cotton, rice, and tobacco fields of their former homes rebuilt as productive grain fields on the valley's vast alluvial plain. All supplies, however, even the smallest items, had to be transported down from Stockton by wagon. Water and fuel were scarce on the barren treeless plains. Stifling summer heat, chilly tule fogs in winter, and monotonous work became their companions. A few built relatively comfortable homes, but most of the settlers lived in tents or small shacks, which sometimes collapsed when fierce gales periodically swept across the plains. In addition, they struggled to protect their grain fields from the depredation of wild horses and equally wild cattle that roamed the unfenced plains. Some gave names to their ranches in jest or in frustration, names like "Hell's Half Acre." The Dixon's called theirs "Refuge," a place of retreat, they thought, from misfortunes generated by the Civil War. Most of the settlers, unable to survive droughts and other challenges, slowly drifted away to other places and different occupations in the valley.

Harry St. John Dixon became Fresno County's first clerk and recorder in 1869,

4. *Fresno*, 1884, California History Section, California State Library

began a law practice, formed a real estate partnership that resulted in the first map of the county, and took an active part in the region's political life (fig. 4). Maynard Dixon remembered that his father might have been more prosperous, but since many of the early settlers concluded their arguments with six-shooters, his law practice was limited. The encroachment on land and water rights sometimes led to gunfights on the city's streets. There was still animosity between those who supported the Union and those who fought for the Confederacy. Sometimes Dixon's father would find a note left at night on his office door; "Get out of town, you Rebel Ass."

The Alabama settlement was probably the first in the area to experiment with irrigation and farming, competing with cattle and sheep interests for the open range. Most of the San Joaquin Valley, 250 miles long and averaging 60 miles across, was still the domain of the vaquero. In the heat of summer, the movement of the herds toward the nearest water could be traced by clouds of dust they kicked up, obscuring the horizon. As the rush for California's land emerged to rival the earlier gold rush, the valley spun in constant turmoil. Quarrels over land ownership, cattle stealing, and especially water rights often ended violently. In the early 1870s, the 8,200 square miles of Fresno County—land that is now Fresno and Madera counties with portions of San Benito and Kings counties—embraced vast areas of flat valley, foothills, and parts of the high Sierra Nevadas. In January 1872, the county seat was still at Millerton, less than twenty-five miles from present-day Fresno. The main way to travel across this wild and undeveloped terrain was by stage. One line ran from Sacramento to Stockton, then to Millerton, and along the edge of the Sierras to Visalia in Tulare County; the other led from San Francisco, through Pacheco Pass, over to Visalia, then down to Los Angeles.

Sectional and political disputes and the struggle with emerging railroad interests provided litigation work for Harry St. John Dixon. He began to spend more time in San Francisco, since many of his cases required court appearances in that city. There, in 1873, at the wedding of Blanche Maynard and William Gwin, where he was best man, he met Constance Maynard, the daughter of Lieutenant Lafayette Maynard. Lieutenant Maynard, once prominent in Washington, D.C.'s social life, had distinguished himself in several battles during the Mexican War. After the war he obtained a furlough and arrived in California during December of 1848. When gold was discovered, he chose to resign his naval commission and quickly became identified with San Francisco's business interests. He was the first person to take a paddlewheel steamer, the *Senator*, up the Sacramento River to Sacramento; later, with two partners, he started the first steamboat service. Although he was a speculator more than a businessman, making and losing several large fortunes, mostly in real estate and mining, Maynard was one of San Francisco's prominent financial figures before he was brought to ruin in the panic of 1873. On Valentine's Day 1874, his daughter Constance married the young, blue-eyed Fresno attorney, Harry St. John Dixon, in the parlor of her father's Harrison Street home.

Late in 1874, Harry brought Constance to Fresno. It was then the county seat, a boom town fueled by land and water speculators, eager settlers, and other people attracted to a new frontier. An informal census in July of 1874 turned up twenty-eight businesses, including two law offices (one of them Faymonville and Dixon), a local newspaper, and twenty-five private residences (among them Harry Dixon's shabby cabin from Millerton, which had been dismantled, moved, and resurrected in Fresno). Some trees had been planted, and they struggled to provide shade while being harassed by wandering cattle, horses, and pigs. People still used wood from the foothills as fuel for their cookstoves and heaters.

In the early 1870s, the natural beauty of the southern San Joaquin Valley was still relatively intact. On the open plains, tall grasses, bright orange poppies, lupines, forget-me-nots, and an array of other wildflowers—if prompted by rich winter rains—carpeted the valley floor each spring to the horizon's edge. Over the landscape whirled antelope, while wild mustangs grazed along the edges of ephemeral lakes. But when summer arrived, the grasses turned brown, the shallow lakes disappeared, the earth dried, and the valley rivers— the San Joaquin, the Fresno, and the Kern—sulked and became part-time streams. Strong harsh winds blew down the valley, shaking the gray sagebrush and dry brittle grasses. By the middle of summer, the wind would stop, and the dust would settle thick and gray under a burnt-out blue sky. In his classic book, *The Octopus*, about the struggle between farmers and railroad interests in the San Joaquin Valley, Frank Norris wrote, ". . . the natural forces seemed to hang suspended. There was no rain, there was no wind, there was no growth, no life; the very stubble had no force even to rot. The sun alone moved."[2]

On January 24, 1875, in this land of harsh extremes, Constance Dixon gave birth to a son. They named him Henry St. John Dixon, after his paternal great-grandfather. However, by the time he was formally christened at San Francisco's Trinity Church on September 8, 1875, his name had become Lafayette Maynard Dixon (fig. 5). One sister recalled that he abhorred his middle name, but absolutely despised Lafayette, discarding it sometime after the turn of the century. There were other children: a brother, Harry Jr., who would follow his older brother into the arts, and three sisters, Rebecca, Eleanor, and Constance. Three more children died either at birth or shortly thereafter and were buried in a little graveyard behind the Dixon house, their tiny headstones surrounded and protected by poplar trees.

5. *Constance Maynard and Maynard Dixon*, ca. 1876–1877, private collection

Harry St. John Dixon always missed the plantation lifestyle. His meager income as an attorney, along with Constance's sometimes-foolish expenditures, prohibited establishing anything nearly like it. But the rapid growth of Fresno provided financial opportunity, so he subdivided some property he owned within the city limits and used the proceeds to build a new home in 1882. The large high-ceilinged house at 1605 K Street—the first in Fresno to boast tarpaper insulation—proudly displayed the Dixon ancestral crest in leaded colored glass on the front windows. Harry's parents, never successful farmers, left Refuge to live with Harry and Constance, and Richard Dixon joined Harry in practicing law.

During the 1880s, Harry St. John Dixon took an active part in civic affairs, serving as Fresno's first city attorney, chair of a vigilance committee, and a board member of the volunteer fire department. He also served in his college fraternity, Sigma Chi, at the national level and organized the Blue and Gray parades in Fresno during the 1880s, which brought together former adversaries as comrades to help heal the lingering bitterness of the Civil War. In times when the Dixon's neighbors practiced conservative politics and religion, the Dixon family, led by Harry and his father, Richard, remained unswervingly freethinking and liberal while retaining the time-honored traditions of family loyalty and aristocratic codes of honor from the antebellum South. Maynard Dixon cherished these values, inheriting from his father and grandfather an uncompromising spirit and idealism. For his father, it was the "damn Yankee." And for Dixon, it became the "damn businessman" or the "damn smarty-arty artists" who ran with whatever current art fashion was in vogue.

Between his grandfather, father, and mother, Maynard Dixon grew up in a progressive family atmosphere. From his father's family he learned pride, stubbornness, and indepen-dence, but his mother tempered these attitudes with a humanistic outlook. Constance Dixon was an omnivorous reader of history, novels (the more romantic the better), and poetry. She bought books freely, subscribed to leading magazines, and surrounded her children with the classics. The house was jammed with books, flowers, a reading lamp, and even a piano. Constance loved to read aloud. She would sit at a table in the wide cen-tral hall of their home, reading of Lewis and Clark's explorations, *Ivanhoe*, *A Tale of Two Cities*, and particularly the poetry of Tennyson. Dixon absorbed it into his soul, using verse as a companion to his painting in later years. One of his sisters remembered that her father worried that Constance's passion for reading aloud would inhibit the children's ability to read for themselves; he finally insisted they be taught "properly."

Maynard Dixon's earliest recollections of the southern San Joaquin Valley included the dark brooding outline of the Coast Range on the west. To the east loomed the "Range of Light," the luminous blue and white ramparts of the Sierra Nevadas. Everywhere— from the jagged arroyos and shallow sloughs to the newly laid railroad line, irrigation ditches, and fences separating immense cattle ranches—everywhere seemed dead level, an endless horizontal plane forever radiating in all directions. The few variants, houses or barns, stood like islands in a prairie sea, the town's lone water tank transfixed in the center. Nature had created an elemental geometry in the long lines of the valley, distant horizontal hills, and cloud-massed skies. And everywhere, men came and went on horses in the dress of the range.

These people intrigued young Dixon: longhaired frontiersmen, hard-riding cattlemen, and Civil War veterans, with their stirring tales of bandits, trappers, and Indians passing through the valley and of battles lost and won during the war. "The atmosphere of Fresno in my childhood," he recalled, "was a sort of hangover from the 1849 era." Rocky Mountain trappers, miners, and adventure seekers abounded in the California towns. A shy sensitive youth, Maynard Dixon listened, looked, and remembered, absorbing impressions of simplicity, low-laid masses of land, and the far-flung decorative sweeps of sky. Such shapes would dominate and give signature to the art of his later years. As a youngster, Dixon never was strong or athletic, suffering constantly from severe attacks of asthma. Barred from rough-and-tumble play with schoolmates, he drifted toward introversion and solitude, dreaming of Kit Carson and Sitting Bull, Stonewall Jackson, Geronimo, and Joaquin Murrieta, whose hideout had been in the willow-fringed sloughs that bordered Fresno. In later years, Dixon brought these people and others to life in countless illustrations.

Dixon's life as an artist began at the age of six, lying on the living room floor, cutting pictures of soldiers and trains out of newspapers and magazines. No professional artists lived in Fresno at this time, nor was drawing taught in the public schools. So he pursued his own self-directed learning. The first drawings seem awkward but possess a raw vitality. They could be found everywhere in the Dixon residence: on the barn doors, the flour barrel, pieces of cardboard, scrap paper, and finally in neatly arranged notebooks. Dixon created drawings of the town, broncos on the prairie, Southern Pacific trains, cattle, cowboys, Indians, and Civil War veterans. He received encouragement from his mother and particularly his grandfather, Richard Dixon, who offered instruction in the fundamentals of accurate drawing by teaching him to observe, not merely to see, and to judge distances and proportions. "He was a stern and picturesque old-time Southerner," Dixon recalled, "one of my heroes, and I think he must have had a kindly understanding of my tendency to shyness and introspection, and felt that sketching and studying nature would be a wholesome corrective. His influence had a lasting effect."[3]

Through the middle and late 1880s, his uncle, George Washington Mordecai, emerged as one of Maynard Dixon's strongest influences. Mordecai had been an artillery captain in the Confederate Army during the Civil War. One of the original "Alabama settlers," he took over the running of Refuge when he married Louise Dixon, Richard and Julia Dixon's only daughter. Along with his brother-in-law, Harry, he helped organize a local chapter of the Veterans of the Blue and the Gray. Young Maynard Dixon marched proudly with his father and uncle as the drummer boy in their parades and reunions. Another influence was his father's buckskin saddle horse, Dandy, who became an important outlet for his emerging artistic interests. His father and uncle taught him to ride, and he rode with the cowboys or scouted the foothills where vast flocks of sheep roamed, trailed by Indian sheepherders. The well-trained horse became both friend and companion on solitary sketching rides across the endless plains, far beyond the fences and people. George Mordecai included him on exploring adventures at Refuge, and for young Dixon, the open ranges filled a special need for solitude and a visible horizon.

In 1889, his father took him on a long camping and fishing trip through the remote wilderness of the Kern River Canyon and into the high, austere Kaweah Range. Dixon made sketches of "this great backbone of the earth" and never forgot the dramatic sight of a group of Paiute etched against the horizon. For this trip, his father had given him his first rifle, a .22 Winchester pump, and Dixon, proud as any fourteen-year-old could be, clutched it close. Far back in the mountains, he and his father encountered a lonely little cabin where two hunters, an old Mono Indian and a French Canadian, had made their summer camp. The Indian carried an old sawed-off English musket; the French Canadian, a huge man with a shock of long black hair and a red-brown beard that reached almost to his waist, had a heavy .50 caliber Sharps buffalo gun. Years later, Maynard recalled the encounter: "Wal keed," he said, "You gon hont the deer now? Was that you got there?" "That's my rifle," Dixon said. "It's a new one." The huge man reached for it and turned it over in his enormous hands. "Vere pretty leel gon," he said. "W'at you shoot we that—flies?"[4]

Dixon spent two more fitful years struggling with intermittent schooling in Fresno, punctuated by numerous rides on Dandy, saddlebags stuffed with sketchpads. By now

6. *Dawn, Coronado,* 1891, watercolor on paper, 7¹/₂ x 10¹/₂ inches, collection of Dr. Richard Paltenghi

his drawing had progressed beyond crude images to something that indicated promise. A few sketches survive from this period and already show signs of a direct and forceful manner. Dixon read popular magazines avidly—*Harper's, Scribner's, The Art Journal,* and others—looking at their vivid romantic illustrations by Edwin Austin Abbey, Howard Pyle, Arthur Burdett Frost, and, in particular, Frederic Remington, carefully studying the illustrators' styles. Graphic images had never before been as pervasive as they were in the years from 1885 to the early 1890s. A popular visual culture was born in this imagery, offering a shared understanding of the latest trends and current events, the country's geography, and the attitudes, ideas, and impressions of a diverse United States during the final two decades of the nineteenth century. What Maynard Dixon found in these magazines would open the window on his dreams.

In 1891, Harry St. John Dixon suffered a nervous breakdown brought on by business and political reversals and a debilitating disease contracted in his early twenties. Constance Dixon, convinced her husband could recover by living in a more moderate climate, moved the family down to Coronado (fig. 6), in San Diego County. Dixon did not last long in the new school. He quit in anger and despair at sixteen, "graduating through the back door," vowing never to return. Again, he was without access to formal art training, so he immersed himself in improving his drawing skills, making studies of the remnants of the Spanish empire in and around San Diego, Mission San Juan Capistrano, and the brown barren hills marching inland from the ocean. Sketching the old adobes and dreaming about the past they represented, Dixon developed a lifelong interest in and appreciation for Hispanic culture.

"At the age of sixteen," he remembered, "I determined to devote my life to illustrating the old West."[5] In 1891, he sent two sketchbooks to the one person he admired most among the illustrators he had studied—Frederic Remington. By the early 1890s, Remington had achieved national fame as the leading illustrator of western subjects, even as the frontier waned. He drew his inspiration from the cowboy, the rancher, and the cavalryman out on the Great Plains and in the Southwest. By 1890, hardly an issue of *Harper's* appeared without a Remington-illustrated article. The famous artist responded to Dixon's overture with a letter on September 3, 1891, holding out a hand "to my dear young man."

> . . . *your letter and books are here and I have quite enjoyed your sketches. I hardly know what to tell you—I do not "teach" and unused to giving advice—the only advice I could give you is to never take anyone's advice, which is my rule.*
>
> *You draw better at your age than I did at the same age—if you have the "Sand" to overcome difficulties you could be an artist in time—no one's opinion of what you can do is of any consequence—time and your character will develop that.*
>
> *Most every artist needs "schooling." I had very little—it is not absolutely necessary—it is best to have it. Be always true to yourself—to the way and the things you see in nature—if you imitate any other man ever so little you are "gone."*
>
> *Study good pictures—do not imitate them—read books and good literature, see much and observe the things in nature which captivate your fancy and above all draw-draw-draw—and always from nature. Do not try to make pictures when you are studying—do the thing simply and just as you see it—use India ink-crayon or some board medium at first—then color, either water or oil—solid simple subjects and work work work.*
>
> *Art is not a profession which will make you rich but it might make you happy—its notaries are all sacrifices but you are master of your own destinies.*
>
> *Another thing—never cheapen yourself—you do not know it but to be a successful illustrator is to be fully as much of a man as to be a successful painter, so I do not think many young men help themselves financially in that way. If you want to get a living while studying, that is very hard—It can be done but circumstances and not men are responsible.*[6]

Remington's encouraging response confirmed Dixon's desire to become an illustrator. However, Constance Dixon knew her son would be successful only if he could secure an appropriate art education and circulate among practicing artists. The center of art in California, home of the state's only important art school, the California School of Design, was San Francisco. In 1893, Constance and the five children moved to Alameda, a ferry ride across the sparkling bay from this art capital. Harry Dixon did not go with them. He had failed to respond to Coronado's environment and had become even more despondent, an old-fashioned Southern gentleman slowly descending into silence. Dixon and the other children would never forget the image of the three tall, grave, bearded gentlemen who came and took their father away to Agnews State Hospital in San Jose before they left for Alameda.

TWO

Fin-de-Siécle Illustrator
1893–1900

I n early 1893, sixteen-year-old Dixon enrolled in the California School of Design, part of the San Francisco Art Association, located in the ornate Mark Hopkins mansion on Nob Hill. The San Francisco Art Association, established on March 28, 1871, was the first formally organized group of artists west of the Mississippi River. The association added the California School of Design in 1873, expanding operations to include a school of art. In 1876, the school of design moved from a rented room at 313 Pine Street into rooms shared with the Bohemian Club over the California Market at 430 Pine Street, in a noisy wholesale district. When offered the Mark Hopkins mansion, which had been donated to the University of California for the use of the art association, the California School of Design changed its name to the Mark Hopkins Institute of Art on March 4, 1893.

By the time of the art association's founding, San Francisco had become a culturally mature and cosmopolitan city with an air of light-headed gaiety. Often termed the "Paris of the West," its physical setting attracted a flourishing artistic colony. By the 1890s, there lived and worked in San Francisco as talented a group of artists, illustrators, and sculptors as existed anywhere in the country. The California School of Design had a strong sympathy with the European neoclassic tradition and developed instruction around that influence. For nearly five decades, the basic courses included drawing from life, drawing from plaster casts, and outdoor plein-air landscape study. This conservative approach continued without notable departure up to the Panama-Pacific International Exposition of 1915, although Barbizon influences and the newer interest in impressionism was brought back by students who went to Paris for academic study. The basic instruction was sound and generally of high quality. The school flourished despite the fact that some quarters of the local art community ignored it, finding the facility tradition-bound and unresponsive to the work of Manet, Monet, Degas, and others in the impressionist movement. Among the early California artists who attended the school were Xavier Martinez, Joseph Raphael, Earl Cummings, Gottardo Piazzoni, Emil Carlsen, Ralph Stackpole, Granville Redmond, Theodore Wores (who painted

Oscar Wilde during his visit to San Francisco in 1882), and John Gutzon Borglum, sculptor of Mount Rushmore.

Much of San Francisco's artistic and bohemian life revolved around the Mark Hopkins Institute of Art and the San Francisco Art Association. The institute converted ground-floor salons and drawing rooms into exhibition galleries and classrooms, using many of the spacious chambers on the top floors as studios. Major art exhibitions were scheduled twice each year in the spring and fall. Every winter the students hosted one of San Francisco's major social events of the season, the colorful and not always sedate Mardi Gras ball. Everyone appeared in costume, including Alice B. Toklas, who once came dressed as Carmen, a high point for the revelers, arriving with the crowning of the King and Queen of Bohemia at midnight.

In 1890, the California School of Design appointed Arthur F. Mathews as director. Mathews achieved mastery in his painting as a European artist would have done, belonging to a generation that viewed France as the world's art center. He served until 1906 and modeled his school on the French example. He would never work anywhere except in the Bay Area, however, where the region's warm, golden-brown colors supported his particular vision. Mathews exerted a dominant influence in early twentieth-century California art; his California decorative style set the tone for art development on the West Coast. He derived his work, primarily a figurative style emphasizing idealized females, but also landscape, from French academic art, muralist Purvis de Chavannes, expatriate James McNeill Whistler, and the Art Nouveau movement. His painting and murals are characterized by flat decorative contours and Art Nouveau colors. Mathews also carried this theme into furniture and the decorative arts. Along with his wife, Lucia, and close friend, Emil Carlsen, Mathews encouraged California art to go in new directions. He was so domineering, however, that he could not permit competing styles to be exhibited at the Mark Hopkins Institute of Art. Three followers, Gottardo Piazzoni, Xavier Martinez, and Eugen Neuhaus, developed the style well into the twentieth century, modifying it to fit their own tastes.

Some of the many changes in the curriculum Mathews initiated included increasing the number of life classes; inaugurating an artistic anatomy class; requiring the teachers to be present only two days a week (an idea he got from Paris's Académie Julian) in order to give them time for their own creative development; and encouraging an independent but self-disciplined approach to student work, which often resulted in harsh professorial criticism. Mathews encouraged students to study in Paris, particularly at the Académie Julian rather than at conservative Munich schools.

Dixon found little reward in the monotonous drawing of uncongenial plaster casts, while the gruff, unsympathetic teaching style of Mathews, noted for severe temper and caustic comments, dismayed him. He recalled, "I was just a timid country kid. Maybe I expected too much—for I was used to sketching living things outdoors. I was too easily disheartened by the favoritism and sarcasm of Mathews. His method was to pounce upon our work, so like a growling dog he scared me out of my boots. He had me too scared to know what he was talking about."[1] Consequently, Dixon spent most of his time avoiding the classroom. He left the California School of Design permanently after three

7. *Piute Indian*, 1893,
pen and ink on paper, 3 x 4 inches,
California History Section,
California State Library

8. *Indian Sign*, 1893,
pen and ink on paper,
7¹/₂ x 4³/₄ inches,
private collection

short months. The California State Library in Sacramento has a biographical card filled out by Dixon in 1915. The first question asked, "Where did you study?" In reply, Dixon wrote "In the Open." The second question asked, "With whom did you study?' Dixon scrawled out an "X."

Dixon did credit one of his instructors, Raymond D. Yelland, with helping him by scholarly criticism and sympathetic encouragement to understand the dynamics of plein-air landscape painting and the use of colors. With Yelland and some fellow students— Edward Borein, Gottardo Piazzoni, James Swinnerton, and Homer Davenport—he went on numerous sketching trips through San Francisco's Chinatown and Telegraph Hill, among the Italian fishermen in North Beach, and north across San Francisco Bay to Mount Tamalpais in Marin County. Fascinated by the color and exotic mystery of Chinatown, he often returned there, making numerous pencil and pen-and-ink sketches of the Chinese and their costumes as he wandered the crowded noisy streets.

As he gained confidence in his drawing ability, Dixon started to submit examples of his work to local newspapers and magazines, particularly San Francisco's *Overland Monthly*. Founded in 1868 by Bret Harte and several others, *Overland Monthly* suspended operation after Bret Harte went east. Revived in the mid-1880s, the magazine became one of the West's leading periodicals, but by the early 1890s, the *Overland's* popularity had started to decline. When Rounsevelle Wildman bought the magazine, he hired Charles S. Greene as managing editor. Greene quickly reversed the magazine's fortunes by publishing more high-quality illustrations and photographs. In its new form, which Ambrose Bierce disparaged as the "Warmed Overland," Greene used so many illustrations that one of his editors declared more illustrators had graduated from its columns to New York magazines and newspapers than from any other publication in the United States. In December 1893, *Overland Monthly* featured an article by Jones Adams, "In the Stronghold of the Piutes"; the eight distinctive pen-and ink-illustrations scattered through the text were furnished by one Maynard Dixon, eighteen years old (fig. 7).

Though he was excited by having his work accepted at *Overland Monthly*, this was also an uncertain period for Dixon. Hurt and disillusioned by his abortive art school experience and missing his father, he would take lonely walks through the quiet valleys and oak-studded hills behind Alameda, drawing anything that captured his attention: horses, Chinese farmers, houses, and trees. He devoted most of 1893 and 1894 to outdoor study, sketching, always sketching, and refining his drawing skills. During this time, he signed his work either L. M. Dixon or L. Maynard Dixon, sometimes Dixon, and almost without exception, each drawing included the date and location. Throughout his lengthy career, Maynard Dixon left evidence about time and place in his drawings and paintings. Seeking additional subject matter, he made pen-and-ink sketches of exhibits at San Francisco's Midwinter Fair in 1893, including some likenesses of Yaqui Deer Dancers, and returned to Refuge several times. Once, in 1894, accompanied by George Mordecai, he made a lengthy horseback sketching trip through Yosemite National

9. *Jackass Meadows*, 1894, pencil and pastel on paper, 9 x 11 inches, collection of Dr. Richard Paltenghi

LEFT: 10. *Overland Monthly* (lithograph poster), 1895, collection of Drs. Mark and Kathleen Sublette

ABOVE: 11. *Overland Monthly,* November 1895, private collection

Park, camping with Portuguese and Mono Indian sheepherders. One of his Yosemite drawings, *Indian Sign* (cut in tamarack) (fig. 8), shows an Indian pictograph carved in a tree. Another sketch portrayed a ramshackle cabin at Jackass Meadows (fig. 9).

Dixon developed his original, fluid illustration style in pencil, crayon, pen and ink, and watercolors by studying the best available work of other artists joined with his constant religious pursuit of drawing field sketches from nature. He thought the works of most illustrators overloaded with detail—"chopped straw" he called it. His own ideals stressed the use of simple, direct forcefulness in drawing. Dixon's early drawings were marred by an awkward perspective, yet were already distinct from the work of other San Francisco illustrators. *Overland Monthly* had noticed the public's reaction to Dixon's illustrations and, during a twelve-months' period starting with the January 1894 issue, used thirty-four of his pen-and-ink drawings in seven stories and small vignettes, and one of his images for their November 1895 cover (fig. 11) and for a poster (fig. 10). The formula for a popular and profitable periodical in the last decade of the nineteenth century consisted of "how-to" articles, exotic travel stories, personality profiles, adventure yarns, and news stories, richly illustrated by artists with fresh innovative styles. Between 1890 and 1925, the American public responded eagerly to this type of informative, entertaining reading. Hundreds of publishers tried to capture that audience. The popularity of the short story, which could be read in one sitting, developed because of periodicals. In addition, serialized novels emerged, which hooked the reader in one sitting and provided him or her with an incentive to buy future issues. The majority of stories in magazines like *Overland Monthly* lent themselves to illustration. Consequently, demand for illustrations soared at the beginning of the 1890s. The older established periodicals had staff artists for illustration projects, but requests for so many pictures forced editors to review the portfolios of young, eager artists like Maynard Dixon.

A prolific school of writers chose to set their stories in the states and territories of the West, which still held the image and allure of a wild region inhabited by steely, rugged individuals. By the 1890s, the West was considerably tamer than the authors' stories, but the American public increasingly demanded "wild and woolly" adventures with dramatic pictures to stir the imagination. Together, authors and illustrators would create an American folklore centered on cowboys, Indians, pioneers, outlaws, and a large romanticized cast of characters. As the folklore grew, an increasingly larger group of artists became identified as purveyors of and creators of the "Old West." *Overland Monthly* noted this development in July 1895, feeling that Dixon had assumed the "mantle" of Frederic Remington. "The readers of the *Overland Monthly* are familiar with the work of Maynard Dixon, perhaps the coming rival of Frederic Remington. His hands are stuffed into his pockets; there is the usual quizzical expression on his face as he walks loose jointed across the plaza and into my view. He has made a national reputation by his designs for posters and cover designs."[2]

That same year, his cousin Will S. Green, editor of the *Colusa Sun*, introduced him to W. S. Leake, editor of the *San Francisco Morning Call* (changed to the *Call* in 1895), who offered Dixon his first regular salaried job—at ten dollars a week. There, he got to work with one of the West's legendary journalists, Wells Drury, who made his reputation on Nevada's turbulent Comstock Lode. Maynard's illustrations on western life for the *Call*'s Sunday supplement attracted immediate attention. In addition to the *Call*, San Francisco's other major newspapers, the *Chronicle* and the *Examiner*, issued Sunday magazine sections, all of them using stories, verse, and articles by local writers.

Whenever Dixon could escape from a publishing deadline, he visited cattle camps around Stockton, French Camp, and Union Island, drawing bronco busting, intoxicated cowboys at country dances, and other scenes of western life. At other times, Dixon traveled into California's foothill country near Nevada City, exploring Indian rancherias and sheep camps, producing drawings with pencil, pen and ink, or watercolor. Besides illustrating Sunday stories for the *Call*, he worked the "morgue detail." Newspaper-illustration staff members were expected to handle a great variety of subjects. In a single day, a newspaper artist might be assigned to sketch the details of an accident, depict the bride and groom at a society wedding, and, toward evening, furnish the sports page with views of a prizefight or a bicycle race. Beginners like Dixon, who could withstand the long hectic hours, discovered they could develop a facility for doing fast, accurate illustrations. However, he found some of the newspaper's assignments clashed with his personal ideals and Southerners' code of justice. He refused to accept "scandal stuff," astonishing his hardboiled fellow artists. They were even more astounded when he received a substantial salary raise. Subjected to the usual razzing and roughhouse pranks

12. *Charles F. Lummis,* 1897, pencil on paper, 12¹/₄ x 9³/₄ inches,
California History Section, California State Library

aimed at new "cubs" by the seasoned staff, Dixon developed his persona: sardonic, ribald, and nonconformist, anchored by an incisive wit that masked a sensitive, sometimes insecure personality.

In 1895, Dixon met an individual who played a major role in shaping the direction his life would take—Charles Fletcher Lummis. In January 1895, Lummis had assumed the editorship of *Land of Sunshine,* a magazine promoting Southern California; and under his energetic direction, the circulation began to increase, tapping into a new literary and cultural identity. Dixon credited Lummis as one of his two or three surrogate fathers, whose advice and ideas had a strong impact on his life. Lummis gathered a large following out of sheer exuberance, incessant activity, and undying fascination for the "Southwest," a term he helped popularize. Lummis excelled at anything he attempted — ethnographer, archaeologist, photographer, linguist, explorer, orator, folklorist, librarian, museologist, and conservationist—looming large in the intellectual history and heritage of the region. Among Lummis's many notable achievements was his tenure as the city editor of the *Los Angeles Times* and founder of the California Landmarks Club and the Sequoia League, one leading the fight to restore California missions, the other helping Native Americans protect their rights. He served five years as the city librarian of Los Angeles and created the Southwest Museum to recognize, interpret, and protect the artifacts and lifeways of Native American and Hispanic cultures.

Although small—only five feet six inches and one hundred thirty-five pounds— Lummis presented a sturdy appearance with a burning, ruddy complexion, large nose, and untamed short hair. His voice and gestures projected a flamboyant, vain personality. In prosperous times, Lummis owned two green corduroy suits, complemented with a red Pueblo sash boldly wrapped around his waist several times, Indian fashion. Lummis never seemed to be without a Stetson sombrero, enjoying them most when they achieved the patina of age, sweat, and use. His pockets often bulged with treasures: flint and steel (he detested matches), blue or red bandannas, a New Mexico hunting fetish, Bull Durham tobacco, brown paper, notebooks, arrowheads, and pamphlets. In August 1897, Dixon drew a pencil sketch of Lummis on one of his visits to San Francisco (fig. 12).

Writing and publishing became constant elements in Lummis's life; his reputation as a writer started with *A Tramp Across the Continent*, published in 1892, seven years after a legendary walk from Cincinnati, Ohio, to Los Angeles. Lummis covered 3,500 miles in 143 days, arriving in Los Angeles on February 1, 1885. He was greeted by Harrison Gray Otis, publisher of the *Los Angeles Times*, who promptly employed him as a city editor for the newspaper. The journey fashioned and shaped Lummis's ideas about "out west," which had a profound influence on his personal beliefs and social values. Many of the themes found in his later writings were conceived on this journey.

In 1893, two more publications appeared—*The Land of Poco Tiempo* and *The Spanish Pioneers*. In them, Lummis explored two of the major cultural influences of the Southwest—the Indian and Hispanic cultures—as he did in more than 450 books, monographs, articles, stories, and poems produced during his lifetime. In particular, Lummis struggled to make Americans aware of the Southwest's Spanish heritage, preaching the message of *poco tiempo*, "soon enough," a Spanish idiom meaning there is a time and place for everything. As historian Kevin Starr suggests, Lummis, a Harvard-trained Yankee, belonged to a generation of educated easterners seeking personal renewal through an imaginative relationship to the western region and to ideals of the frontier. Lummis avoided moderation in whatever he attempted, including his numerous extramarital affairs. Overwork, excessive drinking, and general dissipation while working as the city editor at the *Los Angeles Times* finally provoked a paralytic stroke, forcing him to retreat to the New Mexico frontier. He lived near Isleta, New Mexico, from 1888 to 1892, finding healing for emotional and physical suffering.

Lummis started the construction in 1895 of a stone-and-adobe hacienda in Pasadena, El Alisal, "place of the sycamore," named after the big tree which grew in the patio. He was helped by Isleta Indian artisans, but the home took nearly fifteen years to complete. Dixon designed the iron *rejas*, Lummis's personal brand, on the massive entrance door to El Alisal. Centered on a large patio with a pueblo-style fireplace, unique hand-framed windows, walls decorated with Navajo rugs and California paintings, El Alisal became a mecca for the leading artists and writers of the day. At social evenings — "noises" he called them — Lummis urged his guests to create a new cultural environment from the echoes of the Hispanic and Native American experience in a landscape touched by beauty. Mary Austin remembered she enjoyed and benefited from stimulation received in "the long, dark, barbaric hall." There is little doubt that Lummis influenced and guided Dixon's interest in the landscapes and culture of the Southwest.

Lummis had seen some of Dixon's drawings in the *Call* and *Overland Monthly*, and, on a business trip to San Francisco in June 1895, sought him out at his studio, asking him to contribute illustrations for *Land of Sunshine*. For over five years, the name L. Maynard Dixon would appear on the editorial page of *Land of Sunshine* as one of the magazine's three illustrators. The provocative, sometimes uneasy friendship that formed between the two men would last for thirty-three years until Lummis's death in 1928. Their numerous letters over the years would start with Lummis's salutation, "Dear Kid," or Dixon's "Dear Pop" or "Dear Boss." Lummis relished his surrogate-father status, giving Dixon counsel, advice, encouragement, and occasional cantankerous reprimands. Dixon considered Lummis an egotist who, on the one hand, championed young emerging writers and artists, including Sharlot Hall, Mary Austin, Ed Borein, Eugene Manlove Rhodes, and of course, Maynard Dixon, but would not let those talents compete with him. Lummis had an unimpeachable honesty of his own sort and worked hard and long on behalf of whatever causes he embraced. When he built El Alisal, with different levels and inadequate windows and no particular architectural style, Dixon thought it mirrored Lummis's intellectual eclecticism: part Spanish, part Indian, and part original Lummis. Both intrigued and influenced by Lummis's mysticism, Dixon sensed that Lummis understood the Native American better than anyone else he knew, although he felt Lummis acted out and capitalized on his eccentricities. Finally, Dixon was impressed with Lummis's numerous activities, his "power of mind over fatigue." For the rest of his life, he remembered Lummis telling him, "Do your damnedest. So live that you can look every damn man in the eye and tell him to go to hell. Sell drawings, but don't sell yourself."[3]

After Lummis departed for Los Angeles in the late summer of 1895, Dixon and his friend, painter Xavier Martinez, decided to visit Monterey, attracted by the picturesque but disappearing lifestyle of the old California ranchos and vaqueros. Monterey — its walled gardens, old adobes, vaqueros clattering through the streets, Spanish songs drifting on evening sea breezes — murmured memories of a past era. However, Martinez decided he should return to San Francisco and abruptly departed. Dixon, in agony from encounters with poison oak that grew in profusion among the chaparral, decided to remain. He wandered around Monterey, sketching the old adobes, vaqueros, and fishermen's camps. There, he met a young vaquero, Santiago, who took pity on him, making a brown tea of *yerba oso* and salt, which cured the poison oak in three days. Santiago then invited Dixon "down the coast" to help catch wild horses. "'Down the coast' is a saying in Monterey that attracts a stranger's attention," Dixon noted. "It is a far sad land, with a veil upon it which is not pierced by explanations. If anything is down the coast, that is all that need be said of it. You hear that down the coast is a place of pine trees and fog, and that there are two divisions of it: first, where there is a road, and second, where there is no road."[4]

13. *Vals de Monterey Viejo*, 1897, private collection

Santiago, youngest son of an old California family, had numerous brothers, uncles, and cousins, who among them held a large estate in Big Sur, decrepit with litigation. On a July morning in 1895, Santiago and Dixon started southward down the coast, riding and walking by turns. Wild long-horned cattle scattered on the rocky hillsides watched as Santiago and Dixon scrambled along the capricious trail grown over with sage, lupine, and chaparral. They crossed redwood-filled canyons where small streams dashed downward to the sea. Sometimes they encountered little ranches literally patched to the hillsides. As Dixon and Santiago headed south into the El Pais Grande de Sur, "big country to the south"—Big Sur and the Santa Lucia Range—the trail ran around the bare shoulders of the hills beside the rumbling sea. The hills ended abruptly in great bluffs, yellow and gray against the shimmering water, which seemed to reach away to nowhere. They stopped at the homestead of Don Demas, Santiago's older brother, who had built a house of homemade lumber, split from redwood in a nearby canyon beyond the hill. The home had one room, furnished with a table down the middle from door to door, a bench, two chairs, two beds, two guns, and a tangle of harness, tools, saddles, lumber, riatas, and deerskins. A band of wild horses and even wilder cattle flourished on the surrounding hills and in the deep canyons. Dixon remained there for a week or so, making drawings of Santiago and Don

Demas and a neighbor, Juan Pate, who arrived every evening for a game of cribbage. Juan Pate had hair and a moustache the color of dust and the quiet deliberate way of a man who could handle horses, He spoke Spanish like a Mexican, but his English betrayed an Irish background.

Dixon spent several days busting through dense chaparral, riding down steep dangerous slopes, following his friends and their pack of dogs as they pursued wild horses and cattle. He learned the ways of the California vaquero: a rushing blur of cow, man, horse, dog, rocks, and chaparral, punctuated by good-natured swearing and shouting. In late afternoons, Dixon and the others rested in the shade of a handy manzanita to escape the blazing sun, dozing and keeping watch over the silence of the great canyons below while the dogs whined and explored neighboring gullies for water. Pulling out a sketchbook, he recorded the day's events as the sun stood upon the western rim, sending long shadows into the hills and canyons. When Dixon returned to San Francisco, he was an expert rider, with an increased fluency in the Spanish language and an unqualified admiration for the Californio's lifestyle.

The *San Francisco Examiner* published an article in November 1895 on his Monterey and Big Sur trip. The article, "He Draws the Vaquero," the first widespread publicity his work had received, was illustrated with three Dixon drawings, one of them of Juan Pate astride a horse plunging down a steep slope. The *Examiner* prophetically forecast a positive future for the young artist:

> *Out on Jackson St., beyond Larkin, is the studio of L. M. Dixon, and in this studio many hours daily the young artist works. The studio is not unlike many others in appearance. To the visitor's eye it presents fairly well a picture that might be labeled "chaos" for there is a profusion of color to be seen scattered about with the most absolute disregard of order. There are sketches on the wall in water, charcoal, oil and some engravings tacked up, but not dignified by frame. Open drawers are jammed with studies or completed sketches, many of them of an excellence that does not vent such obscurity, and all of them giving great promise of what the young artist is certain to accomplish with years.*[5]

The years 1896 and 1897 saw Dixon accelerating production of black-and-white illustrations for numerous western adventure stories in *Overland Monthly*. During this time, he became involved with *The Lark*, the first issue of which appeared on May 1, 1895, sponsored by Market Street bookseller William Doxey and published by Gelett Burgess. Burgess belonged to a small group of nonconformists calling themselves Les Jeunes—translated loosely as "the Young"—a group that included sculptor and painter Bruce Porter; architect Willis Polk; printer and bohemian man-about-town Porter Garnett; artists Florence Lundborg, Arthur Atkins, and Ernest Peixotto; writer Carolyn Wells; and poet Yone Noguchi. Despite its diminutive size, the magazine proclaimed a lack of serious purpose, handsome but fragile Chinese bamboo-fiber paper pages, and a short two-year life, but it brought some novelty both in content and format to the publishing world: Gelett Burgess's little, round cartoon "Goops," and the famous verse

"I never saw a Purple Cow, I never hope to see one, But I can tell you anyhow, I'd rather see than be one" appeared on its pages.[6] "To sing a song, to tell a story" was its sole intent, and the little magazine succeeded." Dixon's pen-and-ink drawing of a vaquero playing a guitar, *Vals de Monterey Viejo* (fig. 13), appeared in the February 1897 issue of *The Lark*, accompanied by a ballad he had collected during the Monterey excursion.

A thunderbird, which would become Dixon's trademark sign, now started to appear on his drawings and watercolors at this time. At first, the thunderbird was merely an extension of his signature, then an extension of his personality, and finally a personal totem. Dixon had also started wearing cowboy boots and a ten-gallon hat, a uniform developed to satisfy his public. Not that the cowboy outfit was a poseur's statement, it reflected Dixon's independent spirit, anchored by strong beliefs about what the West or, for that matter, what Maynard Dixon should mean to people.

Aware of Dixon's increasing reputation as an artist and illustrator, the Mark Hopkins Institute of Art invited him to exhibit several drawings, watercolors, and posters, produced as illustrations for *Overland Monthly*, in their 1896 annual exhibit. During the 1890s, there was no distinction between illustration art and fine art. San Francisco's newspapers and periodicals art rooms served as the training ground for a group of cartoonists and illustrators who would later become nationally known artists, among them Homer Davenport, James Swinnerton, Harrison Fisher, Gordon Ross, Rubin (Rube) Goldberg, Henry Nappenbach, Arthur Cahill, Dan Sweeney, Ernest Peixotto, Gertrude Partington, and Grace Hudson.

In early 1897, Dixon received a commission to illustrate two books written by eastern writer Verner Z. Reed. These romanticized mythological tales of the West, *Lo-To-Kah* and *Tales of the Sun-Land*, together contained twenty-nine full-page, black-and-white gouache illustrations. Included in *Tales of the Sun-Land* was *The Cavern of the Dead* (fig. 14). His first book illustrations gave him exposure to a national audience. Lummis criticized *Tales of the Sun-Land* in a review in *The Land of Sunshine*, thinking it "ignorant and pretentious, . . . the one excellence of the book is the illustration, by L. Maynard Dixon, a San Francisco lad of twenty-two. There are anachronisms; but most of his pictures are very effective—and they show remarkable growth over his earlier work."[7] Encouraged by Lummis's support, Dixon continued to increase his production of drawings and watercolors during 1897 and 1898, particularly for *Overland Monthly* stories, including Mary Halleck Foote's article, "The Borrowed Shift," and Charles Howard Shinn's "Northern California Gold Fields." Among the illustrations he made for articles in *Land of Sunshine* were several drawings for George Parker Winship's "The Story of Coronado," which appeared in June 1898.

Searching for other ways of expressing his feelings, Dixon began to write poetry. One of his first poems was the rambling "World's End," which he wrote in 1896 using a lofty, romantic style typical of the era. Lummis reproduced the poem in *Land of Sunshine* in August 1898, as "At the Land's End."

FACING: 14. *The Cavern of the Dead*, 1896, gouache on paper, 10¹/₂ x 6¹/₈ inches, photograph courtesy of Garzoli Gallery

I stand upon the shore of my release;
Out into the immeasurable west;
Far over, down into eternal Space,
Is spread the great blue shining sea of Peace,
Far-glimmering in deep unshaken rest;
A shimmering sleep upon her sunlit face.
The brown and fierce-frowed hills stand bare and bar
The sky's bright rim along the silent east;
And here the yearning land outreaches far
To take the glad sea in his shining arms;
A thousand ages these wan sands
Have shone where men have dared to build few hopes,
Bent like a bow of death between God's hands.

Among the jumble hills sly savages
With keen-cut eyes go wandering in the thorn;
With thirst- and hunger-sharpened sense they steal
Their victual of despair 'tween night and morn, —
And men of stronger hearts appeared. — Forlorn
They came, — who knows through what unspoken pains?
Gauntly they saw with desert-saddened eyes
This sea that reached to Nothing . . . Others built
And taught and tilled, and passes; but This remains.
And over all the vast and hollow skies
Of infinite tenderness from their deep mouth
Vibrate the Song of Silence; and the drouth
Bears hard upon the land and mummifies
These death-contorted ranges of the south.

I am a city's wan unwilling guest;
With three good friends, — a dog, a horse, a gun,
Would I might wander where the great Southwest
Lies throbbing with the pulses of the sun,
And waiting silent with her warm brown breast
Turned up to him; where gray Time for a span
Has dropped the seasons . . . She awaits the best
Soul-singing thought of some great silent man.[8]

Lummis encouraged Dixon to explore poetry as a way to expand his personal vision. "You are really about as much a poet as an artist and that is one reason your pictures are the fine things they are. It will do you good not merely to get them off your mind, but through your mind. Every poem you write is a help to a picture that you paint."[9] Dixon's poetry elaborated deeply held beliefs about important matters: nature, the western landscape, particularly the desert, sexual and romantic passion, and the Native American. A romantic naïveté marked his verse initially; but by 1910, the poems appeared with increasing frequency, showing flashes of insight and emotional depth as Dixon confronted, among other things, a changing West, the emergence after 1915 of the modern art movement, and the erosion of what he considered important American values. Few of his poems appeared in magazines, newspapers, or books. Most were closely held private thoughts and served as an extension for his art or confessionals about his life. The poems varied in subject matter and style. They explored nature, protest, love, and nostalgia, and for several years, between 1915 and 1918, pondered the difference between life and death as Dixon confronted difficult personal problems.

The closing year of the nineteenth century—*fin-de-siècle*, as it was called in the local and national press—brought material prosperity to San Francisco and vitality to its cultural life. Two events contributed to an expansion of work for local writers and artists. One was the discovery of gold in the Klondike in 1896, which prompted thousands of people to outfit and pass through San Francisco on their way to the far north. The other was the outbreak of the Spanish-American War in 1898, which brought a steady stream of men and war supplies into the crowded seaport, bound for the Philippines. San Francisco grew and prospered. Row after row of sun-catching, bay-windowed dwellings spread over the sand hills beyond Van Ness Avenue into the Mission District and toward Twin Peaks, while in the business district, more substantial buildings replaced modest wooden and brick structures erected in the 1850s and 1860s. An increasing pall of dirty smoke marked the emerging industrial area south of Market Street. But despite this rapid expansion, a newly awakened public interest in art and literature, along with the emergence of numerous talented writers, poets, painters, sculptors, actors, and musicians created an exuberant renaissance in the city. "Pre-fire San Francisco," declared Will Irwin in his book *The City That Was*, "was the gayest, lightest-hearted, most pleasurable loving city in the western continent and in many ways the most interesting and romantic."[10]

Besides providing numerous illustrations for *Overland Monthly*, Dixon's work appeared with increasing regularity in the *San Francisco Call* during 1898 and 1899. He worked at the newspaper's 315-foot-high, steel-frame building at Third and Market Streets or in his Pine Street Studio (fig. 15). Once he created a small watercolor of his small room (fig. 16). Dixon produced illustrations for full-page Sunday feature stories along with assignments to the "morgue detail," covering court trials, society events, prizefights, and the violence among the bars and brothels of the city's Barbary Coast waterfront. A sampling of his drawings and watercolors for stories in the newspaper reflected a wide range of topics: the Spanish-American War (especially in the Philippines), a Chinese New Year, Mexico's Seri Indians, the Klondike gold rush, the first missionaries to enter Tibet, San Francisco's fascination with Chinatown and anti-Chinese sentiment, and cowboys, cattle rustling, and outlaws. San Francisco still placed one foot in the Old West, the other in the rising turn-of-the century aestheticism and interest in world affairs. Often he illustrated fiction articles such as "The Shipwreck" by Gertrude Atherton. Dixon also did the illustrations for Rudyard Kipling's jingoistic hymn to American

Above: 15. *Pine Street Studio*,
1898, private collection

Right: 16. *The Corner of the
Room*, 1898, watercolor on paper,
12³/₄ x 9¹/₂ inches,
W. Donald Head,
Old Grandview Ranch

imperialism in the Philippines, "The White Man's Burden," published by the *Call* in February 1899. There was one sad interruption in his work when he learned his father had died in the state hospital at San Jose on August 27, 1898.

Dixon apparently started to experiment with serious oil painting during this time, although long erratic hours at the *Call*'s art room and freelance illustration work kept painting efforts to a minimum. Several art styles overlapped during the 1890s and into the early years of the twentieth century. Artists like Thomas Hill, painter of grandiose canvases of Yosemite, and William Keith, whose serene paintings celebrated the grandeur of California's natural beauty, still flourished alongside painters with Munich and Barbizon styles. Arthur F. Mathews' California decorative style was prominent, and there were even hesitant approaches to the new and radical impressionism. Many artists like Xavier Martinez, intrigued with California's distinctive coloration and exceptional light, also worked in tonalism, a painting style rooted in an idealism drawn from the experience of nature, which favored intimate expressive themes in a limited color scale with delicate light effects creating suggestive moods. Dixon did oil paintings between 1897 and 1900, but few have surfaced. If his watercolors are an indication, the paintings probably reflected the tonalist style favored by many California artists. Most of his work was in pen and ink or crayon such as *Hopi Girl* (fig. 17).

Lummis, more interested in Dixon's progress as an illustrator than in his paintings,

17. *Hopi Girl*, 1898, crayon on paper, 9¹/₂ x 8¹/₂ inches, private collection

offered a critical review of his work in the December 1898 issue of *Land of Sunshine*:

> A man who can do much work as this at twenty-three, and between the upper and
> nether millstones of newspaper routine, has a right to knock with some confidence
> at the door of the future. The striking development in Dixon's work within the last
> two years is of deeper import than even its present standard. To have widened so in
> feeling, as well as in technique, with so little time and so much of disadvantage,
> puts him in an uncommon category; and to draw such figures at any stage of life's
> game is quite as rare. . . .

18. *Hopi Ceremonial,* 1899, mixed media on paper, 12 x 14 inches, private collection

Mr. Dixon's largest talent has to do with humanity and the horse. He paints and draws good landscapes; but is at his strongest in type and drawing action. The subjoined studies of the northern California Indians—particularly "the bride"—are admirable work, good "art," and (what is rarer and even more important in this case) good truth. There are so many who can show us, most artistically, how they think an Indian or a Mexican or any other picturesque type ought to look; so few who seem able to portray him as he does look. And when one pretends to represent a racial type, the first duty of art is truthfulness. The second is to translate the face into forms of grace, without losing the typical character.

Mr. Dixon's place should be as an illustrator of Western books. Not a tenth of the New York artists who now practically monopolizes this work—who draws things they never saw and know nothing about—show either his conscientiousness or his spirit, to say nothing of his familiarity. Remington, Lungren, and a very few other Eastern illustrators who have learned their West in fact, have a right to draw Western illustrations; but I know few artists in the United States who have shown that they could satisfy the type so fully; while none of them need be ashamed of the vitality of the drawing in these figures. An artist so young and already so distinctive will, it seems to me "bear watching."[11]

Journalism and the illustration arts flourished in turn-of-the-century San Francisco. The city's major newspapers competed fiercely with each other, and all of them—the *Call, Examiner, Chronicle,* and the *Bulletin*—tried to employ the best writers and illustrators. For over a decade Dixon would supply countless illustrations for all four publications, such as *Hopi Ceremonial* (fig. 18) and several in an article about the Chinese New Year (fig. 19) for the *Call.* Sin, crime, corruption, politics, and the public's growing fascination in Western outlaws, Indians, cowboys, or, for that matter, anything that smacked of sensationalism drove editorial decisions and any story that would give a newspaper the edge. Mining tycoon George Hearst had presented his son, William Randolph, with the *Examiner* as a gift; young Hearst took journalism seriously, much to the public's surprise and to the other San Francisco newspapers' alarm. In August 1899, lured by Hearst's offer of nearly double his salary at the *Call,* Dixon accepted the position as art director of the *San Francisco Examiner Sunday Magazine,* working in the Hearst Building on the corner of Market and Third streets or in his studio at 2311 Jackson Street. The *Examiner* seemed like a hectic madhouse, inhabited by talented young people like Dixon, drunk

19. *Joy of the Chinese New Year,* February 12, 1899, California History Section, California State Library

on life. The *Examiner*'s frenetic pace with constant deadlines and flashy emotionalism forced Dixon to work virtually nonstop. Through Hearst's relentless pursuit of news and his promotion of the paper as the "Monarch of the Dailies," the *Examiner* appeared a never-ending source of fury and sounds, part pirate ship and part three-ring circus. Reporters and illustrators darted in and out of the offices at all times in fierce pursuit of stories that would produce the newspaper's coveted benchmark, the "gee-whiz." Readers were expected to exclaim "Gee-Whiz!" when they saw the front page, "Holy Moses!" when they turned to the second page, and "God-Almighty!" as they encountered the third page.[12]

During the next year, Dixon created numerous illustrations for the magazine, frequently full-page and sometimes reproduced in the new color process printing.

When Hearst wanted talent, he simply bought it, staffing the *Examiner* with the best reporters, editors, and illustrators he could find, including Bud Fisher, creator of "Mutt and Jeff"; Winifred Black ("Annie Laurie"), who offered advice to the lovelorn; Arthur McEwen, militant muckraker, who wrote editorials with an acid pen; Ambrose Bierce, whose column was both eagerly awaited and dreaded; and Frank Norris, who died young at thirty-two in 1902 but left noted books like *McTeague* and *The Octopus* as powerful examples of his writing. In addition, Hearst employed Edwin Markham, best known for *The Man with a Hoe and Other Poems*, who, as he sketched out this famous poem that the *Examiner* printed on January 15, 1899, was encouraged by Dixon, who shouted suggestions across the noisy pressroom. James G. Swinnerton, another illustrator at the *Examiner*, became one of his lifelong friends. Employed as a cartoonist at age seventeen for the *Examiner*, Swinnerton first drew weather cartoons featuring a little California grizzly. He eventually became nationally known for several cartoon series—"Little Jimmy," "Canyon Kiddies," and "Little Tiger,"—and for his desert paintings.

As Dixon's fame spread, many Bay Area writers clamored for him to illustrate their books or articles. Jack London, a vigorous, brash young writer on the edge of his fabulous career, wrote to his friend Cloudesley Johns, "The Overland has taken a fancy to my Northland tales. The Son of the Wolf was sent to them a week ago; they will have it out in the April number, if possible, illustrated by Dixon. I have seen some of his Indian work and think he's just the man for my types; but I do not know him."[13] Dixon, in fact, painted several gouache illustrations for London's three Malamute Kid short stories, "Men of Forty Mile," "In a Far Country," and "Son of the Wolf," which appeared in the April, May, and June 1899 issues of *Overland Monthly*. London did meet Dixon shortly thereafter. In a letter to San Francisco writer Elwyn Hoffman, he asked, "So you have met Maynard Dixon. What do you make of him? I have only met him a couple of times, and those times perfunctorily. While I liked him at once, I at the same time drew the conclusion that he was sort of hyper-sensitive. Did he strike you in this way?"[14] London was perceptive about Dixon's personality. By 1900, he had emerged from San Francisco's artists and writer's community as a colorful and complex individual. He was also one of the most respected and admired illustrators in the West by then, pursued by noted writers as well as by those authors on the threshold of fame.

In April, Houghton Mifflin published Jack London's first book, a collection of *Overland Monthly* stories titled *Son of the Wolf*. Dixon furnished the frontispiece. His drawings and watercolors appeared as illustrations for the *Examiner*, bringing additional recognition. Among his illustrations for articles in that newspaper during 1900 was one on "Liver-Eating" Johnson, famous Indian fighter and mountain man who had recently died in California; a depiction of the rescue of Guaymas, Mexico, from filibusters; and several watercolors for a lengthy story, "He Was The Wildest Man in All the West," about Bert Alford, a noted Arizona lawman turned outlaw.

Whenever possible, Dixon entered his art in local exhibitions, including three Spanish-American War images originally drawn for the *Examiner* and submitted to the 1899 winter exhibition of the San Francisco Art Association. In March 1899, he joined San Francisco's Press Club, and several of his works were shown in the club's annual exhibition. Searching for improvement in his compositions, Dixon started reading the European art periodicals, particularly *Jugend* and *Simplicissimus*, with their emphasis on current art developments, studying how Europe's leading artists conceived of and composed their images. When 1900 arrived, Dixon decided to expand his exhibition schedule, in particular to participate in the twice-yearly exhibitions of the San Francisco Art Association. He submitted a watercolor of a California Indian, three newspaper illustrations, and a design for a magazine cover to the association's first exhibition of the century. However, the high-pressure atmosphere at Hearst's *Examiner*, and long, hectic work hours discouraged him to the point that he complained, "Only large doses of clean and far-off desert could restore my health." Perhaps he should "go East to see the West." "Dear Boss," he wrote Lummis on May 26, 1900, "I quit the Examiner to-morrow and will be with you toward the end of the month."[15]

Dixon's comment about "going East to see the West" was well within the context of new thinking about the region. By the end of the century, a small part of the restless tide settled along the continent's western edge began drifting eastward into the desert regions; some sought conquest through mining or irrigation or building railroads, while others longed for escape from civilization, searching for a new American spirit. A desert literature emerged, shaped by the intense encounters of some exceptional individuals with an arid domain: John Charles Van Dyke's *The Desert* (1901), Idah Meacham Strobridge's *In Miners Mirage Land* (1904), George Wharton James's *The Wonders of the Colorado Desert* (1906), and *The Land of Little Rain* (1903) by Mary Austin, who stood apart in her power to convey the land's spiritual feeling.

East away from the Sierras, south from Panamint and Amargosa, east and south many an uncounted mile, is the Country of Lost Borders. Ute, Paiute, Mojave, and Shoshone inhabit its frontiers, and as far into the heart of it as a man dare go. Not the law, but the land sets the limit. Desert is the name it wears upon the maps, but the Indian's is the better word. Desert is a loose term to indicate land that supports no man; whether the land can be bitted and broken to that purpose is not proven. Void of life it never is, however dry the air and villainous the soil. This is the nature of that county. There are hills, rounded, blunt, burned, squeezed up out of chaos, chrome and vermilion painted, aspiring to the snowline. Between the hills lie high level-looking plains full of intolerable sun glare, or narrow valleys drowned in a blue haze. The hill surface is streaked with ash drift and black, unweathered lava flows. After rains water accumulates in the hollows of small closed valleys, and, evaporating, leaves hard dry levels of pure desertness that get the local name of dry lakes. Where the mountains are steep and the rains heavy, the pool is never quite dry, but dark and bitter, rimmed about with the efflorescence of alkaline deposits. A thin crust of it lies along the marsh over the vegetating area, which has neither beauty nor freshness. In the broad wastes open to the wind the sand drifts in hummocks about the stubby shrubs, and between them the soil shows saline traces. The sculpture of the hills here is more wind than water work, though the quick storms do sometimes scar them past many a year's redeeming. In all the Western

20. *Sycamores, El Alisal,* 1900, pencil and charcoal on paper,
9 ¹/₂ x 12 inches, private collection

desert edges there are essays in miniature at the famed, terrible Grand Cañon, to
which, if you keep on long enough in this country, you will come at last.[16]

The desert literati would soon be followed by artists attracted to the special challenges
of barren landscapes, stark mesas and buttes, and a limitless horizon. California artists
like Carl Eytel, Conrad Buff, Victor Clyde Forsythe, and James Swinnerton would paint
in the southern California deserts, while numerous other painters in and around Santa Fe
and Taos drew their inspiration from the clarity and forms of New Mexico's landscapes.
Dixon was among the first of the twentieth-century American artists to discover that the
West's arid lands lacked neither beauty nor power to inform the spiritually perceptive.
Like Mary Austin, he came to believe people were tied to their environment, and those
who had lost this basic contact could resurrect and renew themselves through close
observation of lives lived harmoniously as part of the land.

When Dixon arrived at El Alisal (fig. 20) in mid-May 1900, he excitedly started
preparations for a lengthy trip through Arizona and New Mexico. During the next two
weeks, Lummis offered suggestions on various routes and wrote introductions to people
who could assist him in his travels.

THREE

Going East to See the West
1900—1907

O n a hot June day in 1900, twenty-five-year-old Dixon crossed the Colorado River at Needles, California, leaving a temporal home and entering a spiritual place important in his struggle to express his personal vision (fig. 21). For seven years, Dixon had illustrated a West that he had never encountered firsthand. This first journey into the Southwest initiated a long search for the understanding of a region—a place of challenge, inspiration, and, ultimately in the last years of his life, refuge. Lummis sent him off with this prediction in *Land of Sunshine:* "L. Maynard Dixon, for some time chief artist of the *San Francisco Examiner,* and by odds the most promising illustrator on this coast, has gone out to grow in the waiting country—the New Mexico and Arizona which are such bonanzas for the artist but bonanzas almost untouched. He is likely to do good over there. His striking power, which grows rapidly and soundly, is directly in line for a material there wonderfully abundant, picturesque and worthy. It

21. *Maynard Dixon,* May 1900,
private collection

is the first time this young, earnest and competent illustrator has gone to the Mother Lode. It will be a wonder if he does not 'strike it rich.'"[1] When Dixon crossed over the Colorado River to Arizona in 1900, he would discover that out in the desert where the

The Centre of Creation at 122° in the Shade

Fort Mohave, Ariz.

22. *The Centre of Creation at 122 Degrees in the Shade,*
1900, pencil on paper, 10½ x 8 inches,
collection of Drs. Mark and Kathleen Sublette

winds never stop the defining revelation that the landscape had the power to inform the spiritually perceptive.

Dixon first stopped at Fort Mojave along the Colorado River, eighteen miles northwest of Needles. Originally a military post built in 1859 to protect travelers from Indian depredations, the post lay abandoned by 1890; subsequently, some of the buildings had been taken over by Ben Spear, who established a trading post (fig. 22). By 1900, Spear, a seventy-five-year-old, white-bearded, soft-spoken individual, had lived at Fort Mojave for over thirty-five years. After Dixon arrived on the daily mail wagon from Needles, Spear invited him to stay and use the trading post as a base while exploring the surrounding area. Dixon asked Spear to help him establish contact with the Mojave Indians. The Mojave, largest of the Yuman-speaking groups along the Colorado River, then lived in an intersection of humid, narrow river bottom and a surrounding arid landscape of mesquite, cactus, and greasewood. Cane, arrowroot, thick groves of willow, and large cottonwoods grew in and along the edge of the Colorado River floodplain. In July and August, the heat could be staggering, often reaching 120 degrees. Mojave life centered on farming the floodplain but was augmented with fishing, hunting, native plant foraging, and selling their crafts to tourists passing through Needles.

Each morning before the heat descended, Dixon would arrange his sketching materials on a small table under the post's big overhanging roof and, before long, Mojave individuals would appear. Introducing himself, he would shake their hands and then invite them to sit in a chair where he could sketch them. Most of the Mojave liked to pose, particularly when offered twenty-five cents for a sitting. When sketching

23. *Desert Ranges, Roberts Ranch,* 1900, pencil on paper,
8 x 10 inches, private collection

24. *Roberts Ranch,* 1900, pencil on paper, 8 x 11 inches, private collection

individuals, he used heavy paper, a soft lead pencil, and white chalk; he identified each subject on the drawing with a simple phonetic rendering of his or her name, the date, and the location. Sometimes he added his thunderbird design. Dixon made numerous portraits of the Mojave men and women who frequented the trading post. The Mojave at this time wore Anglo clothing but still retained ancient customs such as face-painting, chin-tattooing, and shoulder-length hair. In his portraits, the striking features and steady calm gaze of the Mojave render them both powerful and sensitive, creating poignant ethnographic and documentary images of people forced to live in a rapidly changing world but determined to retain their identity. Dixon made over thirty portrait sketches of Mojave Indians at Fort Mojave, sending two of the drawings to Lummis, who eventually published them in the September 1901 issue of *Land of Sunshine*.

Occasionally, Dixon borrowed Ben Spear's buggy on an early morning before the heat arrived, riding down into the Colorado River bottomlands to visit and sketch among the Mojave, then perhaps going over to the ranch of John Roberts, drawing cowhands, ranch buildings, and the arid landscape bordering the river (figs. 23 and 24). Once he went as far as Black Mountain, some fifteen miles out of Fort Mojave. "I find the country full of good stories, a few of which I cribbed. I went up to the mines, and back into the east range and down again with the ore-teams. . . . Though it is too hellish hot to chase much—but my brush don't hanker after much here but Indians."[2]

As hot afternoons brought life to a standstill, Spear entertained Dixon with exciting stories about the old days when Mojave City served as a steamboat destination, catering to the needs of soldiers and miners. Spear showed him the bullet holes along the outside of the trading post, telling how the store was sometimes used for target practice by bored miners. Dixon was thrilled with the sights he had seen: "Arizona—The magic name of a land bright and mysterious, of sun and sand, of tragedy and stark endeavor. So long had I dreamed of it that when I came there it was not strange to me. Its sun was my sun, its ground my ground."[3] These early visits to Arizona with its remoteness, dramatic landscapes, antiquities, and Indian cultures were like traveling to an exotic and distant port of call for Dixon.

After completing some final drawings around the Fort Mojave trading post, Dixon took the mail wagon down to Needles, then went on to Prescott. The business district of Prescott had recently burned, and the place buzzed like a new mining camp, with stores, banks, saloons, and gambling places doing a thriving business under raw pine boards and canvas. Artists were rare in turn-of-the-century Arizona, Dixon recalled. "In those days in Arizona being an artist was something you just had to endure—or be smart enough to explain why. It was incomprehensible that you were just out 'seeing the country.' If you were not working for the railroad, considering real estate or scouting for a mining company what the hell were you? The drawings I made were no excuse and I was regarded as a wandering lunatic."[4]

At Lummis's suggestion, Dixon stopped and visited Sharlot Hall and her father, James Hall, at their orchard ranch, fifteen miles southeast of Prescott. Hall, who came to Arizona in 1882, had started gaining recognition as a poet through Lummis's encouragement and publication of her poems in *Land of Sunshine*. During the evenings,

James Hall told him rambling tales of life on the old frontier, increasing Dixon's inventory of character sketches and stories of a disappearing West. "Miss Hall," Dixon wrote to Lummis, "is one worth knowing. Next time you buy some port have a gallon sent to Mrs. J. K. Hall and charge to my account."[5]

He spent a week sketching in the area, and upon leaving, he presented an inscribed sketch of a cowboy on a running horse to Sharlot Hall. The sketch hung on her bedroom wall for years. Dixon did not stay long with the Halls, and he never returned, but the visit left him with indelible memories.

The Agua Fria Valley near Prescott was Dixon's first look at mesa and benchland country. The grassland valley had suffered through four years of drought. "The country looks like hell," he remarked, "dead cattle everywhere—punchers gone

25. *Montezuma's Castle*, 1900,
pencil on paper, 10 3/8 x 7 3/4 inches, private collection,
photograph courtesy of Medicine Man Gallery

out or gone to mining; all the infallible streams and springs gone dry, farmers on the verge of starvation." Even though the rains had started to return with the dark drama of cloudbursts, the grasslands still sported mummified cattle carcasses. The valley gave him his first experience with carefree Texas cowboys—"rim fire" saddles, tied rope, batwing chaps—different from the vaqueros he rode with in the San Joaquin Valley. One of his drawings shows a cowpuncher on a tired-looking horse, gazing down at a dead steer. Dixon named it *Drouth* and submitted it to *Harper's Weekly*. The editor returned it with the comment, "not serious enough."[6]

Leaving Hall's ranch, Dixon went on to the mining town of Jerome, which perched precariously on the side of Mingus Mountain—"about played out," he thought—then rode down the Verde Valley's long rift to Old Camp Verde. From there, he walked to the ruins of prehistoric Montezuma's Castle (silly name, he thought) (fig. 25) above the Verde River. Crawling through tiny rooms cut in cream-colored cliffs, picking up pieces of pottery around the ruins and at nearby Montezuma's Well, Dixon dreamed of a far and forgotten past, sensing dim Indian ghosts around him. "I knew them again at old

26. *Phoenix*, 1900, pencil on paper, 10 x 14 inches, private collection

27. *Phoenix, Arizona Territory,*
1900, pencil on paper, 6¹/₂ x 6 inches,
private collection

28. *Tempe, Arizona,*
1900, pencil on paper, 7 x 8¹/₂ inches,
private collection

Oraibi, at Walpi, at Mishongnovi, at Shipaulovi and at silent Betatakin—and through them I have reached to something I cannot name, yet more than half believe. Somehow, it seems, you may not understand Indians until you make friends with the ghosts."[7] Some Tonto Apache, fierce hawk-faced people from the chaparral, lived near Old Camp Verde. The local storekeeper cautioned Dixon to avoid their camps, so he made quick sketches from a safe distance. He told Lummis in a letter, "the Verde Valley is a great thing to paint, but it would take a couple of weeks of settled down works to get at it. The Tonto are a dead hard game but I managed to sneak a few little sketches around the store."[8]

29. *Pima Village*, 1900, pencil on paper, 9¹/₂ x 13³/₄ inches, private collection

30. *Isleta, New Mexico*, 1900, pencil on paper, 9³/₄ x 12¹/₂ inches, private collection

In middle August, Dixon made his way into Phoenix, torrid in its irrigated valley, but arrived broke and had to send a telegram to Lummis: "Send check to Phoenix I am busted."[9] Dixon called Phoenix "Chihuahua Town," and it was not a particularly great city in his opinion (fig. 26). Most of the buildings were adobe, but brick buildings were sprouting, and the city boasted a population of over 5,000 and an electric streetcar system. Still, Phoenix seemed colorful and vibrant with wagons, buggies, and saddled horses tied next to awnings on the streets. Pima, Papago, and Maricopa Indians, arrayed in bright silks and calicos, lounged along the sidewalks (fig. 27), while cowboys, miners, and adventurers swaggered in and out of saloons. Dixon found it difficult to get acquainted, even though he tried "chumming with the town dads and drinking at the best saloons." Attracted by Arizona's Hispanic and Indian cultures, he moved over to nearby Tempe, where he made numerous drawings of the people and their dwellings (fig. 28). Dixon stayed in the residents' homes for several days, enjoying their simple hospitality, and in the starlit evenings they taught him to sing Spanish songs. It was an indolent, sentimental existence, oriented to half-fabulous tales of ancient days.

Dixon made his first Sonoran Desert camp near Sacaton on the Pima Reservation, where he confronted the saguaro cactus (fig. 29). "Close to my bed stood the tall shaft of one devoid of branches. All the long sleepless night it dominated me, a dark finger of doubt pointing ominously forever upward into an unknowable universe of stars."[10] Nor would he forget the sight of a Pima Indian riding a pony down a gentle slope, looking straight into the descending sun, clad only in an undershirt stretched tight over the great arch of his chest, his long gray hair hanging straight down his back, not bothering to look at Dixon as he rode by. In a letter to writer Elwyn Hoffman, Dixon declared, "For me it has been for the past two months a checkered layout of Indians, cactus, rocks, sunlight, antiquities, mesas, Mexicans, adobes, Spanish songs—and salt pork . . . and tomorrow I start for the goal, Isleta, New Mexico."[11] In mid-September, Dixon left Phoenix to meet Lummis at Ashfork, west of Flagstaff. There they boarded an eastbound Santa Fe train for Albuquerque, New Mexico. From there they rode on a rented buggy down the dusty road to the Tiwa-speaking pueblo of Isleta (fig. 30)—where Lummis had stayed while he

31. *Old Barracks, Santa Fe, New Mexico,* 1900,
pencil on paper, 7 x 9¼ inches, private collection

recovered from his stroke—located on the west bank of the Rio Grande, a dozen miles
south of Albuquerque.

The town revolved around a large plaza, surrounded by clear-standing, one-story
homes. A Spanish colonial church, San Antonio de Padua, anchored the plaza. While
Lummis lived at Isleta, the pueblo's leader, Juan Rey Abieta, had sponsored and protected
him. The Abieta family still held a notable position in the community by 1900. They
also extended a welcome and friendship to Dixon, who was eager to document the daily
life activities of Isleta's inhabitants. Both Dixon and Lummis knew Isleta culture would
change in the future. With pencil, crayon, watercolor, and oil, Dixon depicted religious
rituals, hunting, games, house and church architecture, and the pueblo's social life in
a quick illustrational style, all with strict attention to ethnographic detail. Since women
performed many of the tasks, a large proportion of his Isleta pictures illustrate women's
roles: portraits of unmarried women with their hair in wrapped buns; other women
preparing food in their kitchens, weaving on backstrap looms, or making pottery. While
Dixon stayed at Isleta, he made numerous pencil and crayon drawings, some large pastels,
and a few oil paintings, "not very good," he thought. When Lummis left for Los Angeles,
Dixon decided to visit Santa Fe, where he made drawings of the city's architecture as he
wandered the quiet, history-filled streets, savoring an ancient past (fig. 31). Afterwards,
he returned to Isleta and, in mid-November, departed for San Francisco. Just before

he left, one of Juan Rey Abeita's daughters, braving the wrath of the community, presented him with a rare and sacred katchina.

Back in San Francisco, Dixon resumed working for the *Examiner* but was abruptly fired when the newspaper suspected he was considering the *Call*'s offer to return to that competitor. Most important, until 1900 Dixon had illustrated a West he had not seen first-hand. Now excited by the experiences from his recent travels, his work grew in range, strength, and vibrant realism. Undaunted by his termination, he produced numerous illustrations for articles in the local newspapers, including *Murrieta's Gold* (fig. 32).

32. *Murrieta's Gold*, 1901,
California History Section, California State Library

But in May 1901, uncomfortable with his personal life and hearing the call of desert lands again, he decided to accompany his friend Edward Borein, who wanted to head for Montana on horseback. "I am dammed glad we are going," he told Lummis. "I have been through one particular kind of hell continuously ever since I got home. There was a girl in it. That accounts for my trance."[12] Leaving from Oakland on May 6, 1901, Borein and Dixon averaged twenty-five miles a day until they reached Echo Summit in the Sierra Nevada, where they struggled through melting snowdrifts six to nine feet deep. Exhausted, Dixon and Borein decided to rest their horses in Carson City, Nevada, for several days. "We have sumptuous lodging in a box stall, which is preferable to any hotels in sight. This kind of traveling is just to my liking. This is a hell of a country, judging by Ormsby County . . . gray sagebrush flats and ranges. We go to Reno tomorrow from where we'll learn how and where first to strike the ranges. Borein is a good traveling companion and teacher. I may in time even learn to throw a square hitch."[13]

From Reno, the two artists traveled north along the eastern fringes of California's

LEFT:
33. *Alturas*,
1901, pencil on paper,
5 1/8 x 4 1/2 inches,
private collection

BELOW LEFT:
34. *Coleman, Oregon*,
1901, pencil on paper,
6 1/8 x 4 1/2 inches,
private collection

BELOW RIGHT:
35. *Coleman, Oregon*, 1901,
pencil on paper,
6 x 4 1/2 inches,
private collection

Lassen and Modoc counties and into the Warner Valley. At a frontier trial in Alturas, California—actually a murder trial, the result of a "neck tie party" which left four men dead—old rawhiders from remote ranches and lonely canyons had descended upon the town from all directions. "Partisan feeling ran high," Dixon recalled. "There were more real old-timers there than I ever expect to see together in one place again—long haired ones too."[14] Strangers in town, Dixon and Borein did not risk many sketches, although Dixon did some from a discreet distance (fig. 33).

After spending several weeks at spring roundups in the Warner Valley, where he and Borein had their first exposure to large-scale cattle operations at the JJ and Long's ranches, they headed north into southeastern Oregon toward Coleman (figs. 34 and 35). Working their way through the sagebrush ocean of Oregon's high desert country, they spent two long summer months at isolated ranches in the Steen and Alvord mountains, places like the P Ranch, Buena Vista Ranch, Harper Ranch, and Hill Camp, finally stopping at Vale, Oregon. Dixon and Borein stayed longest at the P Ranch, finding the ranch corrals full of just-captured wild range horses being roped and branded, a scene of dust and turmoil: legs broken, gates smashed, riatas snapped. There, Dixon made rapid pencil sketches, trying to capture the frenzied action. This was buckaroo country, where cowboys wore wooly chaps instead of batwing chaps, and Dixon drew an image of one he called *Oregon Cowboy* (fig. 36).

36. *Oregon Cowboy,* 1901, pencil and pen-and-ink on paper, 18 x 23¹/₄ inches, private collection

From Vale, they headed east toward Boise, Idaho, over the long, barren empty stretch of the Snake River plain. Subsisting on cornmeal and an occasional jackrabbit, they arrived in the middle of August. To Lummis, Dixon wrote, "We have been stalled here a week with sick horses—the whole county is full of "pinkeye"—and I hoped to be able to report the continuation of our great exploration into Wyoming and Montana."[15] But Borein and Dixon encountered financial difficulties—although they might also have had their fill of each other—so they decided to terminate the expedition, sell their outfits, and return to San Francisco. "I hate like 47 kinds of hell to turn back at this point—so near and yet so far," he complained to Lummis.[16] On their way home, they stopped at Pocatello, Idaho, where Dixon spent several days sketching Bannock Indians from the nearby Fort Hall Indian Reservation. Outside Pocatello, a group of visiting Chippewa far from their Wisconsin home had camped and invited Dixon to sketch around their encampment as they taught him sign language. Dixon made numerous watercolors and drawings on the journey, among them three drawings showing bronco busting at the P Ranch, which he sold to *Harper's Weekly* as covers for their March and April 1901 issues. "The results of the trip," he wrote Lummis, "were plenty of sketches, no oils, new knowledge of Indians and cowboy and range life in a tough country, and a greater respect for facts."[17]

When Dixon returned to San Francisco, he moved into a studio at 36 Geary Street. With no firm job in sight, he managed to secure freelance commissions for illustrations in the *San Francisco Call,* the *Chronicle,* and the *Examiner.* Some topics in the *Examiner Sunday Magazine* that he illustrated during 1901 included a story by the noted anthropologist W. J. McGee on the Cocopa Indians; Edwin Markham's poem "A Mendocino Memory"; and Emerson Hough's story about Pat Garrett, "The Man Who Killed Billy the Kid," which appeared in the October issue.

As 1902 began, Dixon seemed uncomfortable with the San Francisco art community, particularly the prevailing attitudes emanating from the San Francisco Art Association and the domineering presence of Arthur F. Mathews. Sensing many of the city's younger artists had become isolated from progressive art movements, Dixon, who would always rail against entrenched establishment art, started talking to fellow artists about an alternative art organization. Lummis cautioned Dixon about getting involved with art groups, advising that only what a man does for himself counts. But Dixon countered Lummis's argument, saying that "cooperation seems to be the war-cry of the time, that certainly is the best one for us artists. It is just such a view as you propose that makes this country so bad for art—it is that very thing that forces so many of our best men abroad, to become virtually Europeans—see Sargent, Whistler, Abbey, and others."[18] Other San Francisco artists shared his views. In early 1902, a group of young artists formed the California Society of Artists, declaring their independence from established artistic hierarchies. Dixon became one of the leaders of the group, along with Xavier Martinez, Gottardo Piazzoni, Arthur Putnam, Leslie Hunter, Matteo Sandona, C. P. Neilson, W. H. Bull, and Blendon Campbell. "As for my nerve," he wrote to Lummis, "I reckon it will hold 'till we pull the first exhibition through, anyhow, pray for the minority."[19] The society wanted to offer an alternative to the conservative San Francisco Art Association and encouraged younger, less-established artists in their manifesto.

As the California Society of Artists wishes to enlist your interest and co-operation in the movement for which it is organized, the objects of the Society are here set forth:

1st—To benefit local art and artists by stimulating interest in art. To benefit equally the members of this Society and all other artists who may exhibit with it, by bringing them into closer contact with the public by holding independent semiannual exhibitions which shall be more accessible to the public at large than those previously held here.

2nd—To bring artists themselves into closer and friendlier contact with one another by maintaining an independent society of artists, conducted exclusively by and for artists.

3rd—To give the younger artists a freer opportunity of showing what they can do,— providing always that their work be of good quality.

Local artists are asked to exhibit with this Society; the work of our own members being subject to just as searching criticism and careful selection as that of non-members. The intention of the Society is to enlarge its membership to the fullest extent upon the basis of good work.[20]

The California Society of Artists held their initial exhibit in the studio of Charles P. Neilson at 207 Sutter Street from April 26 to May 3, 1902. Dixon designed the handsomely printed cover for the exhibit catalog. The exhibit included fourteen of his drawings and watercolors, among them Mojave Indian portraits from his 1900 Arizona trip and cowboy images from the 1901 excursion. Twenty-two other artists also exhibited their work, but the California Society of Artists was short-lived as the group drifted apart after the first exhibition.

In the late summer of 1902, Dixon was anxious to return to the solitude of the desert and accepted a commission from the Santa Fe Railway, heading for the Southwest, traveling down the coast to Los Angeles to visit Lummis, then accompanying photographer-lecturer Frederick I. Monson on his way east to Arizona to photograph the Hopi.

En route, Dixon made sketches of the Colorado Desert along the Santa Fe Railway tracks at Mojave and Needles, then left the train at Winslow, Arizona, hitching a ride on one of the ponderous freight wagons that serviced the far-flung trading posts. What Dixon saw before would be similar to Harold Colton's observation: "Beyond the valley of the Little Colorado, as if on stage, the land lifted in a series of steps to the horizon. As mesa rose above mesa, cliff above cliff, the uptilted strata of rock showed as alternating bands of color across the sky; bands of vivid red, of yellow, of blue, of bone white, of vermillion bands of color softened by distance, shimmering in the warm air that rose from the desert valley, and constantly changing in tone and intensity as the sunlight became more and more slanting."[21]

37. *Women of Oraibi*, 1902, pencil on paper,
10 x 9 inches, private collection,
photograph courtesy of Medicine Man Gallery

At Oraibi, Dixon made quick pencil sketches of individual Hopi (fig. 37), their alluvial farms and fortress-like villages almost imperceptible against the rock on top of the high mesa, then worked his way down Oraibi Wash and past Burro Spring. He then backtracked the route toward Oraibi, doing some sketching around Polacca and Walpi. Traveling on to John Lorenzo Hubbell's trading post at Ganado, he arrived there in late August after another jolting ride by freight wagon from the Hopi mesas.

Ganado stood like a fort in a vast, but not empty, wilderness. Bare ground slanted gently down to the thin winding trickle of Pueblo Colorado Wash. Miles beyond stretched a pink-and-white line of level mesas drawn against a vacant horizon. The massive stone walls of the buildings at Ganado were a foot-and-a-half thick, laid in the red mud of Navajoland. The doors were solid, the windows small and iron-barred, with ten-foot ceilings supported by ponderous vigas under a flat roof (fig. 38). On one end stood Hubbell's office, then the store with high counters and double doors, next the rug room piled shoulder high with products of Navajo looms, a storeroom, and finally the barn. Corrals of juniper posts, stock sheds, and the stable angled out from these, forming an L shape. A little way behind the trading-post building and of similar construction stood "the house," finished in 1902: kitchen, dining room, five bedrooms, and a white-washed privy perched precariously on the edge of the wash. A massive stone fireplace dominated the living room, colorful Navajo rugs covered the floor, and Indian baskets lined the walls. Numerous books, government reports, and technical works were shelved haphazardly around the room.

Navajo traded in the store, taking the post's brass tokens, *seco*—"dry money" they called it—or *pesh-tai*, "thin metal," in exchange for their wool and blankets, and spending it over hours making small purchases one at a time. The gamblers and shiftless ones came in to pawn their turquoise and silver. Small groups lounged in the bright

38. *Ganado*, 1902, pastel on paper, 8 x 10 inches,
private collection, photograph courtesy of Medicine Man Gallery

sun. Horses, their high native saddles covered with brightly dyed goatskins, circled the old juniper in front of the post or wandered among battered freight wagons scattered around. Numerous sounds floated in the air: the murmur of Navajo voices, the noise of a blacksmith's hammer, the creak of harness and wagon, and a child practicing the piano inside the house. These were the Navajo Dixon had come to see: women in wide swinging skirts and velveteen blouses; men in colored shirts and cotton pants split at the leg; all with pointed Asiatic-looking moccasins, their hair knotted at the back of their necks. The sun brightened blankets and glinted on silver and turquoise worn by the Indians. And everywhere he looked lay Navajo country, brick-dust red, reaching away to the far blue mesas and the empty sky beyond.

Here too he met the man already a legend in Navajo country—John Lorenzo Hubbell (fig. 39). Born in 1853 in Pajarito, a small village near Albuquerque, New Mexico, the son of a Connecticut Yankee who had gone to New Mexico as a soldier and married into a family of Spanish descent, Hubbell had explored and wandered through the Southwest working as a clerk and Spanish interpreter in southern Utah, New Mexico, and northern Arizona. About 1876, Hubbell rode west from Fort Defiance upon the urging of Ganado Mucho (Many Cattle), head of the Big Water Clan and subchief of all western Navajo, who promised Hubbell a lucrative trade if he would promise to run a small post on the banks of Pueblo Colorado Wash. Hubbell agreed and homesteaded the tract, calling it

Ganado after his friend Ganado Mucho. The trading post empire grew, including stage and freight lines, and Hubbell acquired other posts, as many as twenty-four, at Chinle, Black Mesa, Cornfields, Nazlini, Keams' Canyon, and other locations.

When Hubbell started trading at Ganado, he was twenty-four years old. The Navajo nicknamed him Nak'eznilih, "Double Glasses," because of his thick-lensed spectacles. As they came to know and trust him, the Navajo began calling him by the affection-ate term Nankaii Saani, or "Old Mexican." When Dixon met him in 1902, he saw a great barrel-chested bear of a man, heavy shoulders, thick neck, square jaw overgrown with bristling beard, and strong gray eyes. Hubbell had strong convictions too, doing nothing partway or half-way. The friendship that formed between Dixon and Hubbell be-came strong and lasting. Dixon never referred to Hubbell as anything but

39. *John Lorenzo Hubbell*, 1902, National Park Service, Hubbell Trading Post National Historic Site

"patron." They corresponded for many years, with Dixon's correspondence often begin-ning "Querido Patron" and sometimes written in Spanish. Dixon might discuss his art, mention sales of Hubbell's Navajo weaving, or explain some depressing episode in his personal life. For several years after this first trip to Ganado, Dixon peddled Hubbell's Navajo rugs and Hopi pottery, including work by the famed Hopi potter, Nampeyo, to friends and acquaintances in San Francisco.

Dixon spent more than two months at Ganado. When not out drawing or painting the Navajo (fig. 40) and the surrounding country, he spent time at the "bull pen," center of Ganado's trading activity, a dark, smoky, tobacco- and pinyon-smelling room where the Navajo gathered to warm themselves, talking about weather, clan gossip, or sheep and wool prices. They squatted on the floor or leaned against the walls, smoked, and chatted quietly in Navajo, their words soft as the desert wind. In time, Dixon learned to speak passable Navajo. When Navajo friends visited, Hubbell opened cans of peaches, tomatoes, and sardines to ward off the tiredness of traveling. An open tobacco can sat on the counter, free for all to help themselves, nails driven up through the can's bottom to prevent the taking of too much. Hospitality is the characteristic of a *haciendado*, and Hubbell's graciousness became legendary; he denied no one. Ganado was located fifty-five miles north of Gallup—a trip that could take ten days during the winter at the turn

40. *Lorenzo Hubbell's Trading Post, Ganado*,
1902, pencil on paper, 14 x 10 inches, private collection,
photograph courtesy of Medicine Man Gallery

of the century—nevertheless, he entertained presidents, eastern tourists, writers, bull whackers, archaeologists, scientists, Indians, and artists like Dixon, who were attracted to the country's stark beauty. During the early years of the century, some of the famous men and women who visited Ganado included Generals Lew Wallace, Nelson Miles, and Hugh L. Scott; writers Mary Roberts Rinehart, Hamlin Garland, and Charles F. Lummis; scientists Adolf Bandelier, J. Walter Fewkes, and Stewart Culin; and artists Elbridge Ayer Burbank, Carlos Vierra, and Bert Phillips. At the long dining room table, Hubbell treated everyone with equal courtesy. When offered payment, he responded, "No sir, not a cent. I don't run a hotel. I'm in the blanket business. I'm the mildest mannered man that ever scuttled a ship or cut a throat. If you want to spend your money just come over in the blanket room with me and watch me knock your eye out."[22]

Hubbell told Dixon that over 30,000 Navajo lived in the surrounding vastness of mesas, plains, and canyons, which few white men had explored. To a man on horseback or in a wagon, this country ran on a large scale, with roads only trails or rutted wagon tracks. Most of the time the Navajo stayed apart, almost invisible in the sprawling landscape. Dixon learned that finding his subjects meant hanging around one of the trading posts or attending the dances or sings where hundreds might congregate. Everywhere Dixon looked he saw the enormous scale of the Navajo geographical space, an impression recorded not only in drawings and paintings but in his writings. Deeply moved by the Navajo environment, Dixon recalled his impressions forty years later in an article for *Arizona Highways*:

> On the map of Arizona, Navajoland appears as a great empty place, decorated with a scattering of curious names: Jeditoh Springs, Skeleton Mesa, Canyon del Muerto, Aga-thia Needle, Nach-tee Canyon, Monument Valley, the Mittens, Pei-ki-ha-tsoh Wash—all hinting a far strangeness. A vast and lonely land it is, saturated with inexhaustible sunlight and astounding color, visible with unbelievable distinctness, and overspread with intense and infinite blue. Its long drawn levels are a setting for the awesome pageant of gigantic storms advancing under sky-built domes of clouds, trailing curtains of rain and thin color-essence of rainbows.
>
> This is the land of mesas, laid down in layers of colored sandstone, red, yellow, pink, and creamy white; carved and hollowed by the recession of forgotten seas; their sides often sheer, or broken into strange isolated slabs, turrets, buttes—the blind blunt architecture of a pre-human world. Afar they dwindle away, small and sharp, into clear blue distance and stop short; or in the long yellow slant of late sun their intricate forms are revealed in bewildering patterns of shadow; or seen only as low-lying bands of purple or sombre blue, remote in the shadow of rain clouds.[23]

Dixon sketched and painted the Navajo at the trading posts of Ganado and Chinle; the twisting recesses of Canyon de Chelly and Canyon del Muerto with their massive water-stained walls; cloud formations over the Chuska Mountains; broken, brilliantly colored badlands country around Chinle Creek; the great dark wall of Black Mesa under a thunderstorm; and the mesas and bench lands that dip west to the Painted Desert and the valley of the Little Colorado River. Often he visited Sam Day's place at Chinle, near the mouth of Canyon de Chelly. Established in 1902, it had been built as a log house with wide eaves, mud floor, small dusty windows, its corral and haystack isolated on a nearby bare knoll. An astonishing assortment of Navajo weaving and Ute beadwork of all ages, kinds, and conditions covered the walls, floors, and furniture. Dixon thought it old-timey to the limit, with the Navajo around the post wilder than at Ganado, not "railroad Indians." Once a group of Chinle Navajo tried running their horses at him, all in a group, yelling and laughing as though to run him into the ground. Dixon kept walking, knowing he could not escape. Finally, the Indians backed off when they sensed he would not flinch and run. One time, Dixon accepted an invitation from pioneer photographer Ben Wittick to explore the remote upper reaches of Canyon de Chelly and out into the badlands of western New Mexico, almost as far as Chaco Canyon. Wittick died of a rattlesnake bite only ten months later. In a letter to Lummis, Dixon wrote: "I left here with Ben Wittick a week ago for d. Chelly and got back last evening by the bad lands trail from Chinlee. We made it between noon and sunset and I had a couple of Navajo travelling. I had a fine Indian packing for me. The old boy is still up here and he's a great old braggert. But for me the trip was a failure. When we got out into the Llano de la Laguna Larga (named for the water that the Navajo call Pei-k-ki-hat-soh) we ran up against a north wind that put me out of business for five days."[24]

In early November of 1902, Dixon left Ganado for Isleta, his bags stuffed with drawings, pastels, and a few small oil sketches, visual memories of the Navajo and their country. Among all of the Native Americans Dixon encountered on numerous journeys throughout the West, he would remember these people and their land.

Tsinadzini in the east; Tsotsil in the south; Dhokoslid in the west; Dhepentsa in the north. In all the vast region between these four sacred mountains, you will not find a single village of the Navajo. Their hogans, those odd igloolike huts of logs and earth, stand far and lonely, singly between tall rocks or three together at most, perched high on a ledge, or hidden among the junipers. The herds of goats and sheep and the bands of slender long-tailed ponies must be moved from grass to water, from water-hole to brush browse; clans and families are scattered; so to visit his kin or care for his herds the Navajo must ride. Twenty-five miles to the trading post is for him a jaunt before breakfast, and forty miles home for supper of sheep's head is a mere pasear. *Riding—they are always riding, high in their curious native saddles, padded with bright-dyed goatskins,—wiry, freebodied, swaying, these hawk-faced Mongol nomads. Those close-fitting red moccasins with turned up sole and pointed toe, the dark velvet shirt of the women with its row of silver buttons down the breast, the black hair looped low on the neck, the wide pleated skirt with its band of bright color below: silver bracelets and folds of sun faded blankets—the color, the form and the manner—the cheek bone, the sharp lip and slant of the eye—surely all these are descended here from old Asia.* [25]

When sketching in the field, Dixon used anything that could be drawn upon— scrap paper, sketch paper, wrapping paper, backs of bills, announcements and cards—

41. *San Francisco Men,* 1902, pencil on paper,
5⁷/₈ x 4¹/₂ inches, private collection

to record images in pencil, charcoal, or conté crayon. Dixon also produced some small oil sketches, several large pastels, and a few watercolors. Many drawings showed the Navajo and the trading posts at Ganado and Chinle. He did not find the Navajo easy subjects at first. "Indians have a silent way of being not sketchable when they so will it, though they remain in plain view. The Navajo are all right to paint if you nail them to a post and have somebody hold a gun to 'em while you do it."[26] But the more the Navajo frustrated his painting attempts, the more he persisted, determined to capture their aloofness and proud demeanor. Probably most of the small oil studies Dixon did at Ganado are lost, but two survive in the collections of Brigham Young University. They indicate an increasing understanding of color and an awareness of mood. Maynard painted one large canvas of a Navajo woman weaver in oil upon his return to San Francisco, which he sold to Lorenzo Hubbell for $350. The painting is now in the collection of Hubbell Trading Post National Historic Site at Ganado.

Ganado had an important impact on Dixon's work. There, he experimented seriously with oil painting, developed his pastels and watercolors, and absorbed the lonely shimmering land of color into his imagination. The transformation from illustrator to painter began at Ganado, but Navajo land may have influenced his art in another way. Dixon spent considerable time in the rug room at the trading post, looking through the Navajo textiles of all kinds and periods strewn about. He also liked to explore Hubbell's combination office, museum, bedroom, arsenal, and picture gallery, where Hubbell stored the most outstanding weaving. High on the wall stood more than fifty small, accurate paintings depicting Hubbell's favorite designs, done for Hubbell by artist Elbridge Ayer Burbank, who spent ten months at Ganado during 1898–99. Dixon, impressed with the weavers' sense of color and dynamic design, particularly with that unique rich color called Ganado Red, brought back a number of textiles and displayed them in his studio. When the 1906 San Francisco earthquake and fire destroyed his studio, he left his paintings to the consuming flames but rescued most of the Navajo blankets.

After Dixon left Ganado, he went on to Gallup, New Mexico, and from there to spend a few days at the pueblos of Isleta and Laguna, finally returning to San Francisco in late November 1902. While a considerable part of 1902 had been spent away from San Francisco, Dixon still managed to produce large numbers of illustrations and posters during that year for newspapers, books, and periodicals (fig. 41). For the June issue of *Sunset Magazine*, he painted a striking poster in color. He did illustrations for *Scribner's*, *Colliers*, and *Pacific Monthly*, a Portland-based magazine, and a frontispiece and seven full-page, black-and-white plates for F. H. Balch's book *The Bridge of the Gods*. In 1902, Lummis changed the name of *Land of Sunshine* to *Out West*, reflecting the transformation he felt the West was undergoing. Sharlot Hall submitted a poem to Lummis evocative of those changes, and Lummis requested Dixon paint a full-page illustration to accompany the poem. He promptly reproduced Dixon's illustration *The Genius of the West* (fig. 42) and the poem as a broadside on heavy cardboard, distributing it throughout the United States to announce the new magazine.

THE GENIUS OF THE WEST.

42. *The Genius of the West,* 1902, California History Section, California State Library

The illustrations for *Sunset Magazine* initiated a long productive association with the magazine. When the Southern Pacific Railroad began *Sunset Magazine* in May 1898, a small staff attached to the passenger division produced it with the purpose of exploring the challenges and opportunities of life in the land west of the Rockies. Charles Sedgwick Aikin assumed the editorship in 1902, declaring he would make the publication a combination of *Atlantic Monthly, Outing,* and *McClures,* offering a substantial and entertaining mix of fact along with fiction and poetry. To this end, he attracted such literary figures as Charles G. Norris, Gelett Burgess, George Sterling, Mary Austin, Ina Coolbrith (first poet laureate of California), and Jack London, who had his adventure stories published in early issues beginning in 1903. Other well-known writers for *Sunset Magazine* included Gertrude Atherton, Hamlin Garland, Stewart Edward White, John Muir, Joaquin Miller, Kathleen Norris, and Charles Warren Stoddard.

43. *Bret Harte Jinks*, 1903, private collection

Sometime in early 1903, Dixon received an invitation to join San Francisco's Bohemian Club. Founded in 1872 by newspaper publisher Daniel O'Connell and some other journalists, who enjoyed savoring life as much as work, the organization soon became not only the focus of San Francisco's journalistic profession but also the center for much of the city's literary and artistic life. The membership included such personalities as poets Charles Warren Stoddard, Gelett Burgess, George Sterling, and Joaquin Miller; journalists Prentice Mulford and Will Irwin; painters William Keith, Charles Rollo Peters, Virgil Williams, and Thomas Hill; sculptors Arthur Putnam, Robert I. Aitken, and talented deaf-mute Douglas Tilden; naturalist John Muir; scientist-philosopher Joseph LeConte; historians John S. and Theodore Hittell; and writers like Frank Norris, Ambrose Bierce, Porter Garnett, and Jack London. Dixon's first effort on behalf of the club was designing the announcement for the 1903 Bret Harte Jinks (fig. 43).

By the 1890s, the Bohemian Club had leased quarters at 130 Post Street, between Kearny and DuPont. Their motto was "Weaving spiders come not here"; their totem was the owl, perhaps symbolic of the journalists who worked late into the night. Eventually, membership offers extended beyond writers and artists to influential businessmen and lawyers. The members gathered together monthly for drink and entertainment, producing "high jinks" and "low jinks," comedy and recreation for which an artist member created a commemorative cartoon. Annual encampments in the Bohemian Grove near Guerneville on the Russian River celebrated the combination of outdoor life and elegant living typical of the era. Dixon's association with the club lasted until 1930 and became a natural outlet for his iconoclastic, colorful, occasionally irreverent personality. While Dixon thought the Bohemian Club was influenced by money and was full of sycophants, he enthusiastically embraced the bohemian ideals put forth by people who lived according to their own esthetic standards.

Dixon had moved across the bay to Sausalito by 1903, staying at his mother's home and commuting daily by ferry to a studio at 604 Merchant Street. When he was not working there, he spent much of his time across the street in the big four-story, brick-and-granite building at the corner of Clay and Montgomery streets on the edge of San Francisco's financial district, in the famous Montgomery Block affectionately called the "Monkey Block." By the early years of the twentieth century, the building's ground floor supported lawyers, pawnbrokers, tailors, clothing merchants, and restaurants, of which Coppa's, at the corner of Montgomery and Merchant streets, became the favorite rendezvous of San Francisco's writers and artists. On the upper floors, inexpensive apartments mixed with studio space. Attracted by reasonable rents, nearby local restaurants, and excellent lighting in the big outside rooms, members of San Francisco's cultural colony—painters, metalsmiths, poets, journalists, writers, and musicians—migrated to the building as tenants. Nearly two thousand artists and writers lived in its rooms before the building disappeared in 1959, replaced by the Transamerica Building.

Mark Twain, Bret Harte, George Sterling, Joaquin Miller, Prentice Mulford, Frank Norris, Ina Coolbrith, and scores of other art and literary figures made their homes here at various times, writing poetry, essays, and stories, cooking by the flame of gas rings, passing bottles of cheap red wine around a circle, while talk bounced from the walls of their tiny apartments until sunrise. The Monkey Block became a way of life for generations of aspiring artists and writers, an informal way station for a milling army of the destitute and the successful who pursued various ambitions in the morning, while in the late afternoons and evenings they crowded into Coppa's ground-floor restaurant, where he issued pasta, wine, and credit, fuel for the pursuit of their dreams. Here, Gelett Burgess and friends worked on upcoming issues of *The Lark*, Ambrose Bierce composed his blistering "Prattler" for the *Argonaut*, Jack London stayed in Xavier Martinez's studio after long nights on the town, and George Sterling kept a room for amorous adventures, sometimes irritating other tenants by marching up and down the halls reciting poetry. Life was vibrant in the Montgomery Block with the same hope that energized the rest of San Francisco.

Sunset Magazine featured one of Dixon's paintings, *Navajo Indian from Life*, depicting a silent, blanket-wrapped Navajo Indian set against a backdrop of faraway mesas and an even farther horizon, on its February 1903 cover. The composition of this painting was dramatically different from anything the magazine had featured before. This issue, accompanied by the cover reproduced as a large poster, had wide distribution throughout the western states, creating sold-out conditions wherever the magazine and posters were displayed. The image soon became embedded on the masthead as one of Sunset's primary visual motifs and was used for many years by the magazine in a variety of promotional efforts. By 1907, *Sunset Magazine* had printed 250,000 copies of the poster. Similar images would surface repeatedly in Dixon's art. By the early 1900s, his respect and appreciation for the Native American had evolved into a deepening reverence for the western landscape, with the native peoples as elemental phenomena, like rain on the hills or clouds in the sky. For Dixon, as for many of the other artists working in the American West at the time, the Native American seemed a symbol of the "natural man."

Parley Louis, a Pima Indian, posed as the model for the *Sunset Magazine* cover. Several years later, Dixon came close to being killed by Louis, who, having lost his job as a streetcar motorman, took up the absorption of alcohol in a heroic way and developed a fixed desire to exterminate all white men, especially Bohemian Club artists. Entering the Montgomery Street studio one evening, Dixon felt his own big .45 Colt jabbed

into his neck by the boozy Louis who shouted, "Me goin kill all white men. Might as well begin with you."[27] Dixon argued briefly, grappled with Louis, and maneuvered him through the door, colliding with sculptor Haig Patigian and another artist who had come to investigate the noise. "You too," whooped Louis as he shoved the gun into the surprised Patigian's stomach. Dixon managed to wrestle it away as the gun discharged, puncturing the ceiling. Louis then bolted out the door, vanishing from bohemia's life forever.

Sunset Magazine published two of Dixon's cowboy poems, "In Town" and "Yearlin's," in November 1903, accompanied by two full-page illustrations. The magazine also used four full-page color plates of his paintings to illustrate his article "Christmas on the Range" in the December issue. Other illustrations were made for newspapers or periodicals (fig. 44). According to an article in the *Mark Hopkins Review of Art*, Dixon had returned to Navajo country during the spring of 1903 (fig. 45). The article assessed Dixon's ardor for the land and people of the West:

44. *A Sure Thing Pard*, 1903,
charcoal and pastel on paper, 24 x 18 inches,
private collection

> L. Maynard Dixon has an inborn propensity for drawing the phases and figures of frontier life; it is a constant craving which never lets him rest. . . . Answering this "Call of the Wild" at any, and every, possible opportunity, Mr. Dixon has in the last few years sown the seeds of an intimate knowledge that are now beginning to bear fruit.[28] . . . Mr. Dixon has been frequently urged by those who are interested in his career go to Europe and study, or go to New York where he will not lack plenty of opportunities to make money but his answer is that his work lies here, out West, ready to his hand and why should he leave it? Some day he hopes to go, but he believes that now, while he is young, is his one opportunity to absorb all the impressions possible from his beloved West, the land of his birth. Like Millet, whom he passionately admires and fondly quotes, he "Hears always the cry of the ground."[29]

The Mark Hopkins Institute of Art included several of Dixon's pencil drawings— *Moqui Priest of Oraibi*, *On the Corral Fence*, *Breaking a Hobbled Bronco*, and *Navajo*

45. *Indian on Horseback,* 1903, pastel on paper, 14 x 20 inches,
W. Donald Head, Old Grandview Ranch

Woman—in its 1903 annual exhibition, examples of the vivid pictures of a changing frontier and a virile life of action that he enjoyed. In addition, he exhibited thirty-three drawings in the Newspaper Artists League exhibition, held at the Palace Hotel in October 1903, including sketches from Arizona and New Mexico, and designs for book covers. Dixon also drew the cover illustration for the league's exhibit catalog. In 1904, he moved to another studio at 424 Pine Street. Nearby at 414 Pine Street was the studio of Lillian West Tobey, a diminutive, fiery Irish girl who had come to San Francisco from Chicago at the turn of the century. A painter who also worked in metal and decorative leather, she and Dixon started frequenting each other's studios, discussing art, the local scene, and their own work. Tobey gradually began to push his thoughts toward settling down.

46. *Sunset Magazine,* September 1904,
California History Section,
California State Library

47. *Sue—California Ranch Girl,*
1904, mixed media on paper,
12 x 10 inches, private collection,
photograph courtesy of
Mitchell Brown Fine Art

48. *Ranchero of Old California,*
1904, watercolor on academy board,
12⅛ x 10⅛ inches, private collection,
photograph courtesy of
Owings Dewey Fine Art

Sunset Magazine used Dixon's illustrations and posters extensively throughout 1904. Cover illustrations, all in color, appeared in the February and July issues. The magazine featured an Isleta woman gathering dried chiles from one of the pueblo's structures (fig. 46). In addition, the magazine reproduced several covers as posters. Frequent requests for newspaper illustrations added to a hectic work schedule (fig. 47). The *San Francisco Chronicle* published a large article on February 14, 1904, "Our Friends the Navajo," reproducing several of Dixon's images in color; his illustrations for an article on bronco-busting followed the next week. *Town Talk*, a local weekly periodical, used an illustration on its July cover. The Press Club displayed several watercolors in its April 1904 exhibit, reproducing one of his drawings on the cover of the catalog. Other exhibitions that Dixon entered during 1904 included the annual San Francisco Art Association and Bohemian Club shows. Exhibition records indicate his entries were watercolors and drawings (fig. 48).

Dixon's personal life mirrored the lives of his compatriots: hard work in the studio, hilarious red wine and pasta dinners at Coppa's, long passionate discussions with artist and writer friends about current art theories and literary trends, "girl trouble," and the morning hangover. His closest friends—whom he called the "Fuzzy Bunch"—included Xavier Martinez, Gottardo Piazzoni, George Sterling, Robert Aitken, Porter Garnett, James Hopper, and Arnold Genthe. Xavier Martinez—Mexican by birth, Californian by choice—became known as one of the most colorful of the bohemians. Marty, as they called him, had a shock of jet black hair—someone once called his hair a huge black chrysanthemum—and dark eyes, and preferred dressing in corduroys set off by a bright crimson flowing tie. Martinez had studied in Europe from 1897 to 1901 at Paris's École de Beaux-Arts, adopting a form of tonalism—somber greens, grays, and browns—not an impressionist's palette. Gottardo F. P. Piazzoni, born in Intragna, Switzerland, in 1872, was a little Italian with a porkpie hat, big moustache, and flowing tie, who painted subtle, lyrical interpretations of Northern California's landscapes. Gentle and unassuming, he became the dean of San Francisco painters, a progressive artist who championed modern art movements, particularly futurism. Neither art gossiper nor part of the in-crowd, he disappeared into his studio every day to work methodically on his poetic paintings and murals. Porter Garnett—variously a calligrapher, woodcarver, designer, teacher, critic, and, thereafter, producer and printer—was, of course, an original member of Les Jeunes. Short-story writer James "Jimmy" Hopper, built like a young ox, had played varsity football at Berkeley. Arnold Genthe, a dashing Prussian with a doctor's degree, became San Francisco's leading society photographer, purveyor of the off-focus portrait, eventually famous for his images of Chinatown and the San Francisco earthquake and fire. Robert Aitken, a noted sculptor, developed monumental works, one of which, *Victory*, still stands in San Francisco's Union Square. George Sterling, profligate, melancholy, or charming by turns, was a catalyst for literary activities in the Bay Area, writing strictly rhymed, highly ornamental poetry, the unquestioned poet—symbol of his "cool, gray city of love."

Usually, Dixon would meet them at Coppa's for drink, food, and discussion. Coppa's, presided over by Joseph "Papa" Coppa, became intertwined not only with San Francisco's bohemian scene but with Dixon's life as well. Occupying a narrow high-ceilinged room at 622 Montgomery Street, Coppa's attracted the Bay Area's avant-garde artists and writers. Besides enjoying the ample dinners at the oval central table that Coppa had reserved for the leading bohemians, they knew Coppa would allow them to take meals on credit until the sale of a painting or story improved their finances. The place possessed a soul of its own. When a member of the central table made a sale, everybody feasted, living according to the command "Spend and lend and God will send."[30] Many farewell dinners were eaten in honor of friends departing for the East and just as many welcome feasts given for returning sinners. The conversation at the center table might be philosophical and subdued, or political and argumentative, yet always full of conviviality. Sometimes Xavier Martinez would give a deep baritone rendition of the proud French provincial song, "*Je ne suis pas home; Je ne suis pas femme; Je suis un Avignon*," sometimes mimicking it or other songs with a little marionette. The group often asked Dixon to present his rousing rendition of "Tit Willow."[31]

Usually more men than women could be found at the center table, along with an unrestrained thirst for wine, women, and song. Goaded by desire, the young men exercised every wile to lure new females into Bohemia. Whenever a new one appeared—and only one at a time could be brought to the table, presented after black coffee by the individual who brought her—there would be a silent vote: "all those in favor say 'Aye,' to the contrary 'No.'" Once George Sterling brought Mary Austin. The Coppans rejected her. "She was writing beautiful stuff but wasn't pretty," Jimmy Hopper remembered. "The pretty ones didn't have to write very much to get in again."[32]

Sometime in 1905, the Coppans showed their appreciation to Coppa. Coppa had covered the restaurant walls with red wallpaper in the hopes of pleasing his artistic patrons. Several artists who came in one evening for dinner thought this not the right color, so they offered to redecorate with something more appropriate—inspired graffiti. One Sunday, supplied with free lunch and fortified with all the wine they could drink, they began. Porter Garnett started first, drawing a ferocious-looking, five-foot lobster standing on an island named "Bohemia," with bright-colored chalk. Robert Aitken furnished two near nude figures endowed with heroic proportions. On another Sunday, Xavier Martinez contributed an elegant procession of stalking black cats, a few with gold-painted eyes, extending about the room below the ceiling. Dixon assisted, filling in some of the red wallpaper space with his drawings. Gelett Burgess, Perry Newberry, and others added sketches and phrases. During the next several months, the work continued until every conceivable wall space had been covered.

Strangers who entered Coppa's seemed startled by the pictures piled on pictures, overlapping each other with the whole welded together by the "Temple of Fame," those the Coppans declared immortal. Individuals with a sense of humor laughed when they encountered the line "Ah, well, but is it art?" and further on, Lewis Carroll's "Curiouser and curiouser, cried Alice," along with numerous quotations in English, Latin, Hebrew, medieval French, and wondrous crypticisms. Above the pictures perched names of certain favorites in the Coppa crowd: Aitken, Garnett, Newberry, Martinez, Burgess, Mary Edith Griswold (a freelance writer for the *Chronicle*), Harry Lafler (*Argonaut* editor), and Sterling, whom Dixon's sister, Rebecca Dixon, remembered for the perpetual pose he struck with his profile like a Grecian coin that had been run over by a Roman chariot. The names of illustrious greats—Dante, Shakespeare, Goethe, Kant, Whistler, and others—were included in the roll call. In one instance where an artist misspelled Nietzsche, one of the black cats could be seen returning the missing letter in its mouth. Martinez developed a grand tableau, *Before the Gringo Came*, in chalk, depicting the central table at Coppa's with the bohemians gathered around. In the picture, Gelett Burgess approached the table with a portfolio under one arm. Seated at one end of the table was Martinez, with unruly hair and drooping mustache, next to him Porter Garnett, then Harry Lafler. Standing behind Lafler's chair was a tight-waisted young woman smoking a cigarette. Beside her is Maynard Dixon, somber, mosquito-thin, wearing a Stetson and cowboy boots. George Sterling stood at the back of the group, his head crowned with a laurel wreath. Ultimately, the walls became smothered with drawings and erudite quotations, names of local personalities, nonsense jingles, and caricatures of the bohemians and their cronies.

After working on the Coppa murals, Dixon decided to accompany Xavier Martinez on a painting trip to Guadalajara, Mexico, Martinez's boyhood home, discussing the idea in a letter to Lorenzo Hubbell, "my friend Martinez and I are trying to bunco the Mexican Central into taking us to Guadalajara—don't you want to come with us?"[33] Evidently Dixon and Martinez convinced the railroad to support them; they left for

Mexico during the first week of March 1905. The Southern Pacific issued them artists' passes to Tucson, Arizona; from there, they rode the El Paso and Southwestern Railroad to El Paso, crossing the border and boarding a Mexican Central train destined for Mexico City, then Guadalajara.

Dixon and Martinez spent two months in Guadalajara, visiting Martinez's friends and joining a group of fiery young Mexican revolutionaries who had arrived in the city, attempting to arouse opposition to the autocratic rule of the Mexican president, Porfirio Diaz (fig. 49). Maynard and Martinez found their intense interest in society, art, lit-erature, science, and politics stimulating, and they spent many exuberant evenings in the cantinas, arguing the merits of this or that cause. Excited with the color and passion of old Mexico, Dix-on made numerous sketches and painted several small oils filled with bright color (fig. 50). After they left Mex-ico, Maynard and Martinez stopped for several days at Ganado, where they man-aged to do a little sketching and painting. But Dixon's goal was Lummis's home in

49. *Maynard Dixon, Xavier Martinez, and Friends,*
1905, private collection

Los Angeles. There, Maynard Dixon married Lillian West Tobey on May 7, 1905, the ceremony performed under an enormous sycamore in the patio of El Alisal. "After pay-ing the preacher ten dollars," Dixon recalled, "I had just fifteen dollars left for the hon-eymoon trip to San Francisco."[34] When he returned, he managed to secure illustrations for the *San Francisco Chronicle*'s Sunday Supplement, including *The Goddess of the Wheat*, a full-page color insert (fig. 51).

When he and Tobey returned to San Francisco, Dixon found a letter from *Cosmopolitan* magazine waiting for him. Would he go to Tonopah and Goldfield, booming mining towns in Nevada, and do some illustrations? Dixon rushed an answer back—yes, he would—and departed immediately to join the article's author in Tonopah. She was Winifred Black, "Annie Laurie," the "sob sister" from Maynard's newspaper days at the *San Francisco Examiner*. They spent a week in Goldfield, Tonopah, and Bullfrog, energetic towns sprawling in an arid El Dorado—helter-skelter, hit-or-miss places. Dixon explored the towns and surrounding mines, sketching eager-eyed adventurers, miners, gamblers, and speculators; ponderous freight wagons, each with twenty horses, along with the latest in desert transportation—automobiles. He listened to the rattle of the roulette wheel, high-pitched voices of excited men talking, and the wild wind calling from the desert. However, the magazine included only three of his drawings in Black's

LEFT: 50. *Ranchero, Guadalajara*,
1905, crayon and gouache on paper,
6¹/₄ x 4³/₄ inches, private collection

ABOVE: 51. *The Goddess of Wheat*,
1905, California History Section,
California State Library

article, published in September 1905, deciding to use photographs for the rest of the reproductions. He was disappointed but then rebounded when Chicago publisher A. C. McClurg informed him they would use one of his paintings as the frontispiece for Will Lillibridge's western novel *Ben Blair*, to be published in October.

In the first week of November, Dixon returned to Ganado, accompanied by Tobey, where they spent several weeks. He had a hectic work schedule and told Hubbell before leaving for Arizona that "We are rushed to the verge of insanity."[35] Hubbell's Navajo friends immediately urged Dixon to attend a nine-day Yei Betchai ceremony. Trader Sam Day had two sons participating, and he told Dixon the Navajos called this dance "Giant Grandfather." Three thousand Navajo attended the encampment, their wagons drawn up around the great fires of the dance oval, with only about a dozen Anglo observers present. Medicine men with their sacred meal and pollen; masked and painted dancers with eagle feathers, turquoise, and silver glinting in the firelight; shrill high chants, grating rattles, and sweaty bodies filled the cold November night. There, Dixon thought, "behind those masks, singing out of a twilight past with the voices of eagles, coyotes, bears but wilder, fiercer—were my Indian ghosts again."[36] The Navajo at Ganado knew Dixon by now, assigning him a Navajo name, Bit-tsin-Nez, "hooked-nose man."

After the ceremony, Dixon sketched and painted around Ganado, producing numerous drawings. He took with him a somber memory of this trip to Ganado, one that would shape and define his personal philosophy. Just before he left, a young Navajo girl died. Dixon had seen the girl, called Little Sister, maybe seven or eight years old, with her mother at Ganado a number of times. He thought her a wild and beautiful thing, who bolted every time he tried to sketch her. The girl's family, fearing *chindi*, ghosts of the dead, wanted a Christian burial, so they asked Hubbell to make a coffin and shroud. Hubbell agreed, telling Dixon, who had volunteered to help, "You see, this is a lonesome place. We help these people sometimes. *El costumbre*, the custom of the country and this family . . . they are friends of mine. They are afraid now, like children. *Nada es verdad ni mentera, En este mundo traidor; Todo es sugun el color, Del cristal con que se mira.*"[37] As Hubbell returned to his office, the words seemed to trail after him. Dixon asked Forrest Parker, Hubbell's son-in-law, what the words meant. Parker replied, "It's a favorite quotation of the Old Man's. It means: nothing is true or false in this traitor's world; everything partakes of the color of the crystal through which it is seen."[38] Dixon remembered the words and wrote them down, integrating their meaning into his personal and artistic journey.

On his return to San Francisco, he submitted twelve paintings for the San Francisco Artists Society's annual exhibition held December 18–20, 1905, at the Palace Hotel. A portrait drawing by Dixon was reproduced on the catalog cover, and its contents indicate that for the first time, all of his entries were oil paintings and, with one exception, depicted Southwest subjects. They included *The Town Crier, Moqui, In Navajo Land, Uplands of Pei-ki-hat-tsoh, Navajo Woman, Edge of the Mesa, Tsay-yih, Between the Rocks,* and *Recuerdo de Guadalajara.*

The beginning of 1906 brought him numerous commissions for magazine illustrations, and while the majority of his work revolved around being a commercial artist, he attempted to paint seriously at every opportunity. An assertive palette of southwestern colors had started to emerge in his increasingly simplified compositions, often on *Sunset Magazine* covers. He still worked, however, in an illustrative style, so little pictorial concessions emerged in the paintings. Maynard continued reading the German magazines *Jugend* and *Simplicissimus* and other European publications; their bold, direct images influenced the development of his own crayon, pencil, and pen-and-ink drawing. However, Dixon sensed that something was wrong, puzzled by some mysterious forces that he could not explain. As he would throughout his life, he turned to poetry for an expression, writing the dark "Pueblo de Los Muertos":

The brown-faced children of the sun,
 these people of the plazas bleak,
diminishing their rivers run
from arid bench and barren peak,
(the dry skin on the sunken cheek!)
 they see a vast and hollow place
 where tall poles stark in hungry air
 send starling shadows down the wall
 between the empty corn-bins there

and small dry husks along the eaves,
and brittle twigs of willows small
make dead men's fingers in the leaves.
Cracked and empty in the sun
the oven in the beaten square,
—pale drifting in the vacant air
the thin blue smoke is faintly spun,
a sickly film across the day;
faint-eyed the little children stare
where feeble forms of tribesmen sway
in ritual steps, and there, unseen,
and moving as they move, the gray
of dead men's shadows go between.
Blank wall and open door they stand,
the silent houses of the place;
where meagre strips of meat were strung,
a rawhide shrivels dry in dung
and white bones glimmer in the sand.
The silence of a starven face
turns blindly to the sun
(the feather in the shrunken hand!)
the dancing and the prayer are done
for faded shamans of the past
and wan Koshares of the gloom;
the passing phantom of their breath
makes answer to the ground at last
but ancient shadows that resume
the drifting sunny dust of death.[39]

What could interfere, he wondered, with his career as an artist? "Something Terrible Is Going to Happen," extracted from Oscar Wilde's *Salomé*, had been inscribed on the walls of Coppa's restaurant. Perhaps it was prescience, for in the early morning of April 18, 1906, the first earthquake shock, lasting less than a minute, struck San Francisco. A cloud of dust rose from the city as if someone had shaken a great carpet. Rubble toppled into the streets, and shortly, big columns of smoke fed by ruptured gas lines began rising from the city, signaling the beginnings of fires that would terrify her inhabitants for three days. These fires, unchecked due to broken water mains, surged first up the south side of Market Street, then spread rapidly in a southerly direction like a great tidal wave over the vast section between the Mission District and the bay, traveling up the steep slopes of Telegraph, Russian, then Nob Hill, and winding close to the waterfront.

Dixon and Tobey had been staying with friends in San Francisco. After the shocks subsided, they rushed over to his studio, finding it in chaos, the canvases untouched but all of the Pueblo pottery broken and mingled on the floor with the rest of the studio

litter. A box of matches had been ignited by the earthquake's shock, then extinguished by a vase of water spilling over it. Dixon, his wife, and Mary Edith Griswold, now a *Sunset Magazine* editor, who had stopped by to see how the Dixons fared, started for the *Sunset* building at the other end of Market Street. Dixon thought he should try and save something from his studio, so he and Tobey turned back, appropriating a two-wheeled pushcart to salvage what they could from the wrecked studio before the flames arrived. The next day, Dixon drew a pen-and-ink cartoon of himself fleeing the studio, arms overflowing with whatever he could gather (fig. 52). He was unable to rescue a single canvas. Writing Hubbell afterwards, he commented: "The fire in our part of town started only two blocks away from the studio. I saved only what my wife and I could carry on our backs. I lost a lot of my Indian rugs, all my canvases, and a great many books and sketches, but rescued a few—my most valuable sketches, etc.—the pictures can be repainted some day. . . . I would not have missed that experience for what it cost me—it was one of a lifetime. It was an education. I learned more in those three terrible days than in any ten years of ordinary life."[40] Xavier Martinez made a quick sketch of Dixon and Tobey and he and his wife leaving San Francisco the next day, which he titled *Moving* (fig. 53).

Victims of the earthquake and fire included the presses printing the May 1906 issue of *Sunset Magazine*, but the magazine managed to publish an eight-page pamphlet, called the *New San Francisco Emergency Edition*, printing it on a small platen-press in the still-standing Ferry Building. Dixon designed the cover, *The Spirit of the City*, an image symbolizing hope rising from the smoldering ruins of San Francisco (fig. 54). E. H. Harriman, president of the Southern Pacific and Union Pacific railroads wrote

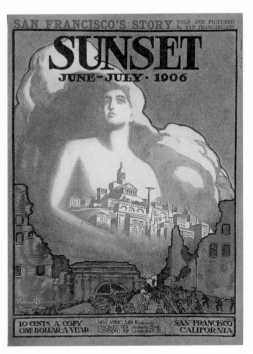

54. *Sunset Emergency Edition,*
May 1906,
private collection

55. *Sunset Magazine,* June–July 1906,
California History Section,
California State Library

the editorial for the little pamphlet. *Sunset Magazine* next assigned Dixon to paint a watercolor for the cover of the June–July issue, representing a goddess-like figure lifting up and embracing the city, looking to a new and promising future (fig. 55). In addition to the cover, Dixon also wrote a poem, "San Francisco's Promise," which the magazine reproduced as an epigraph.

While the fires still smoldered, the little crowd of bohemians, Dixon included, to whom Coppa's seemed a second home, gathered there, survivors in a sea of desolation, standing amidst ashes to bid farewell to the old place. Coppa had decided to move his restaurant. The food and wine, even water for coffee, had to be brought over from Oakland. Permission was secured from soldiers guarding the streets, who told the revelers to remain as long as they liked. With a sentry posted outside, the group recited their memories, hoisted their glasses, and bade farewell. Shortly thereafter, Coppa moved the restaurant to 423 Pine Street, erecting a big electric sign, "Original Coppa," although earthquake rubble still littered the street and sidewalks (fig. 56). The Coppa murals, Bohemia's collective creation, had perished almost on their first birthday. But as soon as the walls of Coppa's new restaurant had been prepared for pictures, Dixon drew a life-size charcoal cartoon on the wall next to the front door, picturing bohemians lured to dinner by Coppa, displaying a gigantic bill of fare. Behind him, perched on a stool, stood

Penelo, the Coppan's favorite waiter, while shown marching through the door were many of the notable people who frequented Coppa's: Jimmy Hopper, Xavier Martinez, George Sterling, Porter Garnett, Harry Lafler, and Charles K. Field. Dixon drew himself in among the group, gaunt, elongated, a cigarette dangling from his lips, tight pants, and the usual large Stetson perched on his head.

The earthquake and fire altered San Francisco's artistic community. Almost all of Dixon's paintings and drawings at his studio were destroyed, not to mention those in galleries and private collections. William Keith lost 1,000 paintings, including forty major Sierra Nevada oils, along with 1,250 drawings. Major private art collections burned or were looted. Many painters lost their life's work. Arnold Genthe lost all of his pre-fire photographs except his Chinatown views. The San Francisco Art Association's Mark Hopkins Institute of Art was destroyed, the contents—pictures, sculptures, library, an accumulation of thirty-five years—swept out of existence. San Francisco's artists scattered; some moved to Oakland, the Monterey Peninsula, and Los Angeles, returning to San Francisco after a few months; others went to New York or Europe, never to return. The city's vibrant art community plunged into a moody silence that lingered for years after the earthquake and fire. For many artists, including Maynard Dixon, they had come to expect the long process of rebuilding frustrated opportunities for their continued success.

Exhausted from the drama of the earthquake and fire, Dixon wrote to Lummis on April 22, 1906: "We are all in, and are coming to L.A. as soon as I can scare up some transportation: I will ask to bum on you for a few days until I can rustle a newspaper job. Nothing doing in the line for me here."[41] When Dixon arrived in Los Angeles, the *San Francisco Chronicle* quickly employed him as an illustrator to work at their temporary

56. *Coppa Restaurant,* 1906, Huntington Library, San Marino, California

editorial offices shared with the *Los Angeles Daily Times*. Dixon dreaded moving to Los Angeles, even though this might mean "longer grass." However, Los Angeles proved "short grass," and he labored in exhausting drudgery for three months. Lummis tried to help, counseling and encouraging Dixon, advising him to keep standards high and let his feelings emerge through poetry. However, Dixon informed Hubbell that "the unsettled state of my affairs, the pressure of work, and this rotten enervating climate they have here, have all kept me in bondage. Do you know, Ganado seems more like home to me now than any other spot!"[42] There was something else. Dixon had met a young woman named Sophie Treadwell when she was working at one of the San Francisco newspapers, and they had become close. Treadwell would become more than just a close friend—their affair would last until 1916.

57. *The Spirit of the Grape*, 1906,
California History Section,
California State Library

Besides assignments for the *Chronicle*, he developed freelance illustrations for magazines and other newspapers, including *Sunset Magazine*, *Pacific Monthly*, *East and West*, and *Ridgeway's*, an eastern magazine. The *San Francisco Examiner* used three Dixon illustrations for an article in June 1906, "A Swashbuckler Out of Time" about the life of Billy the Kid, whose legend continued to expand. The *San Francisco Chronicle* also issued a full-page color insert, *The Spirit of the Grape* (fig. 57), celebrating the state's growing wine industry.

Dixon finally returned to San Francisco in August 1906 and searched for freelance work again, but he found limited opportunities in the post-earthquake city, although he was able to secure a commission from *Sunset Magazine* for a cover (fig. 58). San Francisco was then in the midst of frenetic rebuilding, political graft by local politicians had split the city into quarreling factions, and a violent streetcar strike created further tensions. Many of the city's artists and writers had fled, seeking employment in New York. He managed, however, to secure some illustration assignments from the *San Francisco Chronicle* as well. In December 1906, *Sunset Magazine* published Dixon's article "The Singing of the West," seven pages of praise about the glory of the West with half-a-dozen of his full-page watercolor drawings and several small sketches. The magazine also placed his painting of an equestrian St. Nicholas—with a pistol tucked into his belt—on the cover.

As Dixon struggled to reestablish himself in San Francisco, the art community tried to resurrect the lost sense of community. Since most of San Francisco's artists and their studios had been dislocated, A. D. Shephard, manager of the Hotel Del Monte in Monterey, thought starting an art gallery in his hotel would help revive the careers of Bay Area artists. Shephard called a planning meeting in February 1907, attended by William Keith, Charles Rollo Peters, Xavier Martinez, Arthur Mathews, Eugen Neuhaus, Will Sparks, and Gottardo Piazzoni. From that first meeting emerged the grand opening exhibition of the Hotel Del Monte Art Gallery on April 20, 1907. A jury chaired by Arnold Genthe selected paintings for the exhibit, including Dixon's *Desert Shower*, now in the collections of Hubbell Trading Post National Historic Site at Ganado, Arizona.

58. *Sunset Magazine,* August 1906, California History Section, California State Library

FOUR

The New York Years
1907–1912

During the first month of 1907, Dixon provided an illustration for the cover of *Sunset Magazine* featuring a cowboy with his riata (fig. 59). He also furnished illustrations for the *San Francisco Examiner*, including several for an article by John Muir on the demise of a giant Sequoia (fig. 60). Dixon managed to escape San Francisco, "that monster mad-house," after receiving a commission to create murals for the Southern Pacific's new Tucson, Arizona, passenger depot. He painted four lunette panels in his San Francisco studio for the station's entrance vestibule, illustrating the historical figures or events characteristic of Arizona (fig. 61). The murals illustrated the historical figures and events characteristic of Arizona: *The Prospector*, *The Apache*, and *The Cattleman* (figs. 62–64), as well as *Irrigation*, which is now lost. After finishing the murals, he traveled to Tucson and installed them in the railroad's Spanish Renaissance–style building. "The town took kindly to my work," he wrote Hubbell, "the Americans, they heard it was the proper thing. The first breeze I got from one [of] these was the question 'Are they all hand painted?' The ones who really seemed to understand the pictures were the Mexicans. My fine knowledge of Spanish perhaps saved me some embarrassment."[1] These murals were the first of what became an important segment of his artistic life, when he created numerous murals for libraries, hotels, and post offices from the early 1920s until 1946. After the murals were placed in the station, Dixon wandered through Tucson's streets, making sketches of the Hispanic section's architecture and exploring the surrounding desert (figs. 65–68).

Upon returning to San Francisco, he and Tobey temporarily moved into his mother's house in Sausalito. He quickly secured a commission, illustrations for an article by muck-raker Lincoln Steffens, who came to San Francisco on a national tour, exposing graft in the cities. The article savaged the corrupt regime of Mayor Eugene E. Schmitz and political boss Abe Ruef, who with their followers had sold out to powerful business interests. Steffens asked Dixon to illustrate his forthcoming piece, "The Making of a Fighter," about Frank Henly, an honest San Francisco politician opposing the Schmitz and Ruef machine. Dixon readily agreed and furnished several pen-and-ink illustrations that appeared in

59. *Sunset Magazine*, January
1907, California History Section,
California State Library

60. *When a Giant Sequoia Falls*,
1907, California History Section,
California State Library

the August 1907 issue of *American Magazine*.
Never reluctant to enter the political fray, he drew
numerous illustrations throughout 1907 and early
1908 for *Western World*, a weekly San Francisco
political magazine that had been started by Mary
Edith Griswold and her husband, Colonel Edwin
Emerson, a former Rough Rider commander. In
the magazine's two-year existence, Dixon created
pen-and-ink drawings for six covers, illustrated several articles about San Francisco's political scene,
and even wrote a political poem, "The Gap," for
the magazine's July 27, 1907, issue.

Dixon painted a black-and-white gouache
illustration for a Jack London story in Gertrude
Atherton and Mary Austin's *The Spinner's Book
of Fiction*, published by San Francisco publisher
Paul Elder. That same year, he furnished the
cover design and several pen-and-ink illustrations
for Idah Meacham Strobridge's second book, *The
Loom of the Desert*, a compilation of stories that

61. *Maynard Dixon Painting
Tucson Murals in His Studio*,
1907, California History Section,
California State Library

62. *The Prospector*, 1907, oil on canvas, 31³/₄ x 73¹/₂ inches, Arizona Historical Society: 74.90.2

63. *The Apache*, 1907, oil on canvas, 33¹/₂ x 72¹/₂, Arizona Historical Society: 74.90.1

64. *The Cattleman*, 1907, oil on canvas, 33¹/₄ x 75 inches, Arizona Historical Society: 74.90.3

65. *In Old Tucson*, 1907, oil on canvas board, 9 x 12 inches, private collection

LEFT: 66. *Old Adobe by Moonlight*, 1907, pencil on paper, 11 x 15 inches, private collection

BELOW LEFT: 67. *Tucson Barrio*, 1907, charcoal and conté crayon on paper, 14 x 11 inches, private collection

BELOW: 68. *Adobe Walls, Tucson*, 1907, pencil on paper, 8 x 10 inches, private collection

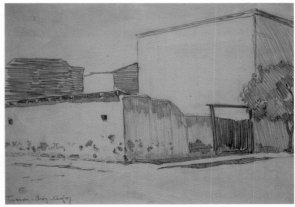

had appeared in the *Argonaut, Out West,* and other magazines. Dixon had met Strobridge through Lummis sometime in 1899, providing an illustration for her article, "Staging in the Sierras," in the February 1900 issue of *Land of Sunshine.* That same year, she had moved to Los Angeles from Nevada and lived near Lummis in the artists' colony in Pasadena's Arroyo Seco. She and Dixon shared a love of arid lands, and her stories expressed desert life as arduous, particularly from a woman's standpoint; she imaginatively conveyed the desert's spiritual beauties with a vision and feeling for place, not unlike Mary Austin's. Strobridge's publications never reached a wide audience since she produced them in limited autographed editions of 1,000 copies each, printed and bound in either fragile pictorial wrappers or morocco leather at her Artemisia Bindery in Pasadena.

Now thirty-two, Dixon (fig. 69) had started thinking about relocating to New York. Most of San Francisco's artists and writers migrated there after the earthquake, seeking the promise of greater opportunity afforded by the center of book and magazine publishing. A commission from the Southern Pacific Railroad for several posters and advertising designs netted him $500 and two tickets good for anywhere in the United States. Dixon and Tobey decided they would go. *Sunset Magazine* declared that "the departure of Maynard Dixon, artist and illustrator, from San Francisco to New York is not cheering news for the reader of *Sunset.* M. Dixon's skillful brush and fertile brain have helped make the covers and posters of the magazines so attractive as to draw praise from all contemporaries. He goes now to establish a studio where demand and reward should be greater."[2] Lummis certainly viewed Dixon's departure for New York with skepticism, cautioning, "I am sorry to see you go to New York. It is like a peach—not that you are one—going from the twig to the cannery. But you are old enough to have acquired permanently in your bones the need of freedom. . . . Only, don't let them swamp you. Don't forget that everybody in the world knows more than you do about something; but that you know more than all the world about your own. The trouble with any such alleged metropolitan center is that it wants to use you. Don't be used. Go hungry first. Don't let any of them buy you. Don't sell anything that isn't you. Don't forget your backbone. And between times, go on writing good honest verse, as an aid to your pictorial art."[3]

When Dixon and Tobey arrived in New York in early January of 1908, they discovered their bankroll, $300 deposited in a New York bank, had been lost in a recent financial panic. However, Dixon promptly landed a commission from *Century Magazine* for a western illustration to accompany Edgar Beecher Bronson's story "A Desert Sport," allowing them to rent a small studio in the Lincoln Arcade building at 1947 Broadway. There was nothing to put in the new studio, however, since his entire cowboy and Indian material had been destroyed in the 1906 disaster. Dixon, as an illustrator of western stories, desperately needed appropriate background artifacts, so he asked writer Eugene Manlove Rhodes, then living in Apalachin, New York, to obtain studio material at the smallest possible cost. Rhodes forwarded the request to Agnes Morley Cleaveland in Silver City, New Mexico, asking for assistance in collecting the material. Cleaveland assembled a stock saddle, saddle blanket, still-usable Stetson hat, runover-at-the-heels-but-wearable cowboy boots, chaps, bridle, spurs, quirt, and leather cuffs, and then shipped them to Dixon in New York.

Once the artifacts were installed in his studio, Dixon made the rounds of the newspaper, book publishing, and magazine offices, discovering a large majority of his bohemian San Francisco friends had also sought opportunities in New York, including artists Harry Raleigh, Arthur Cahill, Harrison Fisher, Ed Borein; sculptors Robert Aitken and Gutzon Borglum; photographer Arnold Genthe; and writers Gelett Burgess, Jimmy Hopper, and Wallace and Will Irwin. Illustrators did not retain representatives at this time, so Dixon and his fellow artists' contacts with editors, art editors, and authors were warm, direct, and personal. The illustrator and author usually discussed picture situations together, often collaborating on book or magazine projects for years. The rapid growth of magazines prompted by the development of new printing technologies enlarged the field of commercial and journalistic art, providing employment for many illustrators.

Dixon became an instant success in New York, spending the next several years working long hours in his studio, filling orders for book and magazine illustrations. Besides *Century Magazine,* his mostly western adventure illustrations appeared on the covers or in articles for some of America's new and important periodicals, including *Scribner's, Colliers, Saturday Evening Post, Hamptons, Life, Cavalier, Outdoor Life, Pearsons, Short Stories,* and *McClures.* By 1912, Dixon would be one of the leading illustrators of western stories in America in a time considered the "Golden Age of Illustration." In the early twentieth century, America's appetite for information and entertainment was served primarily by the illustrated magazine. Publishers, editors, writers, and the greatest heroes—the illustrators—became celebrities. Illustrators enjoyed enormous public recognition, their work eagerly awaited by their fans. There was still no important distinction between fine art and "commercial" art, and many artists pursued simultaneous careers in painting for print and for

69. *Maynard Dixon,* 1907, private collection

gallery and museum exhibition. Important annual exhibitions by Howard Pyle, N. C. Wyeth, Charles Dana Gibson, Frank DuMond, Maxfield Parrish, and a wide array of other noted illustrators often included work originally commissioned as illustration. Few pronounced art styles or movements emerged until 1906 or later; most painting during this period employed variations of realism. Many easel painters used general themes, often illustrative. However, the practical and expedient aspects of book or magazine illustration sometimes relegated their makers to an inferior status as judged by the leading academicians of the period.

Dixon's studio soon became an informal meeting place for artists, writers, actors, Wild West performers, and others with an emotional and intellectual interest in the West and in American art. Artists Robert Henri, Ernest L. Blumenschein, James Swinnerton, and Ed Borein, or writers Eugene Manlove Rhodes, Emerson Hough, and Andy Adams would drop by. Dixon met Charles M. Russell there in 1908, when Russell and his wife came to New York City, bringing an exhibition of paintings on the way to London. Russell made an impression on Dixon, who recalled:

I first began to hear about "Charlie Russell, the cowboy artist" as far back as 1890, and from then on with fair regularity in almost any part of the West wherever pictures of western life might be mentioned. His fame was greatest, of course, among cattlemen and old-timers. He had a poor rating with artists and esthetes—though I believe no one, especially none who had attempted a study of the life he pictured, ever questioned his complete knowledge and truthfulness. For these we all respected him, whatever we thought of the artistic use he made of them. Natural fact and historical accuracy were his aims; imagination, interpretation,—a recreation of the subject matter—to him were non-sense. He said "I do not object to broad free painting—but I want to have sense,—I want to see what it is." Also, "I talk with these esthetic fellows, and I don't believe they know what they want. They don't seem to know a damn thing but painting. They are just 'artists.' I'm not an 'artist'— I'm an illustrator. I just try to tell the truth about what I know." He made such statements always quietly and modestly, even humbly.

He never questioned another man's right to paint as he pleased—but judged him and his works with the literal commonsense of hard experience. (Nothing like long days in the saddle over rough ground in any kind of weather to work the foolishness out of you.)

In appearance he was all an old timer: about five-feet ten inches—heavily boned, wide and solid shoulders, square body, slightly bowed legs; massive head; deliberate of movement, slow of smile. He was the only white man I have ever known whose bone structure of head and conformation of features were really those of an Indian. He had smallish gray eyes and a mane of coarse tawny hair; but if he had been brunette and swarthy you could not have told him from a Crow or a Blackfoot. Also like an Indian, his face was immobile. The gray eyes were kindly; yet looking in them you could realize that he had grown up in a country where "justifiable homicide" was an honored custom. He always wore a cowboy Stetson, the crown not dented, no vest, a northwest "breed sash" and plain cowboy boots; but there was no hint of show business or movie costuming in this;—it was his native garb.[4]

Other visitors to the Dixon studio might include Mart Pickel, a New Mexico cowboy; actor Leo Carrillo; artist Olaf Seltzer; humorist Will Rogers; Annie Oakley and her husband, Frank Butler; and a striking-looking Abenaki Indian from Maine, Tah-a-Mont, or "Dark Cloud," a model used by many of the New York illustrators. Dark Cloud and Dixon enjoyed a close friendship that endured for many years. Lindsay Denison, editor of *Everybody's Magazine*, often hosted parties for the Wild West showmen at his Long Island home when they came to town. There, Dixon met William F. (Buffalo Bill) Cody, Major Gordon Lillie (who called himself Pawnee Bill), and the cowboys and Indians who worked for the shows, discovering "they were the real thing" when not posturing in performances before audiences.

Moreover, what may have set Dixon unswervingly on course as an American realist painter was the stimulating environment at the Lincoln Arcade building. On January 11, 1909, Robert Henri assembled his first class there in rooms 601 and 603, attracting Edward Hopper (back from a year in Paris), George Bellows, Rockwell Kent, Patrick

LEFT: 70. *Prospectors*, 1907;
ink, charcoal, and gouache
on paper; 21 x 14 inches;
private collection

ABOVE: 71. *Dane Coolidge*, 1912,
California History Section,
California State Library

Bruce, and several other aspiring painters. A gripping, captivating vitality permeated 1947 Broadway. George Bellows and another artist sheltered a young writer named Eugene O'Neill during the winter of 1909, members of Isadora Duncan's dance troupe served as models, Healy's Saloon was across the street, while a half block away was Tom Sharkey's Athletic Club. Around Dixon was the emerging evidence of an American realist art tradition in the making. He could not, would not, have failed to absorb an artistic credo proclaiming that expressing the realities of the American scene was worth pursuing. As Robert Henri and his followers found inspiration in the personalities of people, in ethnic types, and in the immigrants and their exotic world within the urban slums and tenements, Maynard Dixon found parallels in the miner (fig. 70), the homesteader, the cowboy, the Native American, and the dramatic physical landscapes of the American West.

As Dixon settled into his New York career, he became closely linked with two individuals who would have a major impact on his conceptions about the West and how his art should respond—Dane Coolidge and Eugene Manlove Rhodes. Famous in his era for fast-paced western novels, Coolidge (fig. 71) grew up in Los Angeles, roaming the surrounding landscape and beginning his lifelong interest in the natural history and people of the West. While an undergraduate student at Stanford University, he became a competent naturalist employed as a field collector for Stanford, the British Museum, and the National Zoological Park. As Coolidge traveled through the remote reaches of Southern California, Nevada, Arizona, and northern Mexico, collecting mammals and reptiles, he also photographed western scenes and gathered information on cowboy life. Along with a substantial part of his generation, Coolidge eventually became intrigued enough with the emerging Western Myth to write forty novels, five nonfiction works, and numerous articles. Maynard Dixon illustrated two of his books, *The Texican* and *Hidden Water*, along with several magazine articles.

Coolidge tried to reconcile fact and romantic fancy. Bernard DeVoto once commented that novelists could have the Old West myth or the historical West, but they could not have both at the same time. Coolidge, more than most of his contemporaries, worried about portraying the historical West accurately, although his sense of romantic drama caused him to drift toward "horse operas." The intellectual level of his work was higher than his competitors. Men fought more with words than with gunfire—and he seemed considerate of his subjects, knowing the West consisted of more complex factors than just rustlers, Indians, and gunslingers. Dixon, who shared this conclusion, developed a close friendship with Coolidge and molded his illustrations to the characters and themes in Coolidge's books and magazine articles.

Eugene Manlove Rhodes (fig. 72) wrote western stories and novels, many of them based on his experiences in frontier New Mexico. His compact slenderness and average height gave the impression of a man smaller than he actually was. Finely sculpted features enhanced by a luxuriant crop of light-colored hair, an abundant sandy moustache, and pale blue eyes that looked through whatever they saw and beyond added to the impression. A cleft palate made him hard to understand and almost incomprehensible when excited. But Rhodes had a poet's feel for description and a scholar's passion for

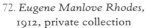

72. *Eugene Manlove Rhodes,*
1912, private collection

73. *Maynard Dixon, Montana,*
1909, private collection

printed words. Charles F. Lummis discovered him and published one of his poems in *Land of Sunshine* as early as 1896. Rhodes left New Mexico in a hurry on the morning of the San Francisco earthquake, April 18, 1906, and did not return for twenty years. The reasons for his leaving are not clear, and the accounts vary. However, Rhodes decided somehow he had "to get out of town."

Although separated from the life and landscapes of New Mexico, he wrote nearly a hundred short stories, serials, and novels, many of them for the *Saturday Evening Post*. Rhodes drew inspiration almost solely from his New Mexico experiences, looking fondly, perhaps wistfully, upon the old days, but never in a misanthropic fashion. With little formal education, he cultivated an exceptional mind, fashioning a literary career unmatched by many southwestern writers. A cowboy and miner before he turned to writing, Rhodes convincingly conveyed a sense of place in his writings with his unparalleled descriptive ability and powers of observation. He possessed an inherent humanity and a westerner's distaste for affectation.

Rhodes and Dixon met at El Alisal in the early 1900s at one of Lummis's artists and writers gatherings. Impressed by his authenticity—he knew Pat Garrett, Albert B. Fall, and other legendary southwesterners—Dixon called Rhodes "Dad" and treated him as another surrogate father, although Rhodes was born in 1869, so only six years separated them in age. From their initial meeting, through Dixon's many illustrations to accompany Rhodes' writings, and up to the time of his death in 1934, Rhodes' thinking about the West helped shape Dixon's personal and artistic philosophy. Dixon named his first son Daniel Rhodes Dixon as a testament to that influence. "I never saw Dad Rhodes often," Dixon said, "but there was a deep understanding between us. I always knew he was there. He was always getting busted and it was my good luck to be able to help out a time or two. He called me banker."[5]

During 1908, Dixon also illustrated a non-western novel, William C. Morrow's *Lentala of the South Seas*, published by Frederick A. Stokes. Morrow had met Dixon in San Francisco while writing for the *Overland Monthly*, *Argonaut*, and other magazines and newspapers. His short stories about the South and the Civil War had a major influence on Ambrose Bierce. Dixon also made a dozen watercolor and pen-and-ink drawings that same year for Amelia Woodward Truesdell's small book of verse, *Francisca Reina*, dedicated to the city of San Francisco still struggling to rebuild.

As their finances became more secure, Dixon and Tobey moved from the Lincoln Arcade studio to a larger one at 17 East 19th Street. When the heavy work schedule permitted, he labored on easel painting, judging results by visiting exhibitions at Macbeth Gallery, Whitney Studio, and other New York galleries, studying the techniques of leading painters such as Robert Henri, Rockwell Kent, John Sloan, and George Bellows. Technically, Dixon thought his painting compared to theirs, but he never absorbed other ideas or styles easily, recalling "I was not analytical and perhaps too stubborn."[6] Besides, Tobey's behavior affected his work, for she had started drinking heavily again, something begun while she still ran with the old bohemian crowd in San Francisco.

Sometime in the late spring of 1909, Dixon received an invitation from Dr. Charles Stuart Moody, a doctor at the Indian Agency in Sand Point, Idaho, who had expressed admiration for his work. Would he like to visit and paint among Plains Indians and participate in a cattle drive? In late June, Dixon arrived at Coeur d' Alene, Idaho. With its cool green colors and vast pine forests, this was country much different from the arid Southwest. With Moody as his guide, Dixon fished in Lake Pend Oreille, visited "old timers" and homesteaders in their log cabins, camped with Nez Perce and Kootenai Indians, and then traveled into the plains of western Montana to St. Ignatius Mission, on the Flathead Indian Reservation (figs. 73 and 74). Dixon enjoyed his rides over the open prairie; it was, he thought, "not strange—old as the world, yet created only this morning."[7] This was the northern plains, treeless, trackless, stretching away in long slow undulations to a limitless horizon. No track, no trail, no fence—only the endless green and brown grass under his horse's hoofs. Now so empty, once it had been buffalo land, and here and there lay reminders: buffalo horns, grey and weathered, in the grass.

In small paintings, Dixon would display his increasing proficiency with brighter colors, but still within the realist manner of the illustrator. He also created numerous pencil and crayon drawings along with watercolors documenting Indian and cowboy life, future notes for illustration assignments or for painting compositions in the New York studio. By this time, he had started to break from the older tradition of pen-and-ink drawing, moving toward sketchier, more powerful realistic pencil, charcoal, and crayon

ABOVE: 74. *St. Ignatius, Montana,* 1909,
pencil on paper, 8 x 10 inches, private collection,
photograph courtesy of Medicine Man Gallery

RIGHT: 75. *Standing Cowboy,* 1909,
crayon on paper, 20 x 9 inches, private collection

76. *Old Adobe, Monterey,* 1909, oil on board, 8 x 9¹/₂ inches,
private collection, photograph courtesy of Medicine Man Gallery

drawing, as in *Standing Cowboy* (fig. 75). When he finished his stay at St. Ignatius, Dixon journeyed to Cutbank, Montana, to join the large C Cattle Company, which had departed for an early fall roundup. Following the chuck wagon tracks in the grass, he found the outfit far out on the empty treeless prairie. The sights elevated his spirit: 150 saddle horses coming in at sunrise every morning or caught and held in a corral consisting of one long rope, cattle scattered over a hundred square miles of lonesome grass, and the good-natured bantering and carefree riding of the cowboys. But, rebuffed in his attempts to paint on the Blackfeet Reservation at Browning, Montana, by the Indian agent, Dixon finally went on to San Francisco. He enjoyed meeting his bohemian cronies again but was troubled by the changes in San Francisco's character and the stale commercialism of the Bohemian Club. Dixon was even more disheartened when he discovered that Monterey's Old California flavor (fig. 76) had "crumbled under the onslaught of fashionable development."

When Dixon returned to New York, he plunged into illustration commissions again and worked on easel painting; evidently his work was noticed, for, according to his records, the National Academy of Design extended an invitation to include two of his western paintings in its 1910 exhibition. Several academies in the United States operated at this time—New York, Boston, Philadelphia, Chicago—but it was the New York National Academy of Design that had pretensions as the national institution. Adherence to strict and accepted standards was its artistic credo. The academy's standards of judgment were based on technical proficiency and conformity to particular traditions, including the Barbizon school of painting, slick portraiture following John Singer Sargent and William Merritt Chase, remnants from the Düsseldorf genre school, impressionism, American proponents of classicism and Renaissance painting, and eclectic combinations of these. By the early twentieth century, however, the academy seemed provincial and puritanical, out of step with major currents in American art. In his autobiography, Dixon indicates he had received invitations for the 1911 annual exhibition as well; however, academy records do not list his name among the artists represented in either of these years. Perhaps he received invitations but for some reason did not submit any paintings to the exhibitions.

As Dixon moved toward increasing national recognition as an artist, Tobey's drinking worsened, resulting in numerous nervous breakdowns. In an attempt to restore harmony to their domestic life, Dixon and Tobey moved to the quiet suburban village of Nepperham, near Yonkers, New York. But his wife continued to drift in and out of despondency. Furthermore, she was now pregnant. Expressing his feelings to Hubbell, Dixon commented, "now listen to the mockingbird—we moved out here in the wood (nice place too) to await the arrival of a little Dixon, who is due in September. Think of me being a dad! That's pretty near a joke, ain't it? The lady is getting along fine, I have good hopes. . . . We are thankful to get out of the crush and noise and confusion of town. I think we'll finally settle down on the desert—where being lonesome is the real thing."[8]

Dixon's career as an illustrator achieved new heights during 1909 and 1910, with book and magazine orders arriving at a furious pace. Scarcely a month passed without

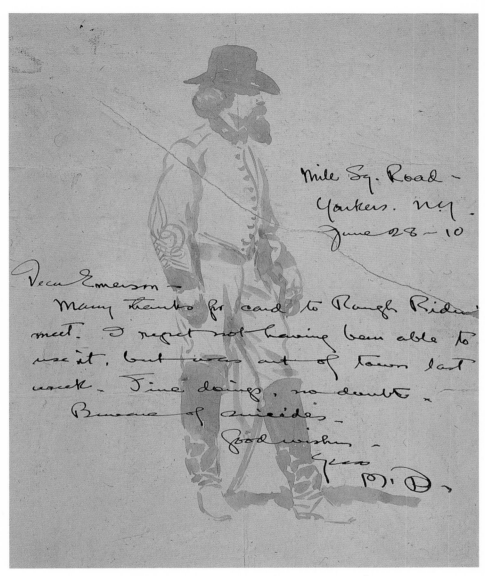

77. *Illustrated Letter to Emerson Hough,* 1910, private collection,
photograph courtesy of Medicine Man Gallery

his illustrations appearing in important books and magazines, and not just in the eastern publications. One of Dixon's closest friends then was the noted writer Emerson Hough, and the two exchanged frequent letters (fig. 77). *Sunset Magazine* continued using his illustrations and covers, including several for Mary Austin's *Blue Moon*, a serialized novelette in six installments that began in January 1909. Later in the same year, *Sunset*

78. *The Texican* (dust jacket), California History Section, California State Library

Magazine published Cyrus Townsend Brady's *The West Wind*, a fictionalized serial account of Plains Indians and military confrontation, to which Dixon contributed illustrations. And in 1909, Idah Meacham Strobridge printed her final book of stories about the life of a woman settler on the southern California desert, *The Land of Purple Shadows*, with the cover design, a frontispiece, and three illustrations by Dixon. As usual, Strobridge issued the book in a limited edition.

Between 1909 and 1913, Dixon illustrated numerous pieces for magazines, among them stories by O. Henry, Stewart Edward White, and Edgar Beecher Bronson. During this time, he also created striking color illustrations for numerous western fiction and nonfiction books, including Dane Coolidge's *Hidden Water* and *The Texican* (fig. 78), Joseph Mills Hanson's *Frontier Ballads*, Edgar Beecher Bronson's *Reminiscences of a Ranchman* and *The Red-Blooded Heroes of the Frontier*, Mary K. Maule's *The Little Knight of the "X Bar B,"* Robert Service's *The Trail of Ninety-Eight*, and Kate Boyles' *The Homesteaders* and *The Spirit Trail*. But of all the books Dixon illustrated, it would be Clarence E. Mulford's *Hopalong Cassidy* series that brought him the most fame.

Mulford created Hopalong Cassidy in 1907, when he was twenty-four. The original Cassidy was a loner, a working cowboy noted for consuming prodigious amounts of tobacco and alcohol, being vulgar, and cheating at cards. Cassidy "hopped along" because of an old bullet wound, possessed the natural irritability of a redhead, and was a two-gun gunslinger with apparent homicidal tendencies (fig. 79). Mulford's Cassidy stories were based upon his perception of reality, and he tried to avoid a romantic orientation. In March 1910, A. C. McClurg published Mulford's *Hopalong Cassidy* with five full-page color illustrations by Maynard Dixon. The book was a roaring success. McClurg also published Mulford's *Bar-20 Days* (fig. 80) in 1911 (dedicated to "M.D.") and *The Coming of Cassidy* in 1913, both illustrated by Dixon. In 1912, he illustrated another Mulford book, *Buck Peters, Ranchman*, that was independent of the *Hopalong Cassidy* series.

The move to Nepperham helped Tobey, and her drinking and their quarrels became less frequent. Dixon was even able to spare a little time for easel painting. In October 1910, he proudly wrote Hubbell, "The eastern coast of our fair land is a-quiver with the great news. On the 4th there was born to the wife of one M. Dixon a girl child of goodly proportions and strong lungs—officially called Constance Maynard, but better known as Mike."[9] Reflecting on his home and work life, he told Coolidge, "poor old dad is up at six and to bed at twelve for no handmaiden is to be had, kept cajoled or put up with and to hell with the working classes. For such is the kingdom of Haven't."[10]

79. *Hopalong Cassidy* (study), 1910, pencil on paper, 10 x 8 inches, California History Section, California State Library

80. *Bar-20 Days* (dust jacket), California History Section, California State Library

But Dixon's painting efforts along with his brilliant success as a leading American illustrator stalled in 1911, interrupted by Tobey's constant despondency, her resumption of heavy drinking, and an onslaught of terrible colds that made their infant daughter desperately ill. He complained to Coolidge, "though we pine for the high places there is no western trip for us this season. . . . So it looks like the Vermont Hills for us."[11] In the summer of 1911, they moved to Royalton, Vermont, near the Green Mountains, hoping this dramatic change would turn their life around. Constance improved, but Dixon disliked Vermont, complaining "I think God must have been soused when he built the eastern summer time."[12] He discovered the distance from New York reduced opportunities for illustration work and interaction with New York's artist's community, so they moved again, to Winsted, Connecticut, within reasonable commuting distance of New York.

Dixon's hectic family life and discomfort with the East's culture and landscape continued to erode his morale. Writing to Dane Coolidge, he remarked, "This last winter has sure put us on the blink, and I don't think we can stand another season of this country without going altogether stale."[13] His dispirited and caustic view of the East, particularly New York's urban life, was communicated in his poem "Thoroughfare."

If you should go a-swagger on the Avenue,
Swaying with its flow,
Taking to yourself some credit for its power—
On penalty of death then beware,—
remember its foundations.
remember you the rock underneath the pavements,
Remember the soil that was scraped from the rock,
Remember the lives that were crushed from the soil,
remember the toil that was squeezed from the lives,
remember the foundations!
To the rushing of this thoroughfare,
To the sucking sluice-way of this multitude
Come many lives from the furrowed lands,
From the woods, from the plains, from the mountains—
On penalty of death then remember
These are the foundations—
Lives-Life itself from the soil![14]

By middle 1911, living in the East and family difficulties had demoralized Dixon. When Dane Coolidge sent him several photographs on Arizona cowboys and range life, he responded, "You don't know how much good those photos have done me. Of course they did not allay my homesickness away but they made me fight for awhile that I was entirely surrounded by New England. Of all the canvases I brought to work on this summer I have put the brush to only one!"[15] The Winsted stay proved short, for by October 1911, the Dixons had returned to New York, living at 57 West 22nd Street. One reason for Dixon's eager return to New York was the presence of Sophie Treadwell, now working as a playwright in the city. Hurt and stunned by Tobey's moods, he increasingly turned to Treadwell for the emotional and physical support he desperately needed. Many of the poems confronting sexual desire and loneliness written from 1911 to 1918 are rooted in his relationship with Treadwell, which lasted until 1916. Dixon pursued illustration commissions and easel painting with renewed vigor, prompted perhaps by the disastrous summer. In addition to his notes about the National Academy of Design, he indicates in his record that the Architectural League, the Salmagundi Club, and the New York Society of Illustrators had all elected him as a member in their organizations by 1911, recognizing his national reputation as one of America's leading illustrators.

His wife's difficulties in combating alcoholism and an increasing resentment toward editorial demands that he portray a violent romantic West prompted him to consider returning to California. Ernest L. Blumenschein, who was then teaching at New York's Art Students League, urged Dixon to join him and several other artists starting to work as a group in a remote village in northern New Mexico by 1912, and which ultimately became the Taos Society of Artists. But Dixon rejected Blumenschein's overture, declaring he was not interested in artist colonies.

By 1910, popular illustrations increasingly portrayed the West as a land of conflict inhabited by only cowboys, Indians, outlaws, and perhaps a few miners and settlers. Americans embraced nostalgia, wanting to forget their present and recent past by focusing upon an earlier, highly idealized frontier epoch. Illustrators, prompted by editors and publishers, in turn exhorted by the reading public, concerned themselves with re-creation, rather than factual recording. The separation of the "western story" from the larger "outdoor action" school, represented by Jack London started in 1902 with Owen Wister's *The Virginian*, accelerated when Stewart Edward White's *Arizona Nights* appeared in 1907. The split was complete when *Hopalong Cassidy* appeared in 1910 followed by Zane Grey's *Riders of the Purple Sage* in 1912. Both Dane Coolidge and Eugene Manlove Rhodes also contributed to the rise of the genre.

Consequently, much of American illustration depicting Western life embodied heroic idealism, helping to create the simplistic myths about the American frontier. Dixon's illustrations were not exceptions, tending to confirm the images of strong heroic people—Indians, lawmen, adventurers, explorers, and self-reliant women. Knowing the historical frontier had passed, Dixon sensed the West as a symbolic concept would persist. Painting, not illustration, must be the mechanism to present the West. The exaggerated western fiction, which he had helped create, finally overwhelmed what he knew and felt about the West. "I'm being paid to lie about the West," he wrote Lummis. "I'm done with all of that. I'm going back home where I can do honest work in my own way."[16]

I have traced, to my own satisfaction—most of these curious misapprehensions, popular and professional, of the west to show business and the moving picture plays. In fact this has gone so far with "our readers" that cowboy, not to say "cowgirl"—costume is reduced to almost uniform, that it is getting hard to sell anything that is not fashioned to the limit. Your art director will seek Eminent

81. *Maynard Dixon in His New York Studio, 1910*, private collection

Talent here and in Europe who will model white men's bodies with Indian faces on them and unimaginable combinations of costume, and the painters follow suit.[17]

Dixon informed Lummis he thought about going to Paris but decided that San Francisco seemed the best choice since he and Tobey were "a trifle unstrung with confinement and overwork. Homesick too, when we get the time to think on it."[18] As he made preparations to close the New York studio, the National Academy of Design notified him they had accepted one of his western paintings, *The Lone Trail*, for their winter 1912 exhibition, following this with inclusion of his *Navajo Country* and *Navajo Journey* for the summer 1912 exhibition (fig. 81). In March 1912, Dixon and his family left New York for San Francisco. When their Union Pacific train stopped for water at Green River, Wyoming, Dixon dashed off the train to make some quick sketches of the landscape. Finally, he was back in the West.

FIVE

Turn of the Tide
1912–1920

When Dixon arrived in San Francisco, he found temporary quarters in a small studio-apartment at 1370 Sutter Street and shortly thereafter rented a third-floor studio at 728 Montgomery Street, occupying this studio until 1939. Almost immediately, Dixon departed for the little desert town of Mojave at the foot of the Tehachapi Mountains, where he searched out subjects for prospective illustrations. *Sunset Magazine* promptly engaged him, offering assignments that included a cover for the April 1912 issue and illustrations for several articles: Peter B. Kyne's Mark Twain tale "The Great Mono Miracle" in July and Dane Coolidge's "Sparrow Hawk" in September. In the midst of these illustrations, Dixon started a mural commission for the library of a San Francisco businessman.

Making a living in San Francisco was difficult in comparison to New York. "Hard work here," Dixon wrote Coolidge, "No use—Sage brush far away."[1] His arguments with Tobey about her drinking problem intensified. When tensions mounted, Dixon would escape from the source of his anxiety. One place he went was Sulphur Spring Ranch near Mt. Diablo. Dixon visited the ranch repeatedly over the years, riding horseback with the owner, John M. Walker, through the rolling hills and open rangeland. In another letter to Coolidge, Dixon commented that "Walker was 'an old-timer,' the last of the wild bunch. He was born here in this valley, was raised a

82. *Anita Baldwin McClaughry,*
California History Section,
California State Library

83. *Victory Song,* 1912–1913, oil on canvas on board, 4 x 18 feet,
California State Library, Sacramento, California

cowman and will never be anything else and he spends his time with me telling me about old California days. His father settled here in 1833."[2]

Near the end of 1912, "a turn of the tide" occurred that brought Dixon closer to the goal of becoming a serious painter, which he had been working toward since completing the Southern Pacific's Tucson murals. Anita Baldwin McClaughry (fig. 82), the accomplished and eccentric daughter of famous mining magnate and horseman E. J. "Lucky" Baldwin, offered him a commission for two sets of wall decorations. McClaughry had purchased two of Dixon's paintings and, after viewing them in her home, asked him to paint four murals for the Indian Hall in her new mansion, Anoakia, located in the Santa Anita Canyon near Pasadena. In addition, McClaughry commissioned eight smaller murals, which would depict a series of old English Yuletide scenes, for the Jinks Room in that mansion. McClaughry initially offered Dixon $8,000 for the murals, including the Jinks Room, but increased it to $10,000 upon their completion. Dixon recalled the impact on his career:

> *My return from New York to the old studio on Montgomery Street marked the beginning of my real development. I was getting a new direction rather than a new manner, and beginning to find myself. And it was Anita Baldwin who gave me my first chance in that new direction. Her encouragement of my ideals, and her purchase of two of my easel paintings, followed by the order for mural paintings to be done as I wanted to do them, gave me the start. I saw and always had seen something wonderful here in America. As a painter, then, I date from 1912.*[3]

Painter—not an illustrator. Painter—not an artist. Maynard Dixon declared his desires early, but not until 1920 would he feel comfortable describing himself as someone devoted

84. *Envoy of Peace*, 1912–1913, oil on canvas on board, 4 x 18 feet,
California State Library, Sacramento, California

to making serious images that stood on their own merit. Dixon completed eight paintings in San Francisco before he began work on the mural commission, among them illustrations for Peter B. Kyne's "The Long Chance," a story that was serialized in the January and August issues of *Sunset Magazine* in 1913. Early in the year, the Dixon family moved into the Osbourne house on Russian Hill, at the northeast corner of Lombard and Hyde streets. This house, designed by architect Willis Polk, had been built in 1900 by Fanny Osbourne, Robert Louis Stevenson's widow, after her husband's death in Samoa. But in Los Angeles, they settled for a combination apartment and studio at 431 South Hill Street near Pershing Square, where Dixon spent the next several months working on the murals.

The two larger panels measure eighteen feet in length and the smaller ones are twelve feet. All four panels are four feet high. One large panel, *Victory Song* (fig. 83), represents a war party returning with captives after a raid; the second, *Envoy of Peace* (fig. 84), placed on the opposite wall, portrays chiefs receiving a delegation from another tribe. *The Pool*, a smaller panel, shows women and children bathing, and in *Ghost Eagle*, warriors are watching "the mystery bird," poised above a huge rock near a grave. Indian models, hired from the nearby movie studios, posed for the figures. While each panel is complete as a picture, Dixon painted a background range of mountains and cloud formations that show a consistent horizon line when the panels are placed end to end. Below the panels ran a wainscoting of curly redwood, dyed smoke gray, completely circling the room. A red-tiled floor pattern from a Navajo design, graced by several priceless Navajo rugs, completed the effect. The door and electric light fixtures were fashioned from copper by hand. A large flat skylight with an arched cove bathed the murals in a diffused natural light. When Anoakia was razed for development, the murals were removed and are now on display at the California State Library in Sacramento.

When he was not working on the murals, Dixon spent much of his time with Lummis and other friends, including author James Willard Schultz, who told him stories about his life among the Blackfeet Indians. George Whitewing, a Winnebago Indian, often came to the Hill Street studio to pose. In fact, he is the central figure in *Envoy of Peace*. After several months of working together, Whitewing and Dixon had become good friends. One day they started discussing the Indian's grievances against the white man, Dixon explaining what seemed to him valid reasons for misunderstandings on both sides. Whitewing remained silent for a while, then remarked, "There must be some way we could kill all these damn white people."[4]

The McClaughry murals generated intense interest in the Los Angeles art community. Asked by an art critic for the *Los Angeles Times* to elaborate on the murals' symbolism, Dixon explained:

> I do not paint Indians or cowboys merely because they are picturesque subjects, but because through them I can express that phantasy of freedom of space and thought, which will give the world a sentiment about these people which is inspiring and uplifting.
>
> In these panels I wished especially to interpret the old life of the Indian who inhabited the prairie lands of northern Montana, Dakota or Wyoming fifty years ago. To bring out the poetic, rather than the harsh, brutal part of their lives, or merely the wild or woolly.
>
> The supernatural in the life of the Indian interests me greatly. It is so appealing, so relatively theirs. They breathe, practice its teachings, and thrive on it. Another fact of interest, and one which has won my everlasting sincere regard is their absolute faith and sincerity in carrying out duties imposed by this belief.[5]

Dixon also had earlier offered the newspaper one of his poems, "The Mystery," as an explication of his feelings about Plains Indian life.

> Sufficient for me is the rhythmical rippling of grasses
> That shine on the prairie, — so low to the earth, humbly bending, —
> Yet how many myriad times their forms are repeated! —
> On the slow solemn soaring of eagles in fathomless blue, and beneath them
> Pale snow of great mountains, — and, veiled, the blue shadows of mountains.[6]

Newspaper and magazine reviews in Los Angeles, San Francisco, and elsewhere praised the murals. Most critics applauded Anita McClaughry for choosing an American artist rather than a European one. The *Los Angeles Examiner* remarked:

> These works are of such beauty and scope of design as to make them notable; a quality which is emphasized because of Mrs. Anita McClaughry's surety of judgment in selecting an American artist who not only copes with but rivals the work done by many more pretentiously lauded foreign comrades. . . . Mrs. McClaughry, a woman

of culture to a degree of erudition, declares she has found here, for all decorations and furnishings—many of which in addition to the murals were designed by Mr. Dixon—a source of supply equal to that of Europe . . .

In Indian Hall to the left is a war party of Sioux Indians returning after a raid, headed by a bonneted chief and a medicine man and followed by a nude white girl captive astride a cayuse, and behind ride warriors and squaws. It is a home going after a raid, with the savage tragedy of those old events eloquently sung by the desperate figure of the white girl. Another mural shows the superstitious terror of a group of Indians as an immense eagle alights on a craggy ledge during a burial ceremony. Here is vigor of space, of immensity rarely equalled in a painting. . . . These are works of lasting and growing worth.

Mr. Dixon, who looks like a rather aggressive Texan more than an artist, is a tall gaunt young man who by sheer vigor of capacity has brought himself to the forefront.[7]

When Dixon completed the murals, he and McClaughry's architect, Arthur B. Benton, held a private exhibition of them at the Hill Street studio. Anthony Anderson, art critic for the *Los Angeles Times*, interviewed him there.

You may tell the readers of The Times . . . that I never was "adopted" nor "initiated" into any Indian tribe, but that I have camped and ridden with them many days and miles. I never "tried prospecting," but I have bunked with old prospectors on the desert and in the mountains. I never "drove a ten-mule team," but I have trailed with freighters on the desert. I never "carried the chain" nor "rolled the log," but I have lived in surveying and logging camps. I never played faro nor "bucked the tiger," though I have lingered many hours in gambling dens for pictorial purposes. I never tried to be anything outside my trade, and never earned a cent except with brush and pencil.

My object has always been to get close to the real nature of my subject as possible—people, animals and country. The melodramatic Wild West idea is not for me the big possibility. The nobler and more lasting qualities are in the quiet and most broadly human aspects of western life. I aim to interpret, for the most part, the poetry and pathos of the life of western people, seen amid the grandeur, sternness and loneliness of their country.

But the big thing is this—that there is something of the West that sings in us— both of the life and of the country that demands to be expressed. It seems to produce both the talent and, in a degree, the means of its own expression. Joaquin Miller's poetry is truly native—so is Sterling's and Sharlot Hall's. And in music you can see the same force at work. Art of purely native growth, lacking foreign education, may not always be "good art," but it seldom fails to be convincing.

Getting back to my own work and what I tried to say about it—the fact that there is something in my native land and its life that seems to breathe a free soul—that impels me to try to express it and what it means—is the same thing, I believe, that has made art great in other countries. It is certain that that feeling has made art national.

And while the West is still American let us make the most of it! Millet touched it when
he said he heard "the cry of the ground." That sense of sun and space and silence—of
serenity—of strength and freedom—if I can interpret that with what I can master of
technical requirements, I will have reached the best of my endeavor.[8]

In the interval between finishing the Indian Hall and beginning the Jinks Room murals, Dixon had planned a study trip to Europe, partly for the purpose of preparing research for decorating the Jinks Room and partly for a survey of European art. Recurrent asthma and confrontations with Tobey intervened. In fact, Dixon would not complete the Jinks Room murals until October 1914.

In the Hill Street studio, he painted another large mural, a triptych called *The Pioneers*. In the center panel, two mounted frontiersmen are posed against a background of blue mountains that extend over the three panels. The left panel depicts a wagon train struggling up the slope of a mesa, while the right panel shows a buffalo herd. The rich yet subdued color scheme gives the mural a hazy atmospheric feeling. In 1913, he donated the painting to the Southwest Museum as a gesture of his friendship for Lummis. Delighted, his mentor convinced the museum's directors to elect Dixon an Honorary Fellow in Art. *The Pioneers* is currently displayed in the Braun Research Library at the Southwest Museum of the American Indian. Before he returned to San Francisco, Dixon also managed to produce five color illustrations for Peter B. Kyne's book *The Three Godfathers*, published by George H. Doran in 1913.

Tobey, Constance, and Dixon returned to their house on Russian Hill in August 1913, and he reopened the studio at 728 Montgomery Street. After his demanding schedule in Los Angeles, he was anxious to head for the desert. He knew there were apparitions or spirits in the lands of light and shadow—perhaps in the image of a dark thunderstorm veiling the Painted Desert; the elegant shape of the San Francisco Peaks, sacred to both the Hopi and Navajo; a dusty herd of sheep drifting across a wide empty valley, trailed by the small, wild figure of a Navajo boy; or the enormous sweep of eastern Oregon's Alford Desert below the Steens Mountains. But as often as the desert summoned Dixon, something in San Francisco's character called too. Here was San Francisco. Out there was the desert. As much as he embraced the desert, he also absorbed the city, as his poem "San Francisco" indicates:

I love the flowing sky-line of your hills,
Blue spaces that encircle you with dreams;
I love the rugged contour of your strength
That points the sky with pinnacles of steel;
*   Your jaunty men make confident with health,*
Their care-free swagger and their careless jokes;
The laughing pretty girls upon your streets,
Keen-eyed and heedless of the dusty winds;
I love the stinging fog that gives them zest,
That wakes ambition in the blood and snaps

The sparkling thought from fact to prophecy;
    I love your round wind-hammered hills of sand
When I can see the sun-gleam on remote
Tremendous weavings of the western main;
    I love your tall gray buildings, garish-new;
Stark flat-faced monuments to Opulence:
Your naughty lights o' night, — your loud cafes;
The stream of strife and merriment that glows
With the blood of people unafraid to live;
But most of all I love your lingering scars: —
Occasional split curbs, — blank-ending steps, —
And grim chaotic gulfs of broken brick,
Where one fierce day the furnaces of Hell
Roared red with courage of a molten race
Remoulded amid shuddering Templors.
Out of those pits of pain now rise serene, —
Upbuilt of hope, — pure shafts of palaces,
White against azure, tipped with domes of Dream;
Yet most I love your scars, our battle ground
Of death and dust and triumph, you are Home![9]

But when San Francisco became pretentious and overbearing, his personal life uncontrollable, the art stale, Dixon yielded to wanderlust, becoming a bohemian westerner, searching for a solitary cosmological experience. "Mind you," Mary Austin wrote in "The Land," one of her stories in *Lost Borders*, "it is men who go mostly into the desert, who love it past all reasonableness, slack their ambitions, cast off old usages, neglect their families because of the pulse and beat of a life laid bare to its thews and sinews."[10]

But after a few days, a few weeks, or a few months in the desert, Dixon would return to the city, reverting to the role as a western bohemian on San Francisco's Montgomery Street. Throughout his life, the desert offered two redemptive qualities: sanctuary from pressures of an urban civilization and direct experience activating the creative drive. San Francisco seemed equally challenging and provocative, a place where he could bring the silence, the loneliness, the feeling of limitless space to appreciative audiences. Dixon enjoyed his role as one of the city's prominent artists, drawing admiring glances and comments as he walked along Montgomery Street, ramrod straight, dressed in his distinctive Old West garb. Of course, Dixon denied he acted out a personality, that "mantle of Remington" thing; but, nevertheless, he enjoyed the stature of his legend. The journeys between here and there, the city and the desert, shaped the contours of his personality and art. The city would eventually fail him; the desert never.

Dixon departed for Pendleton, Oregon, in September 1913 to attend the Pendleton Roundup and then paint in the northeastern Oregon desert. He found the roundup disappointing, "too much professional redshirt stuff in it," he told Coolidge, "the Umatilla were certainly fine in parade. Crook County was not much better, stock men all go in autos and a good saddle horse is as seldom as antelope."[11] But a telegram from Tobey cut the trip short. Felled with an appendicitis attack and a violent cold, she was unable to care for Constance and insisted Dixon return immediately to San Francisco. Dixon came back, though his presence did little to ease the domestic strife.

Near the end of 1914, Dixon prepared paintings and some other work for an important exhibition, November 1–15, 1914, at Vickery, Atkins, and Torrey, located at 550 Sutter Street. The gallery catalog lists thirty-one of Dixon's recent works, representing Arizona, New Mexico, and Oregon subjects, including some watercolor sketches for McClaughry's Indian and Jinks rooms. In addition, and also during November and December, the Hill Tolerton Print Room at 107 Grant Avenue exhibited forty of his preparatory watercolors and charcoal drawings that he used in executing the McClaughry murals. Porter Garnett, who wrote the perceptive introduction for the exhibit, reflected on Dixon's drawing ability:

It may seem like pointing a distinction without a difference to say that the public is familiar with Mr. Dixon's illustrations but not with his drawings, but such is the fact. Mr. Dixon is too much of an artist to confine himself exclusively to illustration, which has been raised to the dignity of an art by only a few masters, but even as an illustrator he has shown qualities of style which gave a certain distinction to his work. The superiority of his drawings as compared with his illustrations is made evident by the fact that a person without ability as an artist but skilled in draftsmanship, might produce a perfect copy of the one but would be quite unable to counterfeit the other. Take, for example, those delightful studies of movement from the nude; note the quality of the line; observe the immediateness of the drawing. Are these things that can be duplicated? Do they not belong only to the hand that executed them? Are they not as much a part of the artist's individuality as the sound of his voice?

In all of his drawings he brings us close to his subjects; by virtue of his free and admirable technique he brings us close to himself—close to the artist, the creator.[12]

But through his wife's increasing extravagance and his own indifference toward financial matters, the money received for the McClaughry murals evaporated. Discouraged, he retreated to his studio, working furiously at easel painting. Sophie Treadwell remained on his mind, and in the quiet studio he wrote numerous poems about his feelings for her. There also he contemplated his own life in "Night":

What storm-gray night-winds wandering about
The dark-subdued blank bastions of my soul!
What gulf reveals these insubstantial walls?
How phantom-like they are—and yet so real
That I can stand thereon and touch the stars
And shout a death-song that reverberates
O'er black imperial peaks that split the sea,
Vibrates the thin white wire of volted thought
And tunes the giant night-winds, wandering!"[13]

By now Dixon wrote poems furiously, reflecting the agonies that plagued him. He had approached the edge of an abyss, and the poems served as self-therapeutic, sense-making mechanisms, pulling him back and helping define his feelings about life. Searching for answers, he read the latest theories in psychology and contemporary philosophy, explored the teachings of Christian Science, even investigated spiritualism and the occult. Unfortunately, the ultimate answers he needed never appeared.

Emotionally exhausted, virtually broke, and desperate for some solution to his marital problems, Dixon wrote to Dane Coolidge about his idea of taking the family to Arizona for six months:

> Now what I need is a dry town in a dry county entirely surrounded by hot air. . . .
> How would Tempe do for a starter? And as the climate increased could we not with
> safety to my wife's temper and my daughter's indigestion work over into the White
> Mts. or Mogollons or Huachucas? My idea is to begin with the simple village stuff
> and end up in plain old camp as isolated and primitive as (for their sakes, both
> ways) it is safe to make it. This may read lightly, but when I say "kill or cure," I
> mean just that. The need is serious—perhaps desperate."[14]

As Dixon struggled with his problems, he and other California artists started preparing for the Panama-Pacific International Exposition, which would be held in San Francisco during 1915. Like the majority of his fellow artists, Dixon had submitted several paintings to be considered for inclusion in the exposition's enormous art exhibition. He wrote Lummis that "more recent work is receiving due recognition. Sent three canvases to P.P.I.E. all accepted."[15] The three paintings listed in the exposition's official exhibition catalog—*The Palomino Mare*, *Navajo Women*, and *The Trail in Oregon*—had been recently painted in his studio. The Panama-Pacific International Exposition started with a proposal in 1904 to celebrate the completion of the Panama Canal in January 1915. After the 1906 earthquake and fire, the exposition also became a tribute to the renaissance of San Francisco. The planners selected a site near the Presidio bordering the marina along San Francisco Bay, nearly ninety-two acres sprawling over seventy-six city blocks. Willis Polk coordinated the difficult task of designing buildings on the site around a central theme. The result was imaginative architecture, night lighting—a first for the exposition—and

85. *First Annual Horse Show*, 1915,
California History Section,
California State Library

innovative landscaping, creating a "jewel city." Local newspapers called the buildings "palaces of peace," although Japanese troop movements in Manchuria, submarine sightings off the English coast, and other war news sent a contrary message to the world.

Dixon was not the only artist inspired by the exposition. A group of five young painters, Selden Gile, Maurice Logan, August Gay, Bernard von Eichman, and Louis Siegrist, were galvanized and liberated by the fair's visual ideas, particularly its treatment of color. Eventually they came together as a group and, when joined by William Clapp, called themselves the Society of Six. While Dixon tried to spend as much time as he could at the exposition's art exhibits, he was also desperate for money and continued, in early 1915, to produce as many illustrations as he could sell, among them a poster for the First Annual Horse Show, a benefit for the People's Place (fig. 85).

Prominent American artists such as William Merritt Chase, Frank Duveneck, Edmund C. Tarbell, and Frank Vincent DuMond, along with California painters Arthur F. Mathews, Francis McComas, Jules Pages, and Eugen Neuhaus, served on the International Jury of Awards (fig. 86). Mathews and McComas, excluded from competition, had their work exhibited in a special gallery. William Keith, recently deceased, had a room devoted entirely to his paintings. The elite of American artists also had one-man rooms, including John Twachtman, Edmund Tarbell, E. W. Redfield, Gari Melchers, John Singer Sargent, Childe Hassam, William Merritt Chase, James McNeill Whistler, and Frank Duveneck. These artists so honored did not qualify for awards except in special cases. Gold medals were awarded to George Bellows, Gifford Beal, Colin Campbell Cooper, Daniel Garber, Ernest Lawson, Louis C. Tiffany, and N. C. Wyeth, among others. The Grand Prize went

86. *Jury of Awards, Bohemian Club Dinner,*
Panama-Pacific International Exposition, 1915, private collection

to Frederick Carl Frieseke and Medals of Honor to Emil Carlsen, Cecilia Beaux, Willard L. Metcalf, Lawton S. Parker, Walter Elmer Schofield, and several others. California artists Henry J. Breuer and William Ritschel got gold medals with E. Charlton Fortune, Carl Oscar Borg, Maurice Del Mue, Armin C. Hansen, Mary Curtis Richardson, Joseph Raphael, Bruce Nelson, and Lucia Mathews receiving silver medals. Anne M. Bremer, Frank Van Sloun, Florence Lundborg, and Perham Nahl received bronze medals, as did Dixon for his painting *The Trail in Oregon*.

Sunset Magazine erected two exhibitions at the exposition, one in the California Building, the other at the Palace of Liberal Arts. The entrance to the magazine's exhibit in the Palace of Liberal Arts was flanked by a palm and a pine tree, symbols of Sunset country. Just inside the entrance stood an enormous poster emblazoned "Sunset: The Pacific Monthly." In the center stood a large poster of Dixon's now-famous *Navajo Indian from Life*. They also displayed the same poster in the California Building, which served to introduce a large collection of original art by the magazine's leading illustrators, including W. H. Bull, Herman G. Struck, and Maynard Dixon. Charles F. Lummis eventually bought the Dixon painting *Departing Glory* that, along with several others, was in this exhibit.

In April of 1915, the Dixons, including five-year old Constance, departed for Arizona. When they reached Los Angeles, Tobey fell ill and they were stranded for a week, an excruciating wait for Dixon. "Arizona at last," he finally wrote Hubbell from Tempe, "in spite of all drawbacks, it looks good."[16] He planned to rent a team of horses and camp wagon, head east and north to the Fort Apache and San Carlos Indian reservations, the White Mountains, perhaps as far as Zuni, and then turn toward Gallup and Ganado.

The Dixons stayed several weeks in Tempe, Arizona (fig. 87), living at the Casa Loma Hotel. While Maynard painted around "Dobe Town" (fig. 88), as he called Tempe, Tobey and Constance adjusted to the climate. Benjamin B. Moeur, country doctor, businessman, community leader in Tempe, and president of the Moeur-Pafford Company, a large ranch and cattle operation, invited Dixon to visit his ranches scattered around the Salt River Valley. Moeur later became governor of Arizona, serving from 1933 to 1937. For two weeks, Dixon sketched and painted cowboy and range life subjects on Moeur's ranches (fig. 89). Afterwards the Dixon's moved on to the copper mining town of Globe, eighty miles east of Tempe, tucked into a narrow valley between the Apache Mountains to the northeast and the Pinal Mountains to the south and west. There he met and traveled with photographer Forman Hanna, who was documenting the life of Arizona cowboys. Dixon wrote to Coolidge about his plans: "Rice and San Carlos. . . . Some climate. We spend maybe 2 weeks at these places—then into White Mts. by wagon—early stages—Ft. Apache, side trip, Cherrycow, maybe, and out by Pinetop or Springerville—beautifully indefinite. Apache men not interesting, but women O.K. Plenty good types and old timers in here. Expect good stuff."[17]

Dixon roamed through the Fort Apache and San Carlos Indian reservations, followed cowboy and trail herds around Rice and the Talkali Mesa near Globe, and wandered along the Salt, Black, and White rivers, eventually arriving in Springerville (fig. 90). At Fort Apache, visiting among Army men and Apache camps, he heard faint echoes of a nasty conflict thirty years hence as he listened to Apache prisoners singing war songs in the post

87. *Tempe Butte,* 1915, oil on canvas, 9½ x 15 inches, collection of David Picerne

88. *Rain in "Dobe Town,"* 1915, oil on canvas board, 11 x 14⅛ inches, private collection

guardhouse. Although he devoted considerable time to taking care of his wife and Constance on the trip, he had still managed to paint over thirty landscape oil sketches and five large canvases, and make numerous drawings by the time they left Springerville. The family then headed to Holbrook, where Dixon spent several days visiting with Lorenzo Hubbell and briefly exploring Canyon de Chelly (fig. 91). From Holbrook, they went to Flagstaff, then to the South Rim of the Grand Canyon.

89. *In the Dust*, 1915, oil on canvas board, 6 x 9 inches, private collection

Dixon enjoyed the Grand Canyon but made only a few small oil and pencil sketches there. Perhaps he considered it visually overwhelming, but more likely, he saw it overrun with tourists, which dampened his desire to paint. It was also likely he felt the Grand Canyon was not sufficiently remote or isolated enough for his purposes. He did respond with the poem "The Grand Canyon":

Look now at this great solid Earth—
Think how old it is—The layered rocks
Laid down and cut by lost receding seas,
And see the little stunted pines that grow
along the canyon's brink, the same to-day,
And shed their little cones into the abyss,
As when the first vague giant emperors

90. *Dixon Family, Northern Arizona*, 1915, private collection

91. *Canyon de Chelly*, 1915, oil on board, 6 x 8 inches, private collection, photograph courtesy of Medicine Man Gallery

Of China ruled,—yes, ages yet beyond
  The same to-day!—then tell me where's the use
To agitate rebellion?—Nations—Art?
What are they? And what difference does it make
Whether this man is crippled, or that wife is true?
The warm immediate commands of life,
  Moist touch of passion—the relief of tears,
The microscopic labors we perform,
The fluctuating borders of our time,
The half-known movements of a century,
The growth of races building from beneath . . .
Cut through like colored layers in the rock,
High over which the moving Spirit sweeps,
  A giant wind along the canyon's rim.[18]

When Dixon returned to San Francisco, he seemed encouraged with his personal and professional life. The Arizona trip appeared to help Tobey's health; in fact, she did not consume alcohol on the trip, which was one of Dixon's goals. National recognition for his easel painting surfaced in 1915 when *International Studio*, an important American art periodical, reproduced *Riding Herd*, a canvas painted in 1914, as the frontispiece in its May 1915 issue. The magazine also featured an article written by San Francisco art critic and gallery owner Hill Tolerton:

Do you know Maynard Dixon? He is an artist who has interpreted the West, and he has interpreted it not superficially nor casually, but profoundly and skillfully, from a knowledge that is thorough and an experience that is wide.

  Executed with careful technique and filled with light and color, these pictures give to the beholder the pleasure of works of art done with truth, with the added joy that is always present when a real artist has put his own personality into what he has depicted. That the artist understands the life of the West, especially the life of the great inter-mountain desert, and that of the Indians, with a very thorough and complete mastery gained from his years of experience and travel in the great southwest, is self-evident. His art reveals the indisputable fact that he is not painting as an onlooker or an outsider after superficial observation, or purely for commercial purposes, but from a love of the life itself, as he has himself known and lived it. His art is expressive of his convictions and reflects absolutely the sincerity of the man. This quality of sincerity is the one to which we especially desire to call attention, and is one of the striking features of his work."[19]

Dixon placed the Arizona paintings in a large exhibit at the Bohemian Club when he returned from Arizona, considering it his first major debut as a painter. Several important sales occurred during that time, including the purchase of *Corral Dust* by the Golden Gate Park Memorial Museum (now the M. H. de Young Museum) and San Francisco collector D. C. Jackling's purchase of *Navajos Traveling*. The Cook Museum in Honolulu had already acquired *The Trail in Oregon*, his bronze-medal-winning painting at the P.P.I.E. In addition, the art gallery at S & G Gump on Post Street sold several Arizona paintings. Because he had painted a large number of canvases during 1915, many of which had been sold to collectors, Dixon decided in November to initiate a master list of his paintings. He kept this record of his work until his death. As he completed each painting, he would put the image's title and number on the reverse of the canvas, and then enter the information in his record book, adding notes about its price and disposition.

After the Panama-Pacific International Exposition closed in December, a Post-Exposition Exhibition, essentially a continuation but more modern in spirit, occupied the Palace of Fine Arts until May 1916. A smaller version of the P.P.I.E.'s Department of Fine Arts, only five-thousand paintings, the exhibition consisted of foreign

92. *Red Paint Restaurant*, 1916, private collection

work stranded in California because of the war, along with American impressionist and some modern works. Included were early cubist works by Max Weber; over thirty of John Marin's works, some painted after his return from Europe; two brilliant canvases by Marsden Hartley; and paintings by Walt Kuhn, Charles Sheeler, Charles Demuth, and Stuart Davis. In addition, Pablo Picasso had four paintings in the show and Henri Matisse was represented by fourteen. Dixon exhibited the same paintings he had at the P.P.I.E.: *Palomino Mare*, *Navajo Women*, and *The Trail in Oregon*.

Prior to the exhibition's opening, Dixon, ill with asthma again, had suffered a physical and emotional collapse, spending a miserable Christmas holed up in his studio. While he struggled to recover, Tobey resumed her drinking. Dixon retreated permanently this time to the sanctuary of his Montgomery Street studio. Tobey had been drinking heavily since 1910 and secretly since 1914, when Dixon forbade alcohol in their home. He had managed to keep her away from alcohol during the six months in Arizona, but within twenty-four hours after their return to San Francisco she was intoxicated. Heartsick, Dixon wrote Lummis, "Christmas day I came down here to write you—but I did not have the heart—The news was too bad. I had hoped to get a trip south and talk it over with you, but instead I have had to take a job with an advertising concern to keep things going. But this is not too bad—this is the road up. Now I am in much better command of myself and the situation then ever before—but the finish must be the same: divorce."[20]

Many of the Dixon's friends rallied around, trying to help. Joseph Coppa, by this time running another incarnation of his restaurant, The Red Paint, now on Washington Street (fig. 92), was particularly supportive, often bringing food to the studio. Dark Cloud, Dixon's Abenaki Indian friend from the New York days, who had arrived in

93. *Savage Tires*, 1916, California History Section, California State Library

94. *Coca-Cola*, 1917, California History Section, California State Library

California to work in the movies, also stopped by. One day, as Dixon stood at his easel working on a painting, he explained his domestic difficulties to Dark Cloud. After a short silence, Dark Cloud replied, "Sometimes your belly is tired. You take a wide piece of cloth and wrap around tight. That hold you up, give your guts a rest. Up here—he tapped his chest—it help get some rest too. But this—he tapped his forehead—it never rest. You stand here and do your work. You think straight and those troubles will fall down in front of you."[21]

In 1916, in an attempt to make a fresh start, Dixon joined Foster and Kleiser, a large commercial art company located on San Francisco's Valencia Street, at the invitation

95. *Pierce Arrow*, 1917, California History Section, California State Library

96. *The Apache Trail via the Southern Pacific;* 1917;
pencil, watercolor, and gouache on paperboard; 10³/₄ x 34 inches;
private collection; photograph courtesy of Christies, Los Angeles, California

of his brother-in-law, Charles Walter Duncan. (Duncan had married Maynard's sister, Constance, in 1910.) To the surprise of other California painters, Dixon credited the five years he spent at Foster and Kleiser as excellent preparation for mural painting. "It gave me not only new experience in design and color but some working knowledge of area and attention value, also an insight into the publicity angle and customer psychology mighty valuable experience," he explained.[22]

Foster and Kleiser hired the best talent available to produce their outdoor billboard and magazine advertising. Their artists made good money, showed up when they pleased, did as they pleased, and became famous throughout the United States for their modern design concepts. Dixon was acclaimed for the bold colorful designs he developed for the Savage Tire Company, originating "Little Heap," the small Indian featured in the company's advertisements (fig. 93). He would also execute successful billboards for the Oakland, Antioch, and Eastern Railroad, Coca-Cola (fig. 94), Pierce Arrow (fig. 95), and the Southern Pacific Railroad (fig. 96). In 1916, he painted a canvas destined for the cover of the *Standard Oil Bulletin*, which would be followed by many others through the 1930s. At the firm, Dixon worked with another close group of friends and colleagues, including photographer and etcher Roi Partridge, Harold Von Schmidt, designer Kem Weber, and Maurice Del Mue, who had, with Dixon, been a founding member of the California Society of Artists back in 1902.

97. *The Prisoners,* 1916,
oil on board, 21³/₄ x 19 inches, private collection,
photograph courtesy of Christies, Los Angeles, California

In addition to his work for Foster and Kleiser during 1916, Dixon painted two covers for *Sunset Magazine* and executed illustrations for Herman Whitaker's serialized fiction story *Over the Border,* including a cover for the November issue about confrontation between Mexico and the United States, showing an American soldier with three captured Mexican irregulars, which Dixon called *The Prisoners* (fig. 97). Dixon encouraged and helped the younger artists at Foster and Kleiser or at *Sunset Magazine,* who often approached him for advice. Harold Von Schmidt contacted Dixon one day in 1916, offering to pose as a model. Dixon, then working on a prospective mural commission, took him on. This gave Von Schmidt the opportunity to observe how Dixon painted and to study his work firsthand. After working for Dixon several weeks, Von Schmidt had painted nearly twenty watercolors, dynamic little depictions of cowboys, horses, and cattle, filled with light, dust, and action. Dixon invited Von Schmidt to bring them over to the studio.

> *He immediately sized up my problems. I was more interested in drawing details than anything else, and they were more like colored drawings than paintings. Dixon was working on the full-scale cartoons for his mural and picked up a handy one-inch square of dark blue chalk with which he proceeded to draw right over my transparent watercolors, blocking in the shadows, connecting them into an organized pattern, putting in a dark figure where it was needed to run across the composition. He went through every one of the pictures, explaining why he put the shadows there, how he was organizing them, how there was no pattern to the things, Again, no silhouette; I'd forgotten that in making the drawings.*
>
> *I was breathless, because I had liked the drawings and was sick to see them ruined. I was leaning against the wall, kind of weak; if the wall hadn't been there, I'd have fallen down.*
>
> *He looked at me when he finished. I guess I had egg on my face and he said,*

98. *Como No* (Sophie Treadwell), 1916,
oil on canvas board, 13³/₄ x 8³/₄ inches, private collection

"Well, you know, son, these are much better than I was doing at your age." I almost cried on the ferryboat going back to Alameda. When I got them home I couldn't stand them any more and put them in the fire. But, I learned a lot from the experience and the working arrangement with Dixon continued for over a year.[23]

Friends of Tobey finally convinced her to obtain a divorce from Dixon. In April 1917, he sadly informed Lummis, "just a line to let you know that I am now divorced. Little Consie stays with her mother—and their future will depend upon C's conduct which is not much in doubt."[24] They agreed that Constance would remain with Tobey if she would place her in a convent boarding school while undergoing treatment for alcoholism. Dixon, already numbed by the recent events, faltered even more when Sophie Treadwell arrived from New York to see him but departed after several days, deciding she would not share his life. Distraught he painted *Como No?* (fig. 98) and expressed his feelings in the poem "Alone":

Now she is gone,—the numb hours turn undirected:
As in a cinema show the people pass dreamily,—
Without color, voiceless, meaningless—now she is gone.
And little cold white thoughts, the snow of my sorrow,
Drift all about me, blinding me,—now she is gone."[25]

In July of 1917, the Great Northern Railway, through the efforts of Foster and Kleiser, offered Dixon an opportunity to paint in Montana's Glacier National Park and among the Blackfeet Indians, the region's two principal tourist attractions. According to the railroad, some of Maynard's paintings were intended for exhibit at Glacier National Park Lodge while others would be reproduced as promotional posters throughout California. Dixon accepted the Great Northern's offer. He then wrote Frank Hoffman, an illustrator he had known while living in New York, inquiring if Hoffman would join him in the project. Hoffman, then living in Chicago, agreed, and told Dixon he would meet him at Missoula, Montana. Dixon also urged Tobey to let Constance accompany him. Finally, Dixon wrote to Charles M. Russell, asking if they could visit him at Lake McDonald, where Russell had his summer home. Russell replied, "Friend Dixon, I received your letter and was glad to hear from you. We are now at our camp at Lake McDonald and will be here until the twentieth and from then to the thirtieth. I received the magazine and think your pictures were fine. They looked mighty real to me. Your Indian ponys and lodges were all mighty skookum. I am glad of your success and hope you keep pulling off good things till your light goes out and hope it burns long and bright with out a flicker."[26]

When Dixon left for Montana in early August 1917, his daughter went with him. Upon arriving at Glacier National Park, they found that William. R. Mills, the assistant general manager of the Great Northern Railway, had made arrangements for Dixon, Constance, and Hoffman to meet Chick Grimsley, a noted old-time guide, who would be their packer and trail boss. Jailhouse John, the camp cook, completed the outfit. (No one asked how he got his nickname.) The old cowpuncher and six-year old Constance

99. *Frank Hoffman and Constance
Dixon*, 1917, private collection

100. *On the Plains*, 1917,
private collection

immediately adopted one another. Grimsley let her ride a swaybacked but spirited yellow pony, along with two other horses, and encouraged her to help with some of the camp chores. "Queen of the camp," her father said, and gloriously dirty."[27] For two weeks Grimsley guided their pack train through Glacier's Peigan and Granite parks and on to Red Eagle Lake (fig. 99).

They then visited Charlie Russell at Bull Head Lodge, located along the shore of Lake McDonald in the shadow of Glacier's lofty peaks. From late June until the first snowfall, Russell made the lodge his workshop and study. A buffalo skull fastened onto planks nailed to a nearby tree served as a beacon to visitors arriving by boat. Two figures, a gnome and an Indian, flanked the steps leading to the porch. At one time, the cabin had only one large room. Later, bedrooms were added, along with a special studio with a large north light window where Russell could paint. "When you come," he told Dixon, "the robe will be shared and the pipe lit. There are no Injuns here but there is lots of good picture country and I think we can have a good time."[28] In the early morning, Russell would work at his easel in the studio, devoting afternoons and evenings to guests, either close personal friends from his cowboy days or artists like Maynard Dixon from his trips east. During the summer, guests always stopped by, and when they became numerous, Russell placed white cotton screens around the camp cots to afford some privacy. Each guest signed his or her name on the screen for that year, and artists were obliged to add a little painting or drawing.

The wooded slopes sweeping up and away to the silent mountains, the clear blue depths of Lake McDonald, the smell of balsam cedar and pine, the sound of mountain water running down streams were beautiful. But this was not Maynard Dixon country. In a letter to Coolidge, Dixon stated, "I did not think too much of the mountains, but the Blackfeet are the best Indians I have seen yet, bar none."[29] Dixon enjoyed his stay at Bull

101. *Blackfeet Indian Agency, Browning, Montana,* 1917, private collection

102. *Bearhead and Constance Dixon,* 1917, private collection

103. *Maynard Dixon's Easel,* 1917, private collection

Head Lodge, often talking with Russell into the early morning hours, respecting him as an authentic westerner and for his knowledge of the West. There were things Dixon was unsure about, costume details, for example, or things about the landscape, or matters of feel and mood that Russell helped him understand.

From Lake McDonald the group traveled east, just outside the park, setting up their camp among the lodges of six important Blackfeet Indian families on the north fork of Cutbank Creek, where the mountains intersect the prairies (fig. 100). There they met Owen Heavy Breast, Two Guns White Calf, Old Stingy, Medicine Owl, Curly Bear, Lazy Boy, Old Lady White Calf, and Old Beaver Woman (102 years of age). The Indians sang, told stories, and served as models for Dixon and Hoffman. From the last generation

104. *Mountain and Meadow*, 1917, oil on board, 6 x 8¹/₂ inches, private collection

of skillful hunters and daring horse raiders, many of them could still recall their life in the days of the buffalo. Few had attended school and most did not speak English. Lazy Boy, a noted medicine man, was born on Montana's Judith River around 1855 and had fought in intertribal wars as a young man.

Dixon worked hard for nearly a month at the Blackfeet Indian encampment, admiring the courtly manners and hospitality of his hosts and their response to his interest in stories about old times. He also traveled to agency headquarters at Browning, Montana, to draw and paint the Blackfeet who congregated there (fig. 101). Their leaders invited him to Grass and Scalp dances, and to the initiation of new members into the Brave Dog Society, an unusual privilege (figs. 102 and 103). He and Constance were the only white

105. *Little Sister,* 1917, private collection

guests at a Beaver Medicine ceremony. Dixon made many small oil sketches and drawings in the mountains and among the Blackfeet, notes for future work in his studio (figs. 104 and 105). The paintings were vibrant, quick with a verve that caught a landscape or a Blackfeet Indian teepee or a horse with a fancy blanket over him and cottonwood trees behind. Dixon said they were "painted down the arm," and what he meant was that he painted them by reflex, almost automatically. By 1917, years of experience trailed behind him. But finally, the snows arrived in October. Time to leave. Constance's last memory of Montana was sitting on the tailgate of a wagon, looking back at the wobbly black lines etched across the snow by the wagon wheels. It broke her heart, she remembered. "I wanted to stay and become an Indian."[30]

When Dixon returned to San Francisco in October 1917, he brought back numerous oil studies and drawings, including twelve paintings intended for Louis W. Hill, president of the Great Northern Railway, who had taken a personal interest in the project. These major canvases, ranging in size between thirty-six by forty inches and twenty by thirty inches and including both landscapes and Blackfeet Indian subjects, were apparently sent to the Great Northern's headquarters in St. Paul, Minnesota, for review, then supposedly forwarded to hotels and chalets at Glacier National Park during the summer of 1918. There was a fifty-percent reduction in tourist traffic that year, however, due to the world war, and the United States Railroad Administration had cut off privileges to use pictures for publicity purposes. Evidently, the Great Northern Railway did not purchase the paintings but indicated they would sell them for Dixon at Glacier National Park during July and August of 1918, if he desired. Some of the paintings have surfaced, but others have never been located. Dixon's records indicate prices for each canvas but no final disposition. Other canvases, inspirations from the Montana trip, were painted in the Montgomery Street studio during the next several years. Dixon also brought back a Blackfeet Indian teepee and the poem "Sweat Lodge":

Blue!—ethereal blue
here where the prairie ends the sky begins,
   no less than there on the ultimate peak of the mountains.
Naked and clean to the sky
   the little hills rest along the dark base of the ranges,
sky-biting teeth set deep in the blue.
      Over the northern prairie
deep benediction of sunlight;
   blue air from the edge of the world:
dream-wind warm from the south; from the north the warrior storm-wind;
   dawn-winds chill from the east; sombre ghost wind from the west,
Yellowing cottonwood groves
and rust—red fringes of willows, silently waiting
where swiftly Two Medicine Stream comes down from the mountains
and smoke-tanned cones of teepees stand sharp in the sun,
   my three brown friends,
   throwing their blankets off, stand nude and strong in the sunlight
   deeply inhaling the blue, they rub their bodies over with handfuls of sage—
Slender the willow branches
   fastened in earth, bent gracefully over
   forming delicate arches;
   the blankets spread over and tied to make snug the sweat-lodge;
the fire is ready; the stones heated,
   a sacred thing is the sweat-lodge.
Dark and close in the sweat-lodge
   three strong men of the Blackfeet in unison chanting
   o-he', o-he'—they are calling the spirit
deep-chested and ancient their power of inner conviction.
Mute in the clear-lit morning
   here I, the white man, listening now and believing
All my turbulent heritage, the turmoil and noise of my race
   slips away and is gone, I see anew this reality; see with new eyes
   the sky-stabbing peaks and small bright stones by the stream,
the silent trees, the vast roll and heave of the prairie, the blue volumes of air;
   the pale curling grass, and tangle of red willow stems;
   the coned teepees with sharp crowns of poles pointing skyward
All distinct, inescapable, sharp—Face down, under the sky,
   I hide my tears in the honest grass of the prairie.[31]

The Montana paintings show that Dixon had moved into a postimpressionist
painting style, with vigorous bold brushstrokes and a virile forceful presentation.
He exhibited five Montana paintings at the Bohemian Club's annual exhibition
from December 1 to 15, 1917, and also at the San Francisco Art Association's annual

exhibition from March 22 to May 22, 1918.

Dixon continued to produce advertising art during 1918 for Foster and Kleiser, although on a reduced basis. Meanwhile, he worked on one of his own projects, painting elaborate stage settings and costume illustrations for Bohemian Grove plays, which would appear in three handsome volumes published by H. S. Crocker in 1918 as *The Grove Plays of the Bohemian Club*, edited by Porter Garnett. The books included plays by George Sterling and Will Irwin, and sixteen full-page color illustrations by Dixon. The publisher also issued a collector's edition, limited to thirty-one sets printed on handsome paper.

As Dixon was completing paintings for the Grove Plays, Alice Corbin, the wife of Santa Fe painter William Penhallow Henderson, stopped by his studio one day to request he loan some work for an exhibit she envisioned of his paintings at the recently constructed Museum of Fine Arts in Santa Fe, New Mexico. Corbin and Henderson were then living in San Francisco while he worked on a camouflage project for the government war effort. They returned to meet with Dixon at his studio one evening, discussing the exhibit and his poetry. A poet herself and a member of the national editorial board of *Poetry*, Corbin was attracted by the power and vigor of Dixon verse and promised to send several poems to *Poetry*, although there is no evidence she did so. At Corbin's urging, Dixon loaned a half dozen of his recent paintings to the Museum of Fine Arts, which exhibited them during September of 1918.

Near the end of 1917 and into 1918, Dixon underwent a terrible episode of dark depression, a period in which he sought solace in women, finding and then losing, in two or three quick relationships, the companionship and sympathy he desired. Dixon credited one of the women, a model who twice nursed him through periods of severe illness, as having rescued him from total despair. Shattered by the loss of his family, he retreated further. In addition, he felt that American idealism had collapsed because of involvement in the war; this conviction further eroded his faith in the old-time Americanism on which he had been raised. Finally, severe attacks of asthma confined him for three months in his studio. Crippled with inflammatory rheumatism, worried about Constance and war problems, he still managed to paint a series of watercolors for an exhibition at Helgesen's Galleries on Sutter Street and to write numerous poems. Foster and Kleiser generously paid his full salary during the illness, so there was some income. Lummis tried encouraging him:

> *You may remember that I detected in you twenty years ago an uncommon capacity to do a valuable thing in an uncommon way. You have grown enormously in these years, not only in your technique, but in your soul. And I want to see you go ahead and grow to your full stature! You have the old chastity of feeling toward art.*
>
> *You have a chance to buckle down and work like hell, and keep working your very best. You have an uncommon natural talent; you have developed it in a way which had pleased me very deeply. Keep it up! Don't let any sorrow, or sickness, or worry cut you out from being the really great artist that it is in you to be. Growing — that was one of the wonderful things about Keith and a few other artists I have known — instead of stagnating they did better work the longer they worked.*
>
> *Never mind about the war or the government and dreams of socialism. Draft*

yourself to paint, and try to be a damned sight harder taskmaster than the government would have to be. Hogtie your attention and your intention; and between paintings, turn out poems.[32]

In 1918, Lee Randolph, recently returned from Paris, became the new director of the California School of Fine Arts at the corner of California and Mason streets, and invited Dixon to join the school's faculty. Randolph, who was attempting to make the school more progressive and responsive to modern art, assigned him to teach illustration. The other faculty members, a mixture of conservative and progressive artists, included Ralph Stackpole, teaching sculpture; Emil Grebs, teaching commercial art; Gertrude Partington Albright, teaching figure and costume sketching; Spencer Macky, Gottardo Piazzoni, and Randolph, teaching painting and drawing. Dixon admitted he accepted the position for the salary and finally left the school in 1920. Sometime in January of 1919, he formed the Hammer and Tongs Club, assisted by artists Rinaldo Cuneo, Harold Von Schmidt, Maurice Del Mue, Maurice Logan, Charles Stafford Duncan, and Francis Todhunter. The club, although short-lived, offered the opportunity for criticism and discussion of each member's work. They did not reject any school of painting and welcomed efforts deviating from the traditional, providing the attempt was sincere. The Hammer and Tongs Club held its first and only annual exhibition, June 16–30, 1918. Dixon had nine paintings listed in the exhibit catalog, including several Montana works.

Earlier that year, one of Dixon's paintings appeared in an important exhibition, The California Group of Contemporary American Artists, held at San Francisco's Palace of Fine Arts under the auspices of the San Francisco Art Association. J. Nilsen Laurvik, the museum's director, wrote in the exhibition catalog foreword that some criteria was needed whereby progress in modern art could be appraised so that only artists who had attained some recognizable form of personal expression in modernist painting would be invited to exhibit. Laurvik accepted Dixon's *Rain Wind*, a canvas done in Arizona during 1915. Other artists similarly favored included Carl Oscar Borg, Anne Bremer, William H. Clapp, Armin Hansen, Xavier Martinez, Arthur F. and Lucia K. Mathews, Gottardo Piazzoni, Henry Varnum Poor, Joseph Raphael, and Ralph Stackpole.

Searching for personal and artistic renewal, Dixon decided to explore desert landscapes around California's Owens Valley in September of 1919. He took a Southern Pacific train to Reno, then the Virginia and Truckee Railway to Carson City (fig. 106). From Carson City, he rode the Southern Pacific's standard and narrow gauge railroad 300 miles to the terminus at Keeler near Lone Pine in Inyo County. At Lone Pine, he stayed with old friends, "Dad" Skinner, an early Inyo County pioneer, and his son, William, a mining engineer and surveyor. Looking for solitude, Dixon wandered in and out of the little towns strung along the base of the Sierra Nevada—Big Pine, Independence, and Lone Pine—explored the vast playa around Owens Lake, and rode through the endless sagebrush into the Inyo Mountains fronting the western edge of Death Valley. To the Paiute Indians, this was the "dwelling place of the great spirit." He could think things out in this empty desert. Neither his former achievements nor the new movements in American art satisfied him. Modernism was gaining both popularity and adherents, yet Dixon still could find little in its concepts that corresponded to his own observations and honest vision. He knew he must make a choice between his natural responses and the advancing dogma of modern art. His inner integrity and respect for the scientific approach led him to decide that his art must include an understanding drawn directly from nature and the American cultural experience.

As Dixon prepared to leave Inyo County in October, he wrote Lummis that he would like to visit. When he arrived at El Alisal, he was surprised and hurt by Lummis's apparent lack of interest in his life. They did not discuss his recent work, Maynard remembered, "I went to Lummis as a wounded man and he rewarded me with coldness and indifference. I just walked out."[33] After returning to San Francisco, he worked on several illustration commissions and completed some paintings started during his travels through Inyo County. Before undertaking his desert journey, and perhaps in anticipation of some of his experiences there, Dixon had painted an illustration, *Pack Train*, showing burros loaded with gasoline cans, headed toward the still-active mining camp at Darwin. The painting appeared as the cover for the September 1919 *Standard Oil Bulletin* (fig. 107). In November 1919, the *San Francisco Examiner* offered some of Dixon's thoughts about the impact of Inyo County on his work: "There is no frizzy camouflages in that country. Everything there is vital and positive. And there is no room for half-tones when you paint it. He says he found there, where the corner of the desert abuts on the eastern slope of the Sierras, and especially in the neighborhood of the town of Lone Pine, a remnant of the Old California as he knew it when a boy."[34]

106. *Carson, Nevada*, 1919, oil on board, 10 x 14 inches, private collection, photograph courtesy of Medicine Man Gallery

STANDARD OIL
B U L L E T I N

PUBLISHED MONTHLY BY THE STANDARD OIL COMPANY (CALIFORNIA)

SEPTEMBER   1919

107. *Standard Oil Bulletin*, 1919, California History Section, California State Library

SIX

The City and the Desert
1920–1931

By the beginning of the 1920s, Dixon had worked out painting techniques to express the West as he understood it. But to his dismay, he discovered the region changing under the impact of popular culture. Inexpensive automobiles were destroying the isolation of even the most remote communities, emptying the stables and dousing old campfires. At first, the motion pictures imitated the Old West, and then the Old West began imitating the movies. That Maynard Dixon did not like what he saw is evident in the poem "To an Old Timer," dedicated to Charles M. Russell:

What news, old timer? True that line and fence
　　now subdivide the prairies and the hills,
　　a web of worries and machine-made ills
　　impeded your freedom without recompense;
　　that little people crowd and trade, and pass
nor lift their eyes beyond the day that brings
　　their petty profit of the little things
　　where once the west wind turned the prairie grass.
And yet I know, remote, a country where
God's desert peaks, unmoved, outstare the sun:
and still in lonely unsought valleys
　　run the distant antelope; and flashing
　　clear stampeding mustangs from their dust-clouds dim
　　wheel and are gone across the broken range;
　　the hidden ranch house and the springs are strange;
and eagles perch upon the lava rim.
　　So somewhere faith believes, though sense denies,
　　that while these peaks are free, these heavens pure,
　　still something of their nature must endure
　　in men who meet the silence of these skies;

that here these greater-hearted ones shall find,
where lesser men their lesser fortunes seek,
a mighty upland, clear from peak to peak
*   the free unfenced republic of the mind.*[1]

Lonely and in a self-pitying mood, Dixon frequented the San Francisco galleries, trying to understand the implications of "modernism" in American art. One of the galleries he often visited during late 1919 was Hill Tolerton's Print Room at 540 Sutter Street where, in the rear of the building, an ambitious young photographer, Dorothea Lange, had recently opened a portrait studio. Lange came to San Francisco in May 1918 from New York, where she had studied photography under Clarence White, afterwards working for Arnold Genthe and others in their fashionable studio portrait salons. People who knew her then describe her as attractive though not particularly beautiful. She walked deliberately, favoring her right leg damaged by the polio she contracted as a child, but she possessed a shapely body and carried herself so her gait attracted little attention. Everyone noticed her greenish blue eyes and her eccentric clothes. Lange encountered Dixon in an unusual way:

> *I told you I was in the basement most of the time, very busy working, and all these people were there a lot, many people. . . . I'd hear them (above me) coming in the evening, and some of their footsteps I knew. . . . My darkroom was just below that corridor. One night there came some very peculiar sharp, clicking footsteps, and I wondered who that was. A couple of nights later I heard the same steps. I asked somebody, "Who is that I heard with those sharp heels?" "Oh, that's Maynard Dixon. Haven't you met him? "No, I don't know him." Well, I did meet him up there a few evenings later and six or eight months later we were married. . . . He wore cowboy boots, that was it, with very high heels, Texas boots.*[2]

At first, Lange was uncertain about meeting Dixon, hesitant and a little afraid of him. But one of Dixon's friends, Roi Partridge, who along with his wife, photographer Imogen Cunningham, had become friendly with Lange, introduced them several days later. In January 1920, Dorothea announced their engagement at a tea party in her studio. Imogen Cunningham and several other friends considered Dixon too old for her, pointing out he was forty-five, she only twenty-four. Besides, he had a ten-year-old daughter. But Lange saw him as an original individual: intelligent, witty, a major figure in San Francisco's life, the kind who attracts legends. In turn, Lange's interest in him and his work offered hope and encouragement for a domestic peace that so far had proved elusive.

On March 21, 1920, they were married in her studio. One of Lange's friends, Florence Ahlstrom, served as her maid of honor while Roi Partridge stood as Dixon's best man. The ceremony was brief, led by Reverend Henry Frink from the People's Liberal Church. Only a few close friends attended the ceremony. After a four-day honeymoon, they moved into a small home at 1080 Broadway on Russian Hill. One of several cottages erected after the 1906 earthquake by "Pop" Demarest, a colorful San Francisco character, it contained one main room, a kitchen, and a tiny bathroom. They called it the "Little House on the Hill" and cut a large window into the east wall to give a view of their garden, installed a brick fireplace at the north end of the room to repulse San Francisco's cool, gray fog, dyed the curtains yellow, and painted the floor and one of their chests of drawers a deep indigo blue and the furniture orange or yellow. The house was within walking distance of Dixon's Montgomery Street studio and cable-car distance of Lange's place. To reach the Little House, one had to climb a steep flight of stairs and pass through a wooden gate, emerging on a bricked walkway into a garden, bright with the color of marigolds, Shasta daisies, geraniums, and nasturtiums. The rent was inexpensive, which was helpful since Dixon paid alimony to and hospital bills for his ex-wife, along with child-support and boarding school for Constance. Lange also had a debt incurred from the establishment of her portrait studio.

In a city crowded with colorful personalities, the Dixons rated second glances. They were a striking couple walking down one of San Francisco's streets: Dixon dressed in black, a black cape flung over his back, black Stetson, sword cane in one hand; Lange attired in emerald green, her favorite color, embroidered beret cocked over an ear, with a cape draped over one shoulder. They were centerpieces in San Francisco's artists and writers circle, a group that included (besides Cunningham and Partridge) the young concert pianist turned photographer Ansel Adams; artists Gottardo Piazzoni, Ralph Stackpole, Lucien Labaudt, Rinaldo Cuneo, Helen Forbes, Otis Oldfield, Gertrude Partington Albright; writers and poets George Sterling, Fremont Older, Charles Erskine Scott Wood with his young wife, Sara Bard Field; and Albert Bender, financier and supporter of the city's artists. They were never an organized group nor were they all close friends, but they contributed to San Francisco's vigorous, exciting culture between the two world wars.

After the marriage, Dixon reduced his time at Foster and Kleiser, working one or two days a week, determined to devote his full energy to painting. He finally terminated his employment in 1921. The S & G Gump Gallery exhibited thirty-six Dixon paintings from November 16 to December 1, 1920. The exhibit included some paintings from his 1917 Montana trip and several Arizona subjects; the rest were recent canvases from his 1919 Inyo County expedition. Local art critics agreed that a number of these paintings were different from his previous work, possessing a mural quality that celebrated the freedom and space of the West. After the exhibition closed at Gump's, Dixon sent all of the paintings to the Frank L. Orr Gallery in San Diego during January and February of 1921, then on to the Stendahl Art Galleries in Los Angeles during March of 1921.

In the early 1920s, Dixon and Lange worked apart, he at his Montgomery Street studio, she at her portrait studio. Home they considered "sanctuary." Lange, after returning from the studio, devoted her evenings to housework and getting the meals for her husband and Constance; while Dixon, who often did not arrive home until seven, divided his evenings between reading, the family, and work. Lange helped him with his work whenever possible, taking photographs of his paintings for clients and for their reproduction in newspapers and magazines (fig. 108). "The biggest part of my energy,

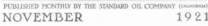

108. *Standard Oil Bulletin,* November 1921,
California History Section,
California State Library

109. *Maynard Dixon, Refuge,* 1921,
private collection

she recalled, my deepest allegiances, were to Maynard's work, and to Constance and the boys."[3] Yet she managed to reserve a portion of her life for photography.

Lange had feared being absorbed into Dixon's life when she entered the marriage, knowing he was already a respected figure on the San Francisco scene. She felt people spoiled him because he suited their ideas of how an artist should look and behave. Years later, Lange admitted that she should have been a more critical and less agreeable wife, holding him to his own standards, encouraging him "to dip his brush in his own heart's blood." Dixon paid scant attention to finances, and his wife tried to shield him from economic difficulties. She knew that Dixon loved her, but he would not share the depths of his life with her. She missed him when he went on his trips and was glad when he returned. But, she recalled, "I wasn't really involved in the vitals of the man, not in the vitals. Perhaps the reason that I was never able to give Maynard an uncomfortable time, which he should have had, at some junctures, was that I never felt courageous enough or felt the need. [Eventually,] it became myself and the little boys . . . not so much he and I, and the boys."[4]

Constance adored her father, thinking him too intelligent to get into another marriage, knowing the first one from an intimate standpoint to have been poignant and devastating. She wanted to live with him even before the divorce from Tobey. He had no room for her in his studio, however, and boarded her out. After his second marriage, he welcomed his daughter into the Little House. But Lange could, at times, be a bit of a tyrant. She demanded Constance help clean the house, cook, and wash, and never seemed able to give the girl the warmth and affection she needed. When Constance resisted, Lange would erupt in rage, hitting out in frustration, but begging her stepdaughter never to inform her father about the terrible arguments between them.

As Dixon settled into family life in early 1921, he received an important mural commission, his first since the Baldwin murals. This was for two lunettes on mining and ranching subjects, each eight-by-sixteen feet, which he painted for the dining salon of the Pacific Mail Steamship passenger liner *Silver State*. The mural so impressed the company that they awarded him another commission, this time for two five-by-six-foot canvas panels in the dining salon of the *Sierra*, the Pacific Mail's other steamship. He completed this mural in 1923, receiving $2,800 for each commission.

Exhausted after completing the first mural and ill with severe asthma, Dixon had to abandon San Francisco in the spring of 1921 for Refuge in the San Joaquin Valley (fig. 109). There he sketched and painted the land of his boyhood, working to refine his compositions and color. Riding over the open rangeland, he made drawings and paintings of cattle and horse herds. He also painted lonely ranch buildings, cowboys herding cattle, dry arroyos, alkali sinks, vernal pools, and the faraway horizon shadowed by billowing white clouds over the higher ranges of the Sierra Nevada (figs. 110 and 111). One of the places he stayed, Sandhill Camp, must have been particularly provocative, for many of the drawings and paintings from this period are annotated with its name. Celebrating the location, he wrote the poem "Sandhill Camp."

Some day I shall make camp at that place:
so far, so lone upon the empty plains!
> *close to that ground there shall be camp for me.*
> *Low against the brightness of the west*
lies the long Coast Range, cut clear
> *from Diablo, faint in the north to the blue southward spur*
> *that ending in mirage hides Coalinga.*
There is bending prairie grass at that place,
and swales where little pools have dried,
> *white-diamonded in rings of alkali.*
And two good saddle horses I will have,
> *and a lean brown cowboy there to ride with me;*
and I will stay awhile, easily, and dream
> *in that place with the sun*
> *and meditate upon the generous largeness of this earth,*
> *the nameless intimacy of grass and sky;*
> *upon the confident placidity of animals*
> *and the wonder of cool water*
drawn up from the deep solid ground, — and then
> *the wailing of coyotes in the night;*
all these, and the innumerable stars.[5]

110. *Erosion*, 1921, oil on canvas board, 10 x 14 inches, collection of Bruce Paltenghi

111. *Ranch House on the Plains*, 1921, oil on canvas board, 10 x 14 inches, photograph courtesy of Mitchell Brown Fine Art

112. *Glacial Meadow, Tuolumne Meadows,*
1921, oil on canvas board, 16 x 20 inches,
Crocker Art Museum, gift of the Elkus Family
in memory of Ben Britton Elkus

After he returned from Refuge, Dixon took Lange on a pack train excursion into the back country behind Yosemite (fig. 112) and around Mount Whitney. Joined by Constance Dixon, Lange's mother, Joan (Dixon called her "the Wuz"), Joan's new husband George Hollins Bowley, and Lange's brother, Martin Lange, the group enjoyed camping in the spectacular high glacial country of the eastern Sierra Nevada, wandering through the Owens Valley, and exploring the Inyo and Panamint mountains near Death Valley. But Lange soon learned, however, that her husband would rarely offer to take her along on his excursions. When the city failed him or when he needed artistic inspiration or when one of his periodic depressions appeared, the desert called with an undeniable force that he embraced to the exclusion of other

113. *Tallac, Lake Tahoe,*
1922, private collection

114. *Mary Austin Lecture Announcement,*
1922, private collection

needs. Lange eventually viewed their frequent separation as a mark of failure in their relationship.

Between 1921 and 1922, Dixon exhibited his work frequently, especially at the San Francisco Art Association and the Bohemian Club. At the First Southwest Museum Competitive Exhibition in Los Angeles, he was awarded first prize for *The Navajos*. In addition, he continued his commercial work, such as the cover for Anita Baldwin's Tallac Lodge at Lake Tahoe (fig. 113) and a poster for a Mary Austin lecture at the Book Club of California (fig. 114).

115. *Kayenta, Arizona, 1922,* gouache and ink on paper, 6 x 7 inches, private collection, photograph courtesy of Medicine Man Gallery

Responding to an invitation from John Wetherill in June of 1922, Dixon and Lange left for Kayenta, Arizona, on the sprawling Navajo Reservation, a trading post established by Wetherill in 1909. Upon reaching Tuba City, they hitched a ride on the biweekly Ford truck bringing mail and parcel post for Kayenta. Heading eastward past Red Lake, a Babbitt Brothers trading post twenty-five miles beyond Tuba City, the Dixons followed narrow tracks stretching weary miles across slick rock and sand to Marsh Pass, fifteen miles west of Kayenta, which divided the sandstone Tsegi Canyon from the rest of northeastern Navajo country (fig. 115). Then they followed Laguna Wash down into Kayenta. People who traveled through this country proclaimed that the Kayenta post office was the farthest distance from the railroad of any post office in the country.

Hosteen John and Estsan otsossi ("Slim Woman"), as the Navajo called John and Louisa Wetherill, had been at Kayenta for fifteen years. Wetherill appeared a soft-spoken, unassuming man, but his gray-blue eyes hinted at steel underneath the surface, reinforced by his wearing of army-issue khaki breeches and leather puttees. He had guided archaeologist Jesse W. Fewkes to the great cave at Betatakin and spurred his horse in front of Byron Cummings and William B. Douglas to be first under Rainbow Bridge. He possessed extensive knowledge and a deep reverence for this remote country. The Wetherills had built their house from cedar poles and rocks, and it was the only trading post in the western Navajo reservation with a lawn. Their living room, centered on a stone fireplace, served as a gathering place for visitors. Yei-bichei figures gazed impassively from a frieze around the top of the living room wall, Navajo rugs crowded the floor, while prehistoric Kayenta pottery perched on bookcases. Priceless old bayeta blankets hung from walls, and the only light at night came from a Coleman gasoline lantern suspended from a nail in the ceiling. While Dixon and Lange were there, other artists used Kayenta

as a hotel of sorts. Jimmy Swinnerton and his wife Louise; George Herriman, originator of the cartoon series "Krazy Cat"; Rudolph Dirks, another newspaper cartoonist, famous for "Katzenjammer Kids"; and painter William R. Leigh, out from New York—all were drawn, as were the Dixons, by Wetherill's warm hospitality, his expertise as a guide and outfitter, the spectacular landscape, and the Navajo (fig. 116).

116. *Navajos, Tuba, Arizona*, 1922,
pencil on paper, 5 x 4 inches, private collection,
photograph courtesy of Medicine Man Gallery

The Dixons stayed on the Navajo reservation for four months, exulting in the landscape's color and forms. Guided by Wetherill, they investigated the prehistoric ruins of Betatakin and Keet Seel, hidden away in the deep sandstone recesses of Tsegi Canyon, part of the vast network of canyons dropping from the great turtle-backed form of Navajo Mountain. Even by 1932, only slightly over 300 people had made the bone-jarring journey to the site. On other occasions, Wetherill led them on horseback rides through Monument Valley or along the escarpment of Black Mesa, stretching south from Kayenta. In September, Dixon and Lange moved to the trading post at Red Lake, using it to explore the country between the post and Navajo Mountain. Red Lake, known throughout the Navajo Reservation as a "dry post" because the water is so scarce, was located halfway down a sandy mesa, above what might be an actual lake in wet years, a dry lake in others, a bare unattractive location. But as the Dixons discovered, views around Red Lake compensated for this. To the west and north stretched the southeastern rim of White Mesa, pale above miles of green-blue sagebrush. Black Mesa stood brooding and massive on the horizon to the east. Navajo Canyon and unnamed tributaries led north to Navajo Mountain and Rainbow Bridge, an unexplored, wild, lonely country of monumental beauty, where only a few white men had penetrated. Dixon's paintings would record these wide expanses; its swollen thunderous clouds, sometimes hard-edged and bright; its moving figures, incidental in a landscape of towering mesas, twisting canyons, cloud-swollen skies; and the silence. "You feel the presence of fundamental things," he reflected, "it takes your mind from trivialities and gives you a sense of freedom. It obliterates everything—even the desire to read. I took some things along that I wanted to read but I found I couldn't get interested in them. It re-establishes your idea of values; everything human taken in a minute scale."[6] "My Country," he called it in a poem:

> *I love the grim gaunt edges of the rocks,*
> *the great bare backbone of the Earth,*
> > *rough brows and heaved-up shoulders,*
> > *round ribs and knees of the world's skeleton*
> > *protruded in lonely places;*
> *where from ledges of sun-silenced cliffs*
> > *the wild war eagle dips aslant*
> > *blue ecstasies of air*
> > *to the delicate deep fringes of the pines;*
> > *the long-returning curves of solid hills*
> > *that bend the wind along the dappled sky;*
> *or far-drawn levels of red mesa-lands,*
> *receding infinitely, step on step on step*
> > *and grandeur of all grandeurs, over all*
> > *the high commanding glory of the sun![7]*

By early 1923, in spite of his recognition as one of the West's progressive artists, Dixon had become discouraged with San Francisco's art scene, an environment he considered hypocritical and destructive of the artist's self-respect. So he decided to try the eastern art market. Taking seventeen paintings with them, Dixon and Lange stopped first at the Chicago Art Institute, but they were rebuffed with the excuse that no space could be found in the museum's exhibit schedule. Dixon nevertheless encountered a magnificent display of Plains Indian art at Chicago's Field Museum, spending three hours at just one exhibit case. He felt that seeing these artifacts affected his design concepts more profoundly than did exposure to the paintings at the Chicago Art Institute.

They traveled to New York, where Robert Macbeth, director of Macbeth Gallery, welcomed them warmly, scheduling an exhibit of Dixon's paintings, February 13–March 5, 1923. Only three paintings were purchased—a bitter disappointment for Dixon— although local press reviews were friendly and favorable. The paintings exhibited at Macbeth's included *Mystery Stone, Guard of the Cornfield, Iesaka Waken, Ledge of Sunland, The Ancients, Black Mesa at Evening,* and *Toward Kaibito,* some of his best work. Macbeth was enthusiastic about Dixon's work and promoted a traveling exhibit of his paintings to other galleries in the East, but he failed to secure any commitments. Through Macbeth's assistance, however, the National Academy of Design in New York accepted *Desert Shepherdess* and *The Ancients* for their 1923 winter exhibition. Those who attended the show at Macbeth's responded with enthusiasm. Robert Davis, a New York magazine publisher who purchased one of Dixon's paintings, *Matarango Peak, Inyo,* expressed his delight in a letter: "My dear Dixon: It is a startling display. The first time for many years that I have been permitted to walk into an atmosphere such as you have

117. *Clouds of Hopi Land*, 1923, conté crayon on paper,
13¹/₂ x 16¹/₂ inches, private collection,
photograph courtesy of Medicine Man Gallery

created. I felt the warmth of your sunsets, the mystery of your canyons and the majesty of your red men. I was particularly struck by *Prairie Shower*. I wish I had the money to buy it. *September Moonlight, Black Mesa at Sunset*, all, had a similar effect upon me. In fact there wasn't any picture there that did not greatly impress me. The trouble with the New York population is its total lack of understanding. They can't imagine how much nature you have seized and spread on canvas."[8]

Before they left New York, the Dixons explored the city's art scene, including a Georgia O'Keeffe exhibit where they encountered Alfred Stieglitz. A confirmed skeptic about "isms," Dixon commented that Stieglitz's presence created a "hot-house art atmosphere and fake modernism. After listening to exploiter Stieglitz expatiate, and observing so much cleverness and futility, I was glad to quit that stale-air existence and come West."[9]

During the late summer of 1923, Anita Baldwin (she had dropped McClaughry after a divorce) arrived in San Francisco for one of her annual trips, to visit Dixon in his studio and buy paintings and drawings. Unexpectedly, she invited Dixon and Lange to accompany her on a two-month trip to Walpi on the Hopi Reservation. Baldwin, who was interested in American Indian music, decided that she wanted to write an Indian opera. Everything would be taken care of, she said, and shortly thereafter sent a check for $250 to Lange just to buy a pair of riding boots, who made it stretch into a number of purchases.

When they arrived in Los Angeles, the Dixons immediately boarded Baldwin's private railroad car, poised on a siding at Union Station and staffed with two cooks, two chefs, two stewards, and an armed personal bodyguard. The blinds stayed closed so no one could look in, and when they stopped at main stations, no one could get off the car. Baldwin traveled all the way with her handbag held close, a small pearl-handled revolver tucked in it. When they arrived in Flagstaff, Arizona, at 2:00 A.M., two men greeted them, drivers who would take them to Walpi, along with dozens of boxes and cases with Baldwin's initials on them. The entourage followed later that day under pouring rain. They encountered washes full of roiling muddy water near Winslow, finally coming to one that the heavily loaded white trucks could not cross. So everyone pitched in, except Anita of course, unloaded the trucks, and brought the baggage across, piece by piece.

118. *Clouds and Mesa*, 1923, conté crayon on paper, 12¹/₂ x 15¹/₅ inches, private collection

Baldwin did not utter one word. Finally, one of the drivers said, "now we gotta pack the old woman over."[10] The drivers carried her over, umbrella upright, making a saddle of sorts with their hands.

Lange was stunned when they reached the foot of First Mesa below Walpi and set up the camp. The camping equipment was outrageous: ten tents shaped like Chinese pagodas, and all the food in cans, including caviar. Lange, who somehow became camp cook, learned to prepare meals for a combination of tastes, including her husband, Baldwin, the bodyguard, and the two drivers who stayed on as camp helpers. The Hopi came down the path from the top of the mesa each evening after dark, chanting and beating drums, often singing until the next morning. When Walpi's annual Snake Dance commenced, petitioning the Hopi deities for moisture, the people who came to see the Snake Dance flocked to Baldwin's luxurious encampment instead. Dixon managed to avoid the spectacle, working at his drawing and painting, enjoying the hot August winds sweeping over the mesa with the promise of rain (figs. 117 and 118).

When Baldwin left for Los Angeles at the end of August, Lange returned with her. Dixon remained until early December, living with one of the Hopi Snake priests, Namoki, and his blind brother, Loma Himna (fig. 119). He spent solitary hours in

119. *Men of Walpi*, 1923,
pen and ink on paper, 6 x 7 inches,
private collection, photograph courtesy
of Medicine Man Gallery

120. *Walpi*, 1923,
conté crayon on paper, 12 x 15 inches,
private collection, photograph courtesy
of Medicine Man Gallery

Namoki's house, making drawings or oil sketches of the Hopi pursuing their daily activities (fig. 120). Prostrate with a rheumatism attack from the cold weather, he laid a folded blanket on the floor opposite his easel, alternating painting with stretching

121. *Lone Hopi Priest;* 1923; ink wash, pencil, and conté crayon on paper; 20 x 30 inches; private collection; photograph courtesy of Medicine Man Gallery

122. *The Sacred Rock*, 1923,
charcoal on paper, 14 x 16 inches,
collection of Drs. Mark and Kathleen Sublette

123. *Hopi Story Teller*, 1923,
conté crayon on paper, 8 x 9 inches,
private collection, photograph courtesy
of Medicine Man Gallery

periods. Loma Himna tried to cure Dixon by rubbing sacred herbs over his body and offering prayers to the sun.

Whenever his strength permitted, Dixon would ride over to nearby Shipaulovi and Mishongnovi on Second Mesa, observing the fall ceremonies in the town plazas. There, as at Walpi, he sketched and painted Katchina dancers, kivas, the multistoried Hopi villages, and the people, who called themselves Hopitii Shinumu, "the peaceful people" (figs. 121–123). As the geographer James Corner so elegantly writes: "Like navigation and communication rooms stacked on the decks of great ships, the Hopi villages probe the expansive sea of desert below and the sky above for clues regarding changes in weather, season, and fortune. Sited on elongated fingers of rock, the three main villages have a constructed unity through lines of sight and communication. The entire Hopi cosmography is constructed, with restraint, to capture the sacred reality of the landscape and its occupation."[11]

One time in November, Dixon and Emry Kopta, another artist also residing at Walpi, took a long cold wagon ride to Ganado, where they visited Lorenzo Hubbell. They then headed north to Chinle, into Canyon del Muerto (fig. 124), within the vastness of Canyon de Chelly, covered with the first snowfall of the season. While there, Dixon attended a Navajo Fire Dance far back in the Lukachukai Mountains, but found it "a poor show—no class—even looked silly," confiding to Lummis that he found the Navajo more changed then the Hopi, whose culture still retained the flavor of older days. "You ought to be interested in the canvases I bring this time, as they will be, in a way, reminiscent of your own observations of an earlier day. With all the modernization, automobiles, cookstoves and gasoline lamps—the place still holds its charm and sometimes I regret my earlier preference for the Navajos, when I might have known the Hopis 20 years ago. However, as I did not have the background to appreciate them nor the ability to paint them, it comes out about even. It all takes me back to the days in Isleta."[12]

124. *Canyon del Muerto*, 1923, conté crayon on paper, 13 x 16 inches,
collection of Drs. Mark and Kathleen Sublette

Dixon's long stay on the Hopi reservation turned into an intense spiritual experience, where he felt a timeless existence and was preoccupied with work to the exclusion of material considerations. As he gradually overcame bodily pain, the world seemed suspended in space for the unfolding winter solstice. His mystical attachment to the Hopi and their country, a land of dreams, emerges in a letter to Robert Macbeth.

You would suppose that here in the ancient Province of Tusayan (now Hopi Land) that I would have plenty of time for everything. But it is not our kind of time, — you can't count it. It is made only of days, moons and eternity. Then also if I have a date with a rock at a certain angle of the sun and shadow, and another with an Indian who lives 2 miles away up a steep trail and from that down to the house in time to chop wood, carry water and cook my dinner and be through in time to make a drawing afterward and then write 3 or 4 letters—then out in the morning to sketch or maybe go to the store (an Indian store) or perhaps ride 12 miles to Mishong-novi to see a ceremony, get back after dark, cook, wash up and start a canvas of what I have seen—why you can see the days are pretty well filled.

As for the country itself, and the people, they are wonderful—always wonderful!—Now is the real autumn, right on the sharp edge of winter, with the sting of frost in the long blue shadows, and a flood of pale yellow sun like an hallucination coming over the far blue rim of mesas to the south. Away out in the golden-brown flats the few cottonwood trees flame like small orange torches and the dust of a band of sheep follows it, a faint golden ghost. The thin distinct voice of an Indian singing a wild wavering song comes dropping down from the tall rocks,—the small delicate drift of blue smoke and the fine odor of cedar burning;—and above all the endless empty blue sky—the sky where there is no time.

These Hopis are remarkable people. They must have come from the south and brought their corn and their pottery and their weaving with them. Small, kindly, home people, very different from the fierce hunting tribes of the plains and mountains. There lingers something of remote antiquity about them—they feel of the stone age. They still believe and act as our forefathers did 20,000 years ago. They are here in the midst of this age of steel and electricity, a little remnant of the stone age still living!

Many people would come here and not see all this. They might see only that these Indians are poor and dirty and lousy; that the kids go naked and are unspeakably filthy; that they have little water and no sanitation; that they believe in magic and have savage customs. But when you see one of their ceremonies—there for an hour something fine flashes out clear; there is savage beauty in them,—they have imagination. They have dignity and form. These things are for the archaeologist

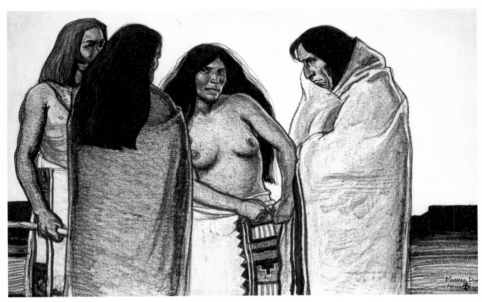

125. *The Witch of Sikyatki*, 1923, mixed media on illustration board, 19 x 30 inches, collection of Donald and Rebecka Hagerty

and the painter to understand. From them the scientist re-creates the ancient world; the artist creates a new one. In these later canvases you will probably see traces of all this. There is something of magic in it, and legends endow it with strange meanings. The imagination moves free and the past and present are one. So the visions of the old days have been as important to my work as things actually seen.[13]

The Painted Desert, below the Hopi mesas, fascinated Dixon, and he spent considerable time exploring the desert landscape and watching as summer thunderstorms crept across the desert floor, taunting the expectant earth with moisture. For Dixon, there was no human presence, only the silent empty terrain interacting with sky and clouds. Mesmerized also by Hopi ceremonies and folklore, Dixon developed several large mixed-media works, one of them a twenty-five-by-thirty-inch charcoal study, *The Witch of Sikyatki* (fig. 125), for an important painting of the same name, a canvas he later destroyed. Sikyatki comes from the name of a ruined pueblo east of First Mesa, abandoned centuries ago. In this particular study, a woman, apparently a ghost spirit, confronts several Hopi men. They are reserved and cautious, but intrigued by her overture.

As soon as Dixon returned to San Francisco, he exhibited the Arizona paintings during early December 1923 in an unusual setting, the Don Lee automobile salesrooms on San Francisco's Van Ness Avenue, which had been converted into ten spacious one-man art galleries. This exhibit was pronounced by some critics as the best California art exhibition since the one at the P.P.I.E. in 1915. Dixon's work was praised in the San Francisco newspapers. Gottardo Piazzoni, Clark Hobart, Bruce Nelson, Armin Hansen, and Frank Van Sloun, among others, were also represented. After the Don Lee exhibit closed, Dixon sent the paintings to an exhibition at the Cannell and Chaffin Gallery in Los Angeles, December 15–31, 1923.

Before they left on the first of their two trips to Arizona, Lange had encouraged Dixon to develop two book projects. The first was *Injun Babies*, a collection of humorous Native American children's tales he included in letters to young Constance from his frequent trips. They were whimsical yet moral stories about Indian children who somehow always got into trouble: "A-Way-She-Go," a runaway girl; "Me-No-Kan," a little boy who said he could not do things; "No-Pah-No-Mah," the orphan; and others. Dixon assembled the stories and provided eight full-page color illustrations for the book. G. P. Putnam published *Injun Babies* in 1923. Robert and Edwin Grabhorn, San Francisco publishers of fine press books, approached Dixon in 1922 about producing a limited edition of his poems. He agreed to their proposal, selecting twenty-two poems and making seven handsome pen-and-ink illustrations for the book. Grabhorn published *Poems and Seven Drawings* in 1923, limited to an edition of 250 copies. Dixon, in a letter to his friend and attorney, Joseph Loeb, said, "The writers say I am a good illustrator, the illustrators say I am a good painter, and the painters say I am a good writer."[14] As a way of recognizing his friends and clients, Dixon designed some striking bookplates (figs. 126 and 127).

Dixon was writing some of his strongest poems by 1923, finely crafted, often

EX LIBRIS

MARGARET LOEB

126. *Bookplate, Margaret Loeb*, 1920s,
California History Section, California State Library

127. *Bookplate, Irving and Beatrice Kahn*, 1920s,
California History Section, California State Library

introspective free verse. *Laughing Horse*, a small literary magazine published by Willard "Spud" Johnson in Santa Fe, New Mexico, included one of Maynard's poems, "Navajo Song," in its December 1923 issue. The magazine had first appeared at the University of California–Berkeley in 1922, begun by Johnson, Witter Bynner, and others as a "horselaugh at the university." In Santa Fe and Taos, Johnson enrolled some of the leading writers and artists to contribute stories, verse, and illustrations, including Bynner, Mary Austin, Alice Corbin, William Penhallow Henderson, Mabel Dodge Luhan, Willard Nash, Will Shuster, and D. H. Lawrence. The artists and writers colonies in Taos, Santa Fe, and the Bay Area were intermingled, and Dixon was recognized as a vital creative participant in those circles. Another of Dixon's poems, the confessional "Visionary," also came in 1923, a response to the search for his own psychic biography:

> *Am I a fool*
> > *in that I am deep-willed to seek*
> > *always a vision*
> > *known never to be reached.*
> *Yet, so having striven, having crushed my heart (and yours)*
> *against the hard will of the world,*
> *and though determination has grown gaunt*
> > *with an immortal hunger,*
> > *I am not yet resigned to wait.*
> *I am deep-willed to strive*
> > *so that if old age, or even death,*
> > *only make answer*
> > *I still can say*
> *out of all the intense devotion of soul*
> > *somehow here I have created beauty.*[15]

The beginning of 1924 saw Dixon embarking on a series of major mural commissions. An American mural revival had emerged during the boom period of the 1920s. Murals were used in libraries, movie theaters, train stations, and other significant structures. These murals embraced a specific subject matter, usually historical, with a readable, clearly understood message drawn from the American experience. Dixon never chose industrial and agricultural themes for his murals; instead, he drew upon American history to validate the efficacy of sacrifice and hard work, as moral encouragement for the public, and to illustrate the march of an American civilization. Many of Dixon's murals showed long chains of events leading to the present, yet they have an up-to-date look; they appear modern and contemporaneous with his time. Dixon avoided the prevailing European theory that mural painting is nothing more than easel painting on a large scale. Instead, he used James McNeill Whistler's argument that an artist is known by what he omits and made a careful study of each building, particularly the wall where the mural would be hung or painted, in order to integrate the mural into a harmonious union with the wall.

A lot of dogma has been peddled around of late concerning mural painting—about significant form, volume, dynamics, golden section, space-division, space-filling and God knows what. Nothing apparently is ever said about the WALL. My own dogma, here offered, is that the wall itself is essentially an element of mural design; that since it is the wall that brings the decoration into existence (hence MURAL painting) the painter can do no less than respect it; that he should put his painting on the wall without crowding or obscuring it, planning open areas of it as integral parts of his design.

The painters of Alta Mira, Egypt and Ajanta had not lost sight of this primary motive, which also finally determines the fitness of the work. They escaped what has now become a foolishly complicated problem by simply spreading their design on the plain surface—and let it go at that.[16]

One of his first murals was an overmantel decoration, which he did not complete until 1925, for the San Francisco workshop of his brother, Harry St. John Dixon, by now a noted metalsmith. Architect Willis Polk then arranged for Dixon to paint *The Sunol Water Temple*, an eight-by-sixteen-foot oil-on-canvas mural for the lobby of San Francisco's Spring Valley Water Company at 425 Mason Street. Dixon also assisted Polk in organizing an Artist's Council, a group of artists and architects attempting to promote stronger ties between the graphic and architectural arts.

During the month of February, Dixon exhibited his work at the Macbeth Gallery in New York, hoping this time sales would be more encouraging. But purchases were again slow, although the exhibit included major canvases, *The Grim Wall* and *The End House of Walpi* among them. Macbeth told Dixon in a letter that he had to start handling only works that sold readily. "Don't think that I don't see it from your side," he told Dixon, "you go out into the desert at a big sacrifice of time, comfort, and money, and do your darnedest to put on canvas as beautifully as you know how, the country, its people, and its spirit. Then you ship them off to us with high hopes, and wait, wait, wait, for good news that never comes."[17]

Dixon told Macbeth he was disappointed in the sales from the two exhibitions but refused to engage in "club stuff" that other painters used to achieve success. "There were two things denying the appreciation and sale of his paintings, he remarked: the architects and interior designers, 'Whispering Nancy-boys,' interested in 'imitation brocade' more than serious painting and the fact that people had been systematically sold to styles, 'periods . . . forms effects,' with no thoughts about the intrinsic qualities and values of pictures as works of art."[18] Furthermore, Dixon let Macbeth know he was trying to correct this, encouraging fellow artists in San Francisco to give lectures before clubs, form groups to pursue common interests. He had even managed to place talks about art and artists with a radio service claiming an audience of three million.

If Dixon was denied success in New York, he found it in Los Angeles, when he joined a group of twenty landscape painters calling themselves the Painters of the West. They included some of California's leading artists: Edgar Payne, Carl Oscar Borg, Frank Tenny Johnson, Charles P. Austin, Aaron Kilpatrick, Arthur Hazard, George T. Cole, Clyde

Forsythe, Jack Wilkinson Smith, DeWitt Parshall, Douglas Parshall, Max Wiezorek, and Armin Hansen. Thomas Moran, by then living in Santa Barbara, served as an honorary member. During the first competitive exhibition at the Biltmore Salon, sponsored by the Painters of the West during May and June of 1924, Dixon received the gold medal and $400 for his dramatic *The Survivors*, a three-and-a-half by five-foot canvas he had started seven years earlier as a result of his Montana trip and only completed in 1922. The painting, which he ultimately destroyed, survives only as a photograph in the Maynard Dixon papers. It depicted a line of buffalo, led by a shaggy bull, coming over a rise, the beasts backed by high mesas bathed in an ebbing sunset glow. *The Survivors* was a nostalgic painting full of symbolic yearning for a lost era.

Earlier that year, during February of 1924, the Biltmore Salon had scheduled a one-man exhibition of his paintings. Anita Baldwin promptly purchased one of the most striking compositions in the exhibit, *Circle of Shimaikuli*, for $3,000. She also purchased *Mystery Stone* and *Iesaka Waken*. The Biltmore Salon exhibit catalog lists twenty of his paintings, most from the 1922 and 1923 Arizona trips. *Circle of Shimaikuli*, *The End House of Walpi*, *Witch of Sikyatki*, *Grim Wall*, and *Pony Boy* were in the exhibit, and almost all of them found eager purchasers. The Painters of the West followed that first exhibition with a second one at the Biltmore Salon during December 1924, where novelist Henry Herbert Knibbs, Charles F. Lummis's son-in-law, purchased one of Dixon's paintings, *Desert Shepherdess*.

Toward the end of 1924, Dixon encountered one of his periodic depressions, struggling with his work, going every day to the studio, and yet, in his mind, accomplishing nothing. Discouraged, he expressed his feelings to Joseph Loeb: "Did you have a nightmare in which you were running like hell and not covering a foot of ground? I have made sketches and they are rotten. The paint won't say what I want it to. You cannot produce a fine work by force alone—there must be the inner urge that gives it life and meaning—and I am compelled to realize that this source in me is for the time being used up."[19]

Active in the San Francisco art environment but still struggling with his attitude toward modernism, Dixon continued to write poetry during the middle 1920s, trying to connect his passion for the western landscape to his art and personal life. In 1925, the Book Club of California published *Continent's End: An Anthology of Contemporary Poets*, with poems by Robinson Jeffers, Mary Austin, Witter Bynner, Ina Coolbrith, George Sterling, and others. Dixon was represented in the book with his poem "Navajo Song." In the midst of writing poems, a busy work schedule, numerous exhibitions, and family life, he found time to support his friend John Collier's efforts to help Native Americans protect their land rights. During the 1920s, he illustrated several articles in *Sunset Magazine* on the activities of Collier's Indian Defense Association and contributed drawings for publications issued by that organization. Through much of the decade, the magazine used Dixon illustrations for western fiction and articles, and several of his paintings for covers. The Standard Oil Company also frequently used his work for the covers of their magazine (fig. 128).

Meanwhile, a new tenant appeared at the "Little House on the Hill." On May 15, 1925, Dorothea gave birth to their first son, Daniel Rhodes Dixon. The amusing birth

128. *Standard Oil Bulletin,* June 1925,
California History Section, California State Library

announcement was designed by Dixon (fig. 129). Lummis wrote, "I was delighted to get your clever card yesterday announcing the new exhibit, glad to note you voted for a boy—and judge that this was the casting ballot and made it unanimous. I hope the young man will be all that he should be; and that, as my Indian friends say, God will loan him to you many years."[20]

As Dixon adjusted to an extended family, one of his friends, architect and designer Kem Weber, a colleague at Foster and Kleiser, invited him to paint two murals in 1925 for the ninety-foot lobby of the Barker Brothers building in Los Angeles, located at Seventh and Figueroa streets. The murals, which are actually woven linen tapestries, portray selected elements of Pueblo Indian ceremonies. Dixon painted the mural hangers, each one twenty by six and one-half feet, by using thinned paint applied on the coarse hand-woven linen to preserve its visible texture. A reviewer for *Western Arts* commented:

> *It is notable that in this over-industrial country of ours, the man who is usually best able to secure the commission to decorate a public building is not always the one best qualified to execute it. But here is a welcome exception. The credit is due to Kem Weber, himself an artist, as well as architect and designer, for having given Maynard Dixon an unusual opportunity to exercise his natural gift for decoration and to make use of the native subject matter he has so long been studying.*
>
> *The color is simple but rich, the dusty tone of the travertine appearing as an under color throughout turquoise, brown, terra cotta, a curious sage-and-turquoise green, ochre, with checks and spots of green, vermilion and flecks of orange, and a dusty purplish brown in lieu of black.*
>
> *The placing and arrangement of the Indian figures, and the pattern of the highly conventionalized forms of rock and bushes is built up in series of step and zig-zag patterns, suggested by designs in the pottery and garments of the Indians, as well as the general form of the interior for which the hangings are designed. The effect is one of slow and stately movement, almost Egyptian in feeling, and a harmonious progression of color areas, with here and there a heightened contrast.*[21]

The BOY born to Dorothea and Maynard Dixon on May 15, 1925, has been named

[ ] Harold   [ ] Calvin
[ ] Wolfgang   [ ] Ezechial
[ ] Cyril   [ ] Gottardo
[ ] Ludwig   [ ] Caleb
[ ] Algernon   [ ] Bozo
[ ] Llwellyn   [ ] Max
[ ] Aubrey   [ ] Jasper
[ ] Balthazar   [ ] Ossip
[ ] Chauncey   [ ] Isador
[ ] Antonio   [ ] Cuthbert
[ ] Eraſtus   [ ] Hans
[ ] Basil   [ ] Alphonse
[ ] Olaf   [ ] Vladimir
[ ] Archibald   [ ] Percy
[ ] Boaz   [ ] Marcus
[ ] Casimir   [ ] Guſtave
[ ] Leander   [ ] Oscar
[ ] Hiram   [ ] Ephriam
[ ] Euſtace   [ ] Sven
[ ] Ambrose   [ ] Haniel
[ ] Julius   [ ] Vivian
[ ] Elijah   [ ] Angus
[ ] Shingo   [ ] Ugolino
[ ] Oreſtes   [ ] Fritz
[ ] Zebulon   [ ] Porter
[ ] Bildad   [ ] Jesus
[ ] Rex   [ ] Ignatz

[ ] --------------------

129. *Daniel Dixon's Birth Announcement, 1925, private collection*

After completing the Barker Brothers mural, Dixon joined Los Angeles architect John Kibbey on a trip through Arizona in late 1925, visiting Phoenix, Tucson, Nogales, and Tumacacori in an unsuccessful attempt to persuade the Southern Pacific Railroad Company to build a tourist hotel on the Apache Trail. Dixon returned to San Francisco "exhilarated but not enriched." In spite of the project's failure, he was elated with the Sonoran Desert's beauty and remoteness. Back in the studio, he found a letter from an art student seeking his guidance, which he gave:

> My advice to you would be to work alone a little longer—don't try too fast. It is not a sound method to attempt the broad effects and generalizations of experienced painters. You cannot begin where they leave off. Each must win his own way from his own beginning.
>
> Work with Nature. Rely on nature and your own observations. Do not begrudge the time or labor to make many drawings. Do not be ashamed to make them accurate. What you need is knowledge of the thing you are working with and its value to you. Do not work for style or to make something handsome or astonishing. Work for Truth. The truth is in you as well.
>
> If I had my life to live over again would I do it otherwise?" For a man to ask himself this question is much the same as asking "Would I (or could I) be a different person than I am?" It would mean starting again with an entirely new set of ancestors and following circumstances—an impossible premise. "I" would not then be I.
>
> However, if a man is inclined to look back into his past (and I believe it is a dangerous indulgence) he can always see where he might have done better,—or thinks he might. But the same old faults travel with him; and at 50 he finds himself struggling with the same shortcomings that he knew at 15. This makes him doubt whether with his given disposition he could have met the circumstances of his life in a much different way or brought others about.[22]

Sometime in 1925, Beatrice Judd Ryan had introduced Dixon to Charles Peter Weeks, a leading San Francisco architect. Weeks was searching for San Francisco artists to paint murals for some of his building projects. In early 1926, he hired Dixon and Frank Van Sloun to put a mural in the Room of the Dons at the newly opened Mark Hopkins Hotel on Nob Hill. Dixon sketched the first ideas on the back of a restaurant menu, but it took three different submissions of sketches that synthesized the two artists' concepts before Weeks approved the final design. Weeks insisted on using Queen Califia as a major theme in the mural. Califia, of course, is the symbolic embodiment of California. Dixon was not taken with this particular symbolism; he thought it a "fanciful, story-book idea." But he reluctantly agreed to Week's wishes. Working shoulder to shoulder, he and Van Sloun executed the murals at the Palace of Fine Arts, which afforded room for the enormous canvases. The painting tasks were divided between the two artists, both developing the theme and color effects in close unison and each accepting the other's modifications. A gleaming "line of gold" is the mural's unifying theme, set against a background of flat gold. The nine panel sections on the room's four walls recall important episodes in California history, from the early Spanish explorers to the gold rush of 1849. The tall panel over the central door is dominated by the robed allegorical figure of Queen Califia, who is flanked by a brace of seminude women warriors. The other panels narrate the inexorable course of empire: the early explorers, the days of Spanish and Mexican occupation, trappers, forty-niners, settlers, and soldiers. Junius Cravens praised the murals in the *Argonaut*:

> *Mr. Dixon and Mr. Van Sloun are to be congratulated not only upon their individual work, but upon the success with which they have surmounted the inevitable difficulties attendant upon this form of combined effort. They have blended their separate personalities into a perfect unified and harmonious decoration, consistent throughout. The creation of this splendidly decorative work is significant. Its importance lies in more than unquestionable merit. This city is becoming a big girl now. It harbors a wealth of latent artistic ability—latent in so far as it has been unemployed heretofore for public benefit. It is to San Francisco's discredit that it has been left to a hotel to take the initiative in commissioning two of her foremost artists to paint a mural decoration. It is high time for this city to recognize the importance of art in public buildings as a necessary element in cultural development.[23]*

Although absorbed with the Mark Hopkins murals, Dixon continued to produce illustration work during 1926. Near the end of the year, the Dixon family left the little house on Russian Hill, moving to a larger home at 1607 Taylor Street. When her own children came in 1925 and 1928, Lange attempted to provide a good home for them and Constance, but, concerned with her flourishing photography business, she could not quite manage it. Tensions increased and quarrels between Dixon and Lange escalated. Constance continued to fight with her stepmother, and finally, in late 1927, Lange and Dixon agreed that since Constance was now seventeen, she could move out and start earning her own way.

Lange desired security, stability, and a gracious social life, with herself as the center. Dixon became edgy when she staged dinner parties at their home, peppering her guests with sarcasm. He never failed to project his contempt for the "fancy life" and would savage even friends and clients if he thought they represented the upper class. On numerous occasions, he took opportunities to embarrass Lange. When Roi Partridge and Imogen Cunningham's four-year-old son, Rondal, visited them once, Dixon pulled him aside, taught him a short obscene verse, and then sent him out among the guests to recite it. A friend recalled another time when his wife had invited guests, mostly her clients, for dinner. Dixon, who generally protested by being late to these parties, spotted a pair of women's undergarments in the street while walking toward their house. He speared them with the sword in his sword cane, triumphantly held them aloft, marched into the dining room, and dropped them into the circle of shocked guests. And when Dixon grasped an opinion, no one could reason with him. He and Lange, who could be just as inflexible, clashed frequently, and soon it became common knowledge among their friends that both had started having affairs.

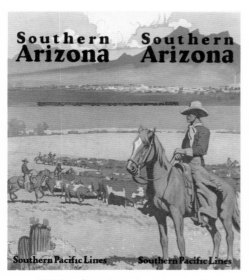

130. *Southern Arizona,* 1927–1928,
California History Section,
California State Library

In June 1927, Dixon completed another large mural, this time for the auditorium at Oakland Technical High School. The mural, which he titled *California, Pais de Sol,* measured sixty-eight feet across by twenty feet at the supports and ten feet above the arch. As was so often the case with Maynard's murals, the main theme was California history. A large golden sun occupied the center; to the immediate right stood a heroic female figure accompanied by the California grizzly; at the extreme right, Indian and Spanish figures portrayed the state's early history; and on the left, Kit Carson, John C. Fremont, and the forty-niners stood for a later period. The mural disappeared in 1959 when the old auditorium was remodeled into a library.

By this time, Dixon's murals, along with his landscape and figure painting, consistently endorsed a personal philosophy that American art should both absorb and free itself from the modern, specifically European, art movements, creating a body of work that is American in both form and subject. In a letter to *The Argus,* he expressed these feelings:

> Artists, being the most sensitive members of the commonwealth, intuitively reflect its temper. So far they have successfully visualized its tension, its neurosis—the breakup of old forms reassembling into new. Hence "modern art." But is this the whole story?
>
> Observers in the world of finance and affairs have seen what the artists apparently have failed to note: that since the war the center of wealth and power has shifted from Europe to the United States, and with it all the cultural implications of a material development rapidly coming to completion. There is here a widespread, though still rather blind, desire for something more than mere size and quantity when it comes to matters of culture, art and beauty. We artists here in America are facing the opening-up of a new set of conditions—psychic and emotional—growing out of material conditions developed here.
>
> Most of our artists (let us say painters) European trained, are fond of saying that Art is universal; that there is no American art (many imply there cannot be any) and that if it should ever develop it will come in some far distant future.
>
> True, the underlying impulses and desires which create art belong to all humanity; but the actual work has been done by individual men, of temperament

strongly marked by race or nationality out of localities and conditions present to them. It would be foolish to deny or attempt to evade our cultural heritage: the great "moderns" of France—the Renaissance, the Middle Ages, Rome, Greece, Egypt, India, Japan and China, and all the "Primitives" of the world. True also that, as a nation, we have not yet arrived at any uniformity of temperament and character; but we have a certain flair, a certain speed and keenness, and these are asking to be transformed into forms that are our own.

This is no plea for one hundred percent Americanism in art. But let me ask what art is vital that does not grow out of the psychic and material life of the country that produces it. . . .

If we are to have anything that can be called a vital American art it must come this way; not by the obedient repetition of European formulas, but through the ability and courage of our artists to take the life and the material of their own country and out of these express their aspirations.[24]

As Dixon worked on the Mark Hopkins murals, that prospecting trip to Arizona paid off with a commission from the Southern Pacific Railroad to furnish a cover illustration for a promotional tourist brochure on the Apache Trail. The trail, located between Globe and Phoenix in a region of dramatic beauty, follows the old route used by Apache Indians as they conducted raids through Arizona and into Mexico. Dixon painted an image for the brochure's cover, *The Apache Trail* (fig. 131), posed against colorful angular cliffs. Its plastic solidity and strong color relationships give it a decidedly modern flavor. The Southern Pacific Railroad issued twenty-five thousand copies for nation-wide release in 1927, reprinted the folder many times until at least 1930, and used the image on a poster for use in the railroad's ticket offices. The

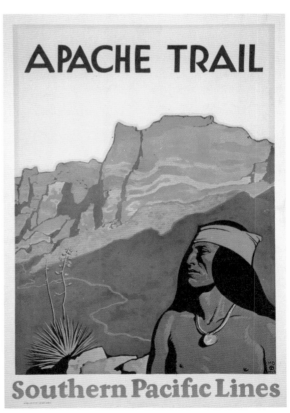

131. *The Apache Trail*, 1926,
California History Section,
California State Library

132. *Maynard Dixon Working on* The Pageant of Tradition, 1928, California History Section, California State Library

railroad also issued a brochure on Southern Arizona graced by a Dixon illustration (fig. 130).

Dixon was not always so fortunate. In 1927, competing with artists Ray Boynton, Dean Cornwell, Augustus Vincent Tack, Albert Herter, William Pogany, Norman Kennedy, and A. W. Parsons, he was rejected in open competition to paint a mural in the new Los Angeles Public Library. His designs were approved and voted for by all the members of the Los Angeles Public Library's board of directors except one, who fought the decision until the board finally awarded the commission to Cornwell, a magazine illustrator with no prior mural experience. Dixon, suspicious and infuriated, was convinced this individual blackballed him at the urging of William Randolph Hearst. After Cornwell won the commission, he promptly sailed for England to study mural painting under Frank Brangwyn. Arthur Millier, critic for the *Los Angeles Times*, reacted: "My own conclusion, reached after viewing all the designs on several different occasions, is that the scheme submitted by Dixon is at once the most original and the one best suited to the building and the particular walls to be decorated . . . and the only one which attempted to stylize the living elements in California history, treating men, animals and trees as symbols, making them timeless and avoiding the perils of actual historical illustration."[25]

Dixon's esthetic did seem invigorated by his experience with murals. He came to the belief that he needed to work in a new medium, something more expressive of the times. He regarded easel painting also as out of step with contemporary attitudes. "Artists," he declared, "should become part of the present day, instead of painting bits of canvas detached from modern living, perhaps working in concrete or stucco or some other 20th century medium, having their art be an innate part of modern life." Arthur Millier thought Dixon's philosophy reflected the tradition of his city of residence. In comments for *The Argus*, Millier compared the art environments of San Francisco and Los Angeles:

> Many things contribute to this impasse, and I propose to enumerate a few of them here. Broadly one may say that the typical art of San Francisco is urban and esthetic, that of Los Angeles rural and naturalistic. San Francisco is a city that, with well established civic traditions, has attracted city people. Los Angeles has drawn the bulk of her people from the agrarian states of the country and most of her artists, even though from the cities of those regions, have their roots in the life of the farm.

. . . Thus one finds that the typical art product of San Francisco reflects that art of the past and the art of the present as it is known in the great world centers, while the typical art product of Los Angeles reflects nothing but Southern California.

The physical structure of either community doubtless has its influence on the artists. San Francisco has a definite artists' center. The Italian quarter, Russian and Telegraph Hills and the California School of Fine Arts may all be enclosed in a small circle within which the majority of the city's artists either live, work or come together for frequent exchanges of ideas. This makes for discussion, spreads new ideas and tends to develop the intellectual side of art.

Los Angeles is physically reversed, decentralized. Here you will look in vain for a cultural center. Artists are scattered through outlying communities and rarely meet. They make their homes and studios where the natural surroundings please them most, by preference insulating themselves from the busy life of the norm and facing the landscapes they enjoy painting. They concern themselves little with abstract theories of art, giving their whole time to the interpretation of nature.

As archetypes of the art of either city, I might cite two artists who have both influenced and been influenced by their respective communities. They are William Wendt of Los Angeles and Maynard Dixon of San Francisco. Both of these men have the same desire: to interpret the West. But their attitudes and final goals are markedly different. Dixon tends more and more to develop a mural, decorative art for urban adornment, sacrificing the subtleties of nature to the aims of architecture. Wendt's painting, on the other hand, is far more concerned with the nuances of atmosphere, the feel of outdoors, and his whole effort is increasingly bent toward enclosing the breath of nature within his frame.

Either of these methods can produce art of the highest order, but it will not be the same kind of art. It is fashionable today to talk about the "fundamentals of art" but no two people describe the same fundamentals. Wherever artists are sincerely working and thinking, art will be produced. To arrive at a sympathetic appreciation of their work it can hardly be amiss to consider their aims and the background against which they create.[26]

Once again tired of the city and wanting "sagebrush inspiration," Dixon left San Francisco in October 1927 to begin a four-month journey through Nevada. Lange and two-year-old Daniel remained behind. Dixon started up in the remote northwestern part of Nevada's Washoe County, guided by noted Nevada cattleman and ex-peace officer Frank Tobin (fig. 133). They explored opal mines around Denio along the Nevada and Oregon border, then afterward rode horseback over the Pine Forest Range and out into the haunting Black Rock Desert, one of the largest playas in the Great Basin (figs. 134 and 135). One place he lingered was Alder Creek Ranch, about forty miles north of the Black Rock Desert. Before he left, Dixon painted a self-portrait mural on one of the ranch's bunkhouse walls, which he called *Bien Venido y Adios* (fig. 136). Wandering through this high desert country, he made drawings and oil sketches of lonely valleys, abandoned mines, dry alkaline lakes, and remnants of

133. *Tobin's Camp*, 1927, ink on paper, 9½ x 15 inches,
photograph courtesy of Medicine Man Gallery

134. *Sage and Rabbit Brush*, 1927, oil on canvas board, 10 x 14 inches,
private collection, photograph courtesy of Medicine Man Gallery

the old California emigrant trail well past Elko. Dixon and Tobin worked their way back through northwestern Nevada to Carson Valley, ablaze with the fall colors of cottonwoods and Lombardy poplars, then traveled to the old mining towns of Tonopah and Goldfield dozing quietly in the bright fall sun. Using Tonopah as a base, Dixon ventured on a 180-mile trip east into the Monitor Range and through the immense Railroad Valley, only to be surprised by an unanticipated early snowfall that forced him to retreat over nearly impassable roads.

From Tonopah he headed for Scotty's Castle but found the legendary Death Valley Scotty "only an old show-man." Dixon lingered a week or two at nearby Beatty, drawn to the spectacular arid land-scapes of the Amargosa Des-ert, the Funeral Mountains, and breathtaking vistas of

135. *Rainbow Ridge, Nevada*, 1927, ink on paper, 10 x 12 inches, private collection, photograph courtesy of Medicine Man Gallery

136. *Bien Venido y Adios*, 1927, oil on panel, 44 x 77 inches, private collection

Death Valley. When he reached Las Vegas, he turned northeast to explore the desert almost to the Utah border, where the Virgin River punches through the volcanic rocks of Virgin Canyon as it heads toward a rendezvous with the Colorado River. The Great Basin landscapes captured Dixon's imagination much like what John McPhee describes in his book *Basin and Range*.

> *Each range here is like a warship standing on its own [some] are forty miles long, others a hundred, a hundred and fifty. They point generally north. The basins that separate them—ten and fifteen miles wide—will run on for fifty, a hundred, two hundred and fifty miles with lone, daisy petalled windmills standing over sage and wild lye. Supreme over all is silence. Discounting the cry of the occasional bird, the wailing of a pack of coyotes, silence—a great spatial silence—is pure in the Basin and Range. It is a soundless immensity with mountains in it.*[27]

Dixon's record indicates fifty-six paintings resulted from this trip, an enormously productive effort. He exhibited many of them at Reno's Riverside Hotel in October 1927, at the Galerie Beaux Arts, November 20–December 3, 1927, and at the Biltmore Salon in Los Angeles, February 1–8, 1928. An art critic for *The Argus*, reviewing the Nevada paintings at the Galerie Beaux Arts, discussed his motives:

> *Approaching his subject with an attitude of absolute submission to it, Maynard Dixon, who recently spent four months in Nevada, shows paintings which are direct renditions of the country visited and seen. In these the artist has not attempted to compose, to organize his subject matter. He has not tried to create problems for his brush, or even to express his own individuality through his work. He sat in front of his models: strangely shaped mountains adorned by green meadows, alkaline beds of pure white running in long stretches at their feet. There lay something greater than his "ego," he thought, something masterly in design and composition, and, letting it guide him, he tried to render it as it is, not to interpret it.*
>
> *Fifty-one oils of mountains, desert and fertile valleys, abandoned mining camps, bits of curious cities, are here to testify to this attitude and manner. It is the work of a man who is conscious of what he is doing and who knows how to restrain his emotions, who has dignity and poise.*[28]

As the vigorous dialogue about modern art continued to rage among San Francisco's artists, Dixon wrote a letter to *The Argus*, declaring,

> *Out of the sanity which usually comes to the artist when he returns to Nature and isolates himself from current fashions in art theory — out of the effort to go direct to his source of interest and interpret subject and sensation with-out reference to the mode in art — there comes an assurance that art is related to something larger than art, that it is, after all, but one of the functions of life. Through some weakness or egotism, artists allow themselves to become detached from the main current of men's affairs. They attempt to build art always upon art — dealing in super-structures — committing sheep-like follies in "schools" and "movements."*
>
> *No one wants to be out of date, of course. To keep in with the direction of thought in one's own generation is essential. But the artist's conformity to the current theories of design which he so uncritically accepts has formed an orthodoxy of "this freedom" — modernism — as narrow, intolerant, and withal as incomprehensible, as any that ever cursed medieval theology. By the devotees of this creed, art is thought to exist for itself, and that it may be meaningless (and therefore purposeless) to the mass of mankind is considered a glory. I do not see that it should lose anything being lucid.*
>
> *Then what?*
>
> *Let us say the Mr. and Mrs. Babbitt have ideas on the subject of art that are intolerable to the artists — and rightly so. Yet here is a hard fact: the Babbitt family has in its control Power, Production, and Publicity, without which not even art*

can exist. These are the vitals of human achievement. Back of these, after all, is a dim idealism, from which the artist has allowed himself to become alienated—and steel, concrete and electricity are its visible manifestations.[29]

During 1927 and 1928, Dixon had one of his largest exhibition schedules: shows in February 1927 at the Ainslie Gallery in Los Angeles, at the Chicago Art Gallery in February and March, at Paul Elder's bookstore in San Francisco and the Art League in Santa Barbara during May, and at the Mark Hopkins Hotel and the San Francisco Art Association in September. He exhibited the painting *Mohave Desert* in the Second Annual Exhibition of the Artists of Southern California in San Diego, June 10–August 31, 1927, then all of his Nevada paintings at the Galerie Beaux Arts to finish the year. In April 1928, the Wichita Art Association in Wichita, Kansas, mounted a major exhibit of his paintings, including *Wild Horses of Nevada, The Wise Men, Eagle's Roost, Tragic Mood, Desert Hill, Cloud World, Tradition,* and *Moon Over the Desert.* It seemed that almost every month during 1928, there was a Dixon exhibition somewhere: the Del Monte Art Gallery and the Oakland Art League in February, the University of California–Berkeley during March, the Pacific Southwest Exposition in Long Beach, July 27–September 3, 1928 (where *Wild Horses of Nevada* won the silver medal), Jake Zeitlin's bookstore in Los Angeles in November, and finally, to round out the year, an exhibition at the Hotel Bigelow Gallery in Ogden, Utah.

Through Charles Weeks' efforts in early 1928, Dixon secured another commission for a mural that would be located in the foyer of Oakland's West Coast Theater. In this seven-by-fourteen-foot mural, which he titled *The Spirit of India,* a Buddha-like figure stood in the center, supported on either side by the images of Tragedy and Comedy. The rest of the mural represented small figures of gaily caparisoned elephants, horsemen, and dancing women. The mural was removed during a later remodeling and apparently destroyed. As Dixon worked on it one day, a message arrived, announcing that Lange had given birth to their second son. "Good news!" Dixon is said to have shouted. So John Dixon, born on June 12, 1928, became John Goodnews Dixon. Later, his middle name was changed to Eaglefeather.

Weeks, delighted with the quality of Dixon's mural work, arranged for him to receive the largest mural commission awarded up to that time in California, destined for the new State Library in Sacramento. The mural occupies the south wall of the library's third-floor reading room and covers a space above the entrance, fourteen feet high by sixty-nine feet in length. Dixon wanted to avoid ancient symbolism and allegory, and chose again the epic story of California for the mural, which he called *The Pageant of Tradition* (figs. 132 and 137). From the left side of the mural march Hispanic explorers and settlers; on the right is the American migration. Both groups move toward the mural's center, indicated by three books representing Philosophy, Science, and Art. On each side of these books are two heroic figures: Beauty, suggesting the values inherent in Hispanic peoples, and Power, showing the industrial machinery of Anglo-Europeans. Arranged in chronological order, each group commences with the 1500s and ends with the 1920s. In a symbolic arrangement, the group design on the right is echoed

by the design of the group on the left. Dixon's murals would and did invariably have a center, with both sides balanced in the overall design. Dixon painted the mural directly on the wall, merging the solid wall and the identity of the mural surface together in a flat perspective.

The Pageant of Tradition required three and one-half months to complete, and Dixon received $9,500 for the commission. He developed the original drawings in his studio on architect's detail paper at a ratio of about six inches to the foot, then used them as guides to paint the mural directly on the wall, executing the design as the building neared completion. "I painted the library mural from a scaffold, to all intents and purposes one of the workmen on the building. I liked this. I liked the craftsmanship it involved. Then, people were constantly coming and going, looking and commenting—carpenters, plasters, visitors. They asked questions and as I worked I answered them. First thing I knew I was giving lectures on mural art, something I had never done before. Out of it all I got a new feeling for my job, something very healthy that has remained with me ever since."[30] While Dixon worked on the state library mural, he took some time to serve as the judge for the 1928 California State Fair 74th Annual Art Exhibition that was being held in Sacramento. Dixon had three of his paintings in the exhibition, including *Cloud World*.

On November 26, 1928, Dixon received a letter from Henry Herbert Knibbs, Charles F. Lummis's son-in-law, which said, "Don Carlos is gone, and you will see the newspapers."[31] Lummis, who opened his heart and mind to countless friends at El Alisal, encountered them for the last time at his funeral on November 28, under the old sycamore, laid on a redwood board, wrapped in his finest Navajo chief's blanket, and covered with deep-red roses, ready for the waiting flame. His ashes rest with those of his first son in a wall niche at El Alisal. Dixon was one of the honorary pallbearers, along with William Wendt, Noah Beery, Douglas Fairbanks, William S. Hart, Edward Borein, Carl Oscar Borg, E. H. Harriman, and other notable figures. For Dixon, it was the end of a thirty-three year friendship; the "Dear Pop" and Dear Kid" correspondence was finished.

In February 1929, poet and writer Sara Bard Field urged Dixon to submit his poems to local and national publications. Dixon responded with insight into the rationale for

137. *The Pageant of Tradition*, 1928, 14 x 69 feet, California State Library

his poems, not dissimilar to that which had prompted Lummis to encourage his poetic endeavors early in their friendship:

> *I should like to have my writings accepted, of course but am no aspirant for literary honors. This versifying is for me a kind of extension of the ego—a way of saying things that can't be expressed in paint. In fact I don't believe much in literary writing or arty painting—there is too much writing about writing and painting on top of painting. We get too far away from the original motives that prompt us to express—too much superstructure. It seems to me great art is generally pretty direct, and that its greatness, broadly and humanly understandable, will redeem its crudities. But here the insinuating isms enter, opening up a God-awful variety show of the arty twins—Hokum and Hooey.*[32]

Early 1929 also found Dixon at work on what he would come to consider his most successful mural. The Arizona Biltmore Hotel in Phoenix was nearing completion, and the building's architect, Arthur Chase McArthur, a pupil and friend of Frank Lloyd Wright, contacted Dixon to urge that he submit designs for a mural in the hotel's main dining room. Dixon and Lange caught a Southern Pacific train to Los Angeles, Dixon working on the preliminary mural designs (fig. 139) in the train's dining car. When they arrived, Kem Weber joined them, and the three drove from Los Angeles to Phoenix. Dixon finished his designs in a Phoenix hotel room. McArthur approved them, giving him wide latitude. When he returned to the Montgomery Street studio, Dixon created *The Legend of Earth and Sun* (fig. 138), a painted hanger on stained fabric, which would be suspended by a steel rod from the dining-room ceiling away from a ninety-foot wall of concrete bricks. Two heroic figures dominate the mural: Father Sun, adapted from the Hopi Sun Katchina, casts light and warmth, while Mother Earth, wearing the head tablet of a Hopi corn maiden, encourages the growth of the corn, symbol of life. Small bluebirds flock in a soft rainfall, and twelve smaller Native American figures kneel along the panel's width at the bottom, each one holding a bowl of corn or a grinding stone.

138. *The Legend of Earth and Sun*, 1928, oil on linen, 8 x 25 feet,
Arizona Biltmore Hotel, Phoenix, Arizona

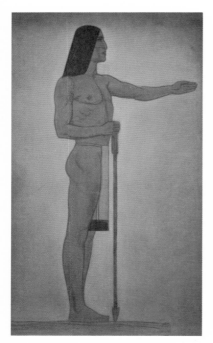

139. *Father Sun* (study for *The Legend
of Earth and Sun*); 1928;
pastel, charcoal, and pencil on paper;
36 x 21¹/₂ inches; collection of
Drs. Mark & Kathleen Sublette

By now Dixon was often used to supply the covers for the *Standard Oil Bulletin*, the magazine that was delighted with his graphic, modern-appearing images (fig. 140). In the midst of commercial projects, Dixon held a series of shows in June 1929 and again in November at Mills College, the University of California–Berkeley, the Galerie Beaux Arts, and the California State Library in Sacramento. Designed for students interested in mural art, the exhibitions included a series of his small and large schematic sketches and cartoons in crayon and watercolors, illustrative of the evolution in his mural decorations. Aline Kistler, writing in the *San Francisco Chronicle*, said, "These are the genius of the finished work. In these drawings, ranging from little larger than a special delivery stamp, to that of an ordinary watercolor, one sees the actual structure of Dixon's art. They are the embryos intact."[33]

During 1929, Dixon also started work on an ambitious book project: illustrations for a new limited edition of Walt Whitman's *Leaves of Grass*. There is some indication Robert and Edwin Grabhorn inadvertently encouraged him in this endeavor. Dixon happened to be in the Grabhorn Press shop when an order arrived from Random House to print Walt Whitman's *Leaves of Grass*. Dixon asked Edwin Grabhorn if he could illustrate the edition. Grabhorn told him he could not do the illustrations. An angry Dixon left but returned the next day with illustrations in hand. He had taken Whitman's line, "I loaf and invite my soul" and made a picture of Maynard Dixon on the top of a hill with the sun shining on his face, his hat over his head—loafing and inviting his soul. Another drawing was "I sing the body electric"—a man and woman standing on a rope over a chasm with sparks going out of their bodies. Grabhorn thought these and the other drawings Dixon showed him were hilarious. Finally, he invited Dixon to do an illustration for the beginning and another for the end of the book. But he refused, informing Grabhorn he had now decided to develop serious illustrations in the promotion of his own deluxe version of *Leaves of Grass*—at one-hundred dollars a copy. The project occupied a substantial part of his time from 1929 until 1933, at which time it was abandoned.

140. *Standard Oil Bulletin*, October 1928, California History Section, California State Library

Anxious to head back to the desert, Dixon paused long enough to start two murals in conjunction with Conrad Buff for the Pasadena and San Francisco offices of the Guaranty Building and Loan Association, but regarded them as a quick and rather superficial job. They were finally completed in December 1929. In the summer of that year, Dixon, Lange, and their two boys went to the Owens Valley, staying with the Skinner family at

141. *Lone Pine*, 1929, ink and watercolor on paper, 10 x 12 inches, private collection, photograph courtesy of Medicine Man Gallery

142. *Lone Pine*, 1929, oil on canvas board, 16 x 20 inches, collection of Diane and Sam Stewart, photograph courtesy of Medicine Man Gallery

Lone Pine (figs. 141 and 142). Dixon sketched and painted in the Alabama Hills near Lone Pine, explored the Panamint Mountains, wandered around the sun-warped buildings of Darwin and Coso, and visited Shoshone and Paiute Indian camps. But "tin-front" progress interfered, even in this remote country. Radios, auto tourists, auto camps, and realtors seemed everywhere, eroding the physical beauty of the landscape and destroying the social structure of the small towns. Turning to the people of this country, he painted

143. *Mrs. Black*, 1929,
oil on canvas, 20 x 16 inches,
collection of
Donald and Rebecka Hagerty

solemn portraits such as *Mrs. Black* (fig. 143) in an attempt to discover unseen but important values in their strong countenances. But as he had before in his life, Dixon experienced a sense of impending doom. Lange, on the other hand, had a positive revelation from nature. One day she was perched on a large rock when a fierce thunderstorm broke, and in the midst of the turbulence, she realized that she should concentrate on photographing people not just in formal portraits, but all kinds of people in the context of their lives. She felt this as one of the great spiritual experiences in her life.

The Dixons returned to San Francisco in September. On October 24, 1929, the stock market fell with an enormous rumble, signaling the onset of the Great Depression. Dixon would paint one hundred and eleven easel pictures, and an equal number of oil sketches in the next four years—and sell only twenty-four. Architects with plans for murals in new buildings canceled contracts, exhibitions were dropped by museums, and collectors abandoned their purchases of paintings. American artists were flattened, and only the WPA projects in the middle 1930s would rescue them.

In March of 1930, concerned with what he saw as worsening times, Dixon sought hard work far from the problems. He decided to explore California's Tehachapi Mountains, between the Mojave Desert and the southern San Joaquin Valley. Arthur Haddock accompanied him, both artists working out of a ramshackle bootlegger's cabin secreted away in a remote canyon near Caliente (fig. 144). Spring rains and thunderstorms had transformed the brown grasses in the landscape into brilliant green; the chaparral, oaks, and scrub pines added a darker hue. Few people ventured through the rugged topography into this desolate region, and deer and cattle seemed the only moving things. As the two painters worked, strong winds pounded the mountains, forcing Dixon to nail one large canvas on a fence post to keep it upright while he painted. He titled the painting *Deer Heaven*. Dixon and Haddock stayed at a little hotel in Caliente, which had a family dining room in it with a large blank wall. After staring at the wall for several days, Dixon pressed the owner for permission to draw a mural on the space. When the owner relented, Dixon quickly drew a life-size horse and rider in charcoal on the wall, explaining to a fascinated Haddock and hotel guests the taxonomy of the horse's joints and muscles as he sketched.

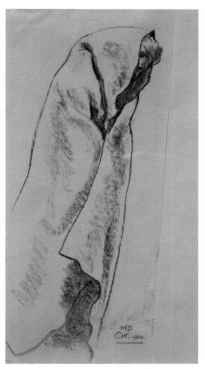

144. *Maynard Dixon,*
Tehachapi Mountains, 1930,
private collection

145. *Study for* Shapes of Fear, 1930,
crayon on paper, 15 x 8 inches,
private collection

At the annual exhibit of the San Francisco Art Association in May of 1930, one of his Tehachapi paintings, *Merging of Spring and Winter,* was awarded the prestigious Anne Bremer Memorial Prize, while *Deer Heaven* received second prize. *Springtime on Bear Mountain* was also singled out for praise by the jury. *Deer Heaven* would later be included in the Corcoran Gallery of Art's Thirteenth Exhibition of Contemporary American Paintings, December 4, 1932–January 15, 1933.

When Dixon returned to San Francisco, he worked on several illustration commissions to resurrect his finances, including a cover for the May 1930 issue of *Sunset Magazine.* Threatening undercurrents in American life, so keenly felt in this first year of the Great Depression, led him to paint a picture that expressed that fear and desperation. Originally, he drew an image in charcoal, calling it *Ghost People.* Consistent with Native American symbolism, he placed a nude female figure in the center, flanked by four blanketed faceless figures. When he exhibited *Ghost People* at the Galerie Beaux Arts, *Art Digest* reproduced the drawing for their August 1930 cover. Dixon then made another version of the drawing, *Study for* Shapes of Fear (fig. 145), as the foundation for a painting, *Shapes of Fear,* this time eliminating the central female. In 1931, the San Francisco Art Association awarded *Shapes of Fear* the Harold L. Mack

Popular Prize at the association's annual exhibition held at the California Palace of the Legion of Honor. Dixon explained the results:

> I still had the sense of being surrounded by vague, ominous, threatening forms—a feeling which became an obsession. Out of the need of freeing myself from it, of eternalizing it, to get it out of my system, grew the idea of painting "Shapes of Fear"—a group of four Indian-like figures, robed, their faces shrouded from view. After making some small drawings of it, I made a full sized drawing on canvas 3 by 4 feet, and exhibited it at the Beaux Arts gallery under the title of "Ghost People." The comment was unfavorable. I made some alterations in the composition, emphasizing the expression of foreboding, then painted it. When I showed it under the title "Shapes of Fear" at the Art Association Annual, to my great surprise it received the popularity prize."[34]

Before he left for the Tehachapi Mountains, Dixon had made preparations to enter a competition for murals at the Luncheon Club, part of the recently constructed San Francisco Stock Exchange building. However, sculptor Ralph Stackpole, one of his closest friends, assured him that no murals would be included. Later, he discovered that Stackpole and several others had for some time agreed to import Mexican muralist Diego Rivera to paint not only the stock exchange murals but a fresco for the California School of Fine Arts. He became even more discouraged when he learned that his brother, Harry, was to provide bronze, silver, and brass hand-pounded elevator doors for the club. Dixon's friendship with Stackpole eroded. "Perhaps," he said, "I had an old fashioned idea of what friendship should be."[35] According to Beatrice Judd Ryan, when the subject of the stock exchange mural emerged in the late 1920s, several Beaux-Arts members, presumably Dixon among them, given his wide reputation as one of California's foremost muralists, were asked to make sketches. But the Luncheon Club president and William Gerstle, president of the San Francisco Art Association, did not favor any of them; they and architect Timothy Pflueger eventually decided to hire Rivera. Ralph Stackpole had earlier presented Gerstle with a Rivera painting after Stackpole's return from Mexico in 1926. Apparently this painting inspired Gerstle to choose Rivera for the fresco at the California School of Fine Arts.

Angry reaction about the choice came, violent and unexpected, from San Francisco's Labor Council and the artists' community. In the midst of the raging debate, Dixon told the press: "The Stock Exchange could look the world over without finding a man more inappropriate for the part than Rivera. He is a professed Communist and had publicly caricatured American financial institutions. I believe he is the greatest living artist in the world, and we would do well to have an example of his work in a public building in San Francisco. But he is not the man for the Stock Exchange Building."[36] Frank Van Sloun and Otis Oldfield went even farther: although they were complimentary of Rivera as a painter, they claimed to oppose importing "foreign" artists under any circumstances. In taking this stance, Dixon, Van Sloun, and Oldfield were branded as "conservatives." In truth, Dixon probably never had any chance for the mural commission for reasons similar to those he thought should disqualify Rivera: his consistent and vocal aversion to big business had continually alienated the city's "money boys."

The hostile reaction to Rivera was defused when Rivera and his wife, Frida Kahlo, arrived in November 1930. Rivera's warm massive personality beamed behind an ever-present cigar, and Kahlo, charming, diminutive, dressed in floor-length Mexican Indian dresses and exotic jewelry, captivated San Francisco's artists. Ralph Stackpole let Rivera use his studio at 716 Montgomery Street, next door to Dixon's. The Dixons met him there several times, and Rivera gave Lange some of his drawings. The city feted and lionized him. The California Palace of the Legion of Honor scheduled his one-man show during November, and the San Francisco Art Association asked him to serve on the jury of awards for the association's annual exhibition in the spring of 1931.

Dixon welcomed Rivera's advice that California painters should paint their own times and country in order to create an authentic American art. Dixon testily pointed out that he had argued this same thing over the past two decades. He became thoroughly disgusted with what he considered "sycophants," those "celebrity hound" San Francisco painters who enthusiastically responded to Rivera not by developing an American art but by imitating his style and subject. Before his involvement in the stock exchange furor, Dixon had angrily resigned his Bohemian Club membership in 1930, protesting the club's conservative policies. Under President James Swinnerton, Haig Patigian, and several others, the Bohemian Club had rejected a "modernist" painting by Lucien Labaudt. "Their action," fumed Dixon, "is unjust and dictatorial. It does not further the aims in which this club was founded—encouragement of artistic progress. Freedom of speech in the arts ought to imply freedom of mind and freedom of expression."[37] Dixon's reaction to both Bohemian Club conservatism and modern art prompted *Watch Your Step*:

> *What is the irreducible minimum of plain common sense needed in any work, art or otherwise, to keep it from being nonsense?*
>
> *Long ago (1918–19) when "modern art" (neo-impressionism, cubism, etc.) was getting under way in the U.S. I had to make a decision. I tried some experiments in non-objective painting, pure expression and whatnot, and then took a turn in the desert to think it over. I came back with the following conclusions; though subsequent work and observation have given me some serious second thoughts I have not seen the need to radically amend them.*
>
> *(1) The artist does not start out to manufacture "art." He tries to tell something seen, sensed or imagined—to state some kind of truth.*
>
> *(2) In this sense art is a language.*
>
> *(3) It should therefore be intelligible. It should have a core of common understanding.*

(4) *The medium form in which it is cast should be chosen with regard to the thought or feeling to be expressed.*

(5) *(And here's where a lot of the fashionable "arty" artists go wrong). The manipulation of that medium should be such as to make it an organic part of the expression, not a thing in and for itself. (The old art-for-arts-sake was therefore mostly sterile.)*

Well, Shakespeare was right: "To thine own self be true . . . thou canst not then be false to any man." If the artist's own observations and experiences are less important to him than an urge to be "Modern," to be always in the mode, then he has dammed little self to express or at best he walks a thin and perilous line between being a genius and a horse's ass.[38]

In July 1930, Beatrice Judd Ryan, in response to an invitation from the Honolulu Academy of Arts, assembled an exhibition of paintings, watercolors, and drawings from Galerie Beaux Arts members and brought them to Honolulu. The exhibition, including work by Dixon, Ray Boynton, Constance Macky, Frank Van Sloun, Nelson Poole, John Langley Howard, Jacques Schnier, and Guest Wickson, attracted considerable attention. Ryan herself gave several lectures at the Honolulu Academy of Arts on modernist trends in art. Dixon's prize-winning Tehachapi painting, *Merging of Spring and Winter*, was praised in newspaper reviews, as were several of his charcoal drawings portraying Native American subjects.

During that summer of 1930, Joseph Strauss, chief engineer of the Golden Gate Bridge project, asked Charles Walter Duncan, his public relations advisor, to recommend a West Coast architect. The rush to design the bridge had started, and Strauss wanted an acceptable individual. Duncan turned to his brother-in-law, Maynard Dixon, who had painted a canvas with an unusual aerial perspective, *Design Study of Golden Gate Bridge* (fig. 146), intended for the promotion of a bridge bond issue. Dixon suggested Irving Foster Morrow. Strauss hired Morrow as consulting architect for the bridge design. Morrow had his own thoughts about developing the bridge's overall design, particularly lighting and color; however, he sought the opinions of other people, including Dixon, individuals he knew combined strong personal ties to the region with proven esthetic sense. A responsive and insightful design emerged, innovative and striking.

Now, at last, Strauss's army had its flag, the image of a bridge unlike any other in the world. From above, the perspective adopted in the Maynard Dixon painting, it was a narrow ribbon, eulogized as though stretched in a tug-of-war between two mountainous and muscular points of land. Viewed head on from the roadway, the towers, with their ladder like rise, carried the eye and the spirit upward; in profile, the towers shrank to slender ellipses, and the great cables and long suspensions turned the bridge into a giant harp, hung in the western sky. There was, in this bridge, no bad side, no unflattering perspective, no camouflaged ugly hodgepodge

146. *Design Study of the Golden Gate Bridge,* 1930, tempera on board, 41 x 57 inches, Golden Gate Bridge District, San Francisco, California

*of mechanistic works. The most powerful emotional argument against the bridge—
its looks—now worked in its behalf.*[39]

The bridge project generated endless controversy among San Francisco's artists. Many viewed it as man's ultimate violation of the natural grandeur of the Golden Gate. Novelist Gertrude Atherton and sculptor Haig Patigian urged San Francisco's citizens not to disfigure the Golden Gate, "one of Nature's Perfect Pictures." Others considered the bridge one of man's premiere technological accomplishments. Winona Tomananczy remembered Dixon held a "pro and con powwow" in his Montgomery Street studio for many of the city's artists. Strauss and Duncan came to the studio, armed with maps, drawings, and models to present their case. Several artists expressed support, but most rejected the project. Dixon surprised everyone by his advocacy. After a prolonged and heated discussion, Tomananczy recalled, the meeting ended, the artists agreeing they would make no protest at that time to the bridge authorities. Dixon's design study itself has an interesting history. In 1937, as cleanup crews started to clear items out of a warehouse, the canvas was taken outside where it might have been carted away had not an inebriated workman fallen through it and, in a panic, pushed it up next to a wall behind other things. The painting survived. Since restored, it now hangs in the foyer of the Golden Gate Bridge District offices at the San Francisco toll plaza.

In mid-November 1930, Dixon received a letter from Roman Hubbell, John Lorenzo Hubbell's son, telling him "El Patron" had died on November 11. The Navajo came from the far corners of the reservation, through cold rain, gathering at Ganado. The first hard storm of winter arrived on the day they buried Hubbell, and in the wind-driven snow, Hubbell's friends and relatives made the long walk to the top of Hubbell Hill and the family graveyard. There, John Lorenzo Hubbell was buried alongside his first wife, Lina, and Manyhorses, a Navajo who had become one of his closest friends. Dixon did not attend the funeral, but his thoughts must have returned to the old days when, as a young man, he had come into Navajo country and been befriended by Hubbell, who encouraged him to seek his spirit and dreams in this red-earth country.

Dixon found little comfort in the San Francisco Art Association's annual show of 1931, a show that received both vociferous praise and condemnation. By then rated as one of the nation's more important exhibitions, it included works by Edward Hopper, George Luks, Charles Burchfield, Guy Pené du Bois, William Glackens, Andrew Dasburg, Willard Nash, Yasuo Kuniyoshi, Lorser Feitelson, Stanton MacDonald-Wright, Millard Sheets, and Diego Rivera. Some artists called the modern works in the exhibit hokum, while others viewed them as a positive harbinger of future years. Charles Stafford Duncan, a member of the jury of awards, called the show "one big banana," perhaps referring to the "Mexican influence," fellow juror Diego Rivera. Even though he won the association's popular prize for *Shapes of Fear*, Dixon, who could blow hot and cold about modern art, blasted the exhibition:

> *Looking over 50 some odd per cent of the exhibition one would think that a yen for the "experimental in art" had robbed our artists of their sense of fitness and of humor. In the ludicrous array can be seen the growth of a cult that makes a virtue of incompetence and takes "self-expression" as an alibi for imbecility. It needs no longer a jury of artists to pass upon the "works of art," but a jury of psychoanalysts to pass upon the "workings" of artists.*[40]

During 1930, Dixon produced twelve cover illustrations, one for each month, as covers for the Automobile Club of Southern California's monthly magazine, *Touring Topics*. The paintings chronicled the history of transportation in the West from 1600 to 1930: Native Americans with burden baskets, a Spanish galleon, a prairie schooner, a clipper ship, the Pony Express, the railroad, the modern automobile, and the airplane. Pleased with the large commission check he received from publisher Phil Townsend Hanna, Dixon urged Lange to consider a place they could escape from a worsening economy and a marriage that had faltered. An extensive stay far from San Francisco might revitalize their relationship. Lange suggested a remote Southwest community— Taos, New Mexico.

SEVEN

From Chaos to Taos
1931—1940

As they made preparations to leave for New Mexico, Dixon decided that he wanted to make the trip by car. He purchased his first automobile, a used black Ford Model A, from the San Francisco Police Department, and—after a fashion—learned to drive. They headed south from San Francisco in early June 1931, through the mountains on their way to pick up Daniel and John in Santa Cruz, but Dixon who preferred looking at the passing landscape to the road, lost control on a steep curve. The car overturned, spilling them out. Lange was unhurt but Dixon went to the hospital with a twisted arm and a broken jaw. Two days later, they retrieved the boys and left for Taos.

Once there, they rented a little New Mexican adobe house at Rancho de Taos, with two rooms, a dirt floor, a well, but without indoor plumbing. Mabel Dodge Luhan let him use a studio in Taos, and Dixon went there every day to work. Dixon established contact again with Ernest Blumenschein and Frank Hoffman, who had moved from Chicago to Taos. Sometimes he went on painting excursions with Blumenschein, Hoffman, and their friend Walter Ufer, but most of the time, he avoided the artists and writers circles, although he did meet Victor Higgins, Emil Bisttram (a proponent of Dynamic Symmetry), and Kenneth Adams. Still, one of the first things he did upon arriving in Taos was to write Mary Austin in Santa Fe:

We are in the neighborhood for maybe 3 months. Sometime, if you are so inclined, I'd like to call on you and crack a nine-year-old bottle with you—if I can hold it out until the day. It's small and was hard to get. I am none too frisky after getting partly squashed in a motor upset—but will soon be right again. We have a nice house 1/2 mile out of Taos. We brought work and materials and the two small boys and look forward to a good summer.[1]

Austin had been considering a book of her poems and had suggested to Dixon that he provide the illustrations. Dixon met with Austin at her home, Casa Querida, on the Camino del Monte Sol in Santa Fe, and stayed with William Penhallow and Alice

Corbin Henderson for several days while he showed Austin prospective drawings. But the book never appeared, probably because by then Austin had decided to write her autobiography. While in Santa Fe, Dixon made arrangements with the Museum of Fine Arts to have one of his paintings, *Men and Mountains*, shown during the museum's annual fiesta exhibit in November.

Back in Taos, Dixon studied dramatic cloud formations exploding over the sweeping southern Sangre de Cristo Mountains and the stark, windswept Taos Valley, translating them into a series of twenty-two oil sketches he called *Skies of New Mexico*. For Dixon, northern New Mexico became a magical land. Nancy Wood describes the spell it casts in her book *Taos Pueblo:*

> *The light in northern New Mexico is pure and crystalline, as if the sun simply exploded from its own intensity. The sun locks the land in dryness, cracks it open and exposes the vulnerability of nature in relentless processes of epochal change. Even in winter, the sun is fierce, searing the landscape as well as the mind; memory is locked in a time when there was only an unspoiled land so vast a man could not reach the end of it in his lifetime. Here the star-filled sky presses down on the blackness of the land, as if to impose its greater power on the fragility of the earth. The land of the Taos Indian sweeps the mind clean of societal clutter and focuses an inevitable confrontation between the dualities of the inner and outer life. One must eventually choose.*[2]

Dixon sent the paintings of cloud studies to the Galerie Beaux Arts in San Francisco, which exhibited them as a group during November 1931. Seeking other locales, Dixon— accompanied by Joseph Sinel, an industrial designer and an old friend from Foster and Kleiser days—went on an ambitious painting expedition along the Chama River to the redrock country around Abiquiu, then west to Coyote, New Mexico (figs. 147 and 148). Other excursions included visits to the pueblos of Santa Clara and Santa Domingo, where he attended various celebrations. Attracted by the sprawling Taos Pueblo, Dixon befriended many of the residents, who invited him to the pueblo's ceremonies: San Geronimo's Day, the Round Dance, and Buffalo Dances. He made numerous drawings of the people and pueblo life at Taos. At other times, he explored the area around Taos Valley, painting in some of the small villages.

The cultural practices of Hispanic Americans had fascinated him from his early experiences in San Diego. He explored *camposantos* ("saint's camps"), cemeteries at Rancho de Taos and Taos, sketching and painting among the decorative grave fences, stone tablets, and ornate crosses festooned with colorful paper flowers. At least once the family came into contact with a more mysterious manifestation of the local religious customs. Los Hermanos Penitentes, the Penitente Brothers, was a religious order that had become an important force in the remote villages. By the 1930s, Penitente rites, which included self-flagellation, had been driven into secrecy by Anglo suspicion and criticism. Dixon must have known their reputation, for when a Penitente group neared the Dixon house one day, he hurried Lange and the boys inside, barred the windows,

147. *Summer Storm*, 1931, ink and conté crayon on paper, 12 x 18 inches, private collection, photograph courtesy of Medicine Man Gallery

148. *New Mexico Juniper*, 1931, oil on canvas board, 16 x 20 inches, private collection, photograph courtesy of Medicine Man Gallery

locked the front door, and stood behind it as the procession passed, his loaded Colt .45 grasped in one hand. Afterwards, he wrote "Tabu":

> Stark and alone, a bare box of boards,
> The small wooden church stands on a mound,
>   and the mound alone on a prairie.
> The hard foot-beaten path leads to the door,
> and the tough native grass to its edge;
>   the gate, battered and scared,
>   and the barbed wire ripped from the post by the vandal boys.
> But the windows, blank in the walls
>   are unbroken, saved by an ancient dread,
> for behind them dwells the dark thought
> of a dead man nailed to a cross. [3]

In the early fall of 1931, Dixon took off on a two-week painting expedition. He started at Española, then turning northeast, he journeyed through Chimayo, Truchas, Las Trampas, and east over the mountains to Mora, absorbing the timelessness, the human qualities, and the artistic expressions of the quiet villages. From Mora, he went on to Las Vegas, New Mexico, and out into the southern Great Plains, responding to an emotional geography of wide-open spaces before returning to Taos. While Dixon worked, Lange took care of the children, cooked and washed, tried to keep things smooth, and drove Dixon to and from his studio every day. Constance joined them at the Ranchos de Taos house. Twenty-one now, she had come to Taos earlier with John Collier Jr., supporting herself by waiting on tables and typing Mabel Dodge Luhan's autobiography, among other jobs. When Lange had opportunities, she photographed local architecture and the people. She remembered that a serious-looking man in a Ford would drive by their house every morning, always at the same time, returning each night, again at the same time. Someone told her he was "Paul Strand, a photographer." Later when she met Strand in New York, he told her that he knew she and Dixon had been in Taos.

Lange felt closer to Dixon in New Mexico. She knew he enjoyed living a simple life. Taos relaxed him and he became less argumentative, less insistent about his points of view. Taos provided a temporary refuge from the uncertainty and unrest of the outside world. Dixon bought a horse for the boys, taught them to ride, and began teaching them Spanish. They told time by the sun. No telephone interrupted their days. Every day brought visual impressions: some for immediate expression, others drawn upon for years. Constance wrote a letter about her father's work to the *San Francisco Examiner*:

> My father has really gotten into his stride now, and is doing some very fine work.
> Strange to say, coming to a country that has been pretty thoroughly painted in all
> its aspects, he seems to have hit on something new, something underneath. I feel
> that he has gone deeper than even the men who belong to the Taos group, and that
> the work that he has done while here is more truly an interpretation of this strange

wild country than that of the men who have lived here for years. There is a little of tragedy of the Indians and Mexicans in it, the dim cycles of their earth-returning lives that seem so hopeless, the little cubical adobes lying flat and low against the earth sleeping, and the sad dark people.[4]

In his New Mexico paintings, Dixon strived to pass on spiritual messages from the region's landscapes and indigenous cultures. Arthur Millier, in an article for the *Los Angeles Times*, conveyed some of Dixon's thoughts, formulated while in Taos:

The west deserves and can have its own culture if it follows through the present trends toward simplicity and honesty, as long as money is our measurement of value, we shall bow, in cultural matters, to the judgment of New York and Paris, but as we learn to live our own life on our own soil we shall be less easily impressed by imported fads which don't belong.

Ever since I began to see and think, I have had a feeling that the west is spiritually important to America. As I grow older it becomes a firm conviction. You can't argue with those desert mountains, and if you live among them enough—like the Indian does—you don't want to. I tried to express this idea in Earth Knower. He is a sage, calm Indian who stands against his own background of mountains, from which he draws his health, wealth, religion and pattern of living.

The artist's job, as I see it, is to try to widen peoples horizons—show them the wonder of the world they live in. To do that the artist had to know about it. I like the depression principally because it brings us back to a realization that integrity is the one thing on which social life can be built. I have tried to paint on that basis and people who come from other lands say that they find a genuinely American art in my work.[5]

When winter arrived, Taos and the other villages in the valley were locked in by deep snow. Dixon struggled with the bitter cold, finding it more difficult to paint in the unheated studio, often working in three layers of clothes and two pairs of gloves. Moreover, the Depression had reached northern New Mexico. Native Americans, Hispanic Americans, and poor whites came into Taos on Saturday afternoons, some in autos but most on horseback or in horse-drawn wagons. Lacking money, they bartered beans, pinion nuts, dried corn, eggs, hides, and weaving, and made exchanges for what they needed. The Dixons shopped in this market too, yet they managed to enjoy a warm family Christmas. Dixon and his son Daniel cut a small pinion pine for their Christmas tree (fig. 149), and stockings hung over the fireplace had presents stuffed in them. The family attended the Christmas ceremonies at Taos Pueblo, watched processions around the plaza, illuminated by great bonfires, and listened as the hymns, the *alabodos*, floated toward the cold star-studded sky.

Dixon was worried, knowing their money was nearly gone. He knew also he would have to go back to the city to earn a living as an artist, even though this meant facing the uncertainties of the Depression. A visit from a Native American friend threw his inner conflict into sharp relief.

My friend Antonio is an Indian; one of the head men of Taos Pueblo, New Mexico. He is a very intelligent man. Besides his native Tigua he speaks Spanish and English fluently. He has travelled, the guest of prominent people—to Chicago, New York, Rochester, Washington, San Francisco, Los Angeles; has made his own observations and drawn his own conclusions. Like most Indians he thinks the white man is a smart fool: and though I am a white man with a deep respect for science I have absorbed enough of the wisdom of the ground to agree with him in many points. So—wishing to make a record of that wise head of his, I painted his portrait; and while I painted we talked. It was winter—a hard winter—in Taos town; harder even than in the Pueblo. There was no money, and the native population, mostly Mexican, were reduced to barter. (The Indians always bartered.) We talked of this and of the ground, the pasture and the corn; and I tried, in crude outline, to give Antonio an idea of the economic jam we white men had got ourselves into. I said I could not see anything ahead for me and my family, but that I was going back to the city and take my chances with the rest of us.

"Well, I guess that's right," he said. "You know I got a little piece of ground over here, pretty good cornfield; and I got that little extra house out this side of the Pueblo. If it gets too tough, come on back and I'll share with you."

He looked at me with steady honest eyes, and I knew that he meant it. But—my God!—if Mr. Hearst is right why—the man ought to be arrested: he's a damned communist.[6]

Finally, the cold winter drove them out. On a clear January day in 1932, they left Taos, the first people to break the road to Santa Fe that year. Dixon and Lange shared the wheel of the Ford, navigating through deep snow in the canyon where veering off the road might cause them to tumble into the Rio Grande below. Finally, they had threaded their way down off the Taos plateau to Santa Fe, and they turned west toward California, choosing the warmer southern route through Socorro, Deming, Phoenix, Yuma, and into Los Angeles. They saw tragic signs of the Depression everywhere: unemployed homeless individuals scattered along the roads. "The Forgotten Men," Dixon called them, uprooted people wandering endless miles throughout the Southwest, their faces turned toward the distance that promised California. "This is my country?" he wondered. After a two-week journey, they arrived in San Francisco.

They gave up their Taylor Street home to save money and enrolled the boys in boarding schools, first in Carmel, and later at San Anselmo in Marin County. Dixon and Lange saw them only on weekends. Daniel and John remember standing by the road, waiting for the old black Ford to arrive, then standing by the road again, watching it depart without them. Dixon moved into his studio at 728 Montgomery Street, while Lange lived in her studio at 802 Montgomery Street, three doors down. The long stay in Taos apparently had not repaired the marriage.

For Dixon, this was a bleak time, "prospects dark," he recalled. The situation was alleviated somewhat when a letter arrived in April 1932 from the National Academy of Design, informing him that *Shapes of Fear*, entered in the academy's 1932 winter exhibition, had been purchased by the Henry Ward Ranger Fund, then placed with the Brooklyn Institute of Arts and Sciences. Besides the award's considerable prestige, Dixon received two-thirds of the fifteen-hundred-dollar purchase price. The painting is now in the collections of the National Museum of American Art in Washington, D.C.

When another in the long line of Coppa's restaurants opened at 120 Spring Street in the early 1930s, Joseph Coppa's son, Victor, invited Dixon to accept a large table for Friday nights, reserved for whomever he might invite. Like its predecessors, the restaurant became a favorite of the city's artists, and, as usual, the walls had been decorated by the patrons, Dixon contributing a particularly ribald cartoon. Winona Tomananczy remembered one night when she and her husband, Paul Tomananczy, went with Dixon and Lange to Coppa's. Present at the Dixon table were Harold Von Schmidt, by then a prominent illustrator for the *Saturday Evening Post*; Albert Elkus, head of the University of California Music department; Roi Partridge and Imogen Cunningham; Kem Weber; Hazel Dreiss, the Grabhorn Press's bookbinder; and Albert Bender. Another time, she recalled, Dixon and Lange invited William Gerstle, Otis Oldfield, Beatrice Judd Ryan, and Alexander Archipenko, the émigré Russian sculptor so closely identified with the Cubism movement, to Coppa's for a celebration. Dixon still wore his tailored black suit on these special occasions but preferred to wear blue denim on his mosquito-thin frame, retaining only the black sombrero and cowboy boots. By the 1930s, his eyes were regulated by wire-rim glasses.

149. *Maynard Dixon and Daniel Dixon,*
1931, private collection

In June 1932, Dixon and Lange took the boys and the twins, redheaded sons of Imogen Cunningham and Roi Partridge, to Anita Baldwin's two-thousand-acre estate at Fallen Leaf Lake near Lake Tahoe, where they spent a leisurely summer in absolute privacy, staying in one of the estate's cottages. Dixon built a sweat lodge, and the boys ran naked all summer, wild as Indians. Baldwin's home itself, no summer cottage, required a multitude of servants to keep it running. The main house had polished hardwood floors covered with bearskins. Suede calfskin lined the dining room. An English butler answered the door, a taciturn Scotsman kept a pack of hunting dogs in order, and another man ran the boats on the lake. Baldwin's personal bodyguard wore a .45 pistol on social occasions, while "line riders" (armed men on horseback) patrolled the strong wire fence that surrounded the property. Dixon did some paintings of the trees and glacial outcroppings, but did so halfheartedly, unresponsive to a country with "too many pine trees." When the Dixons returned to San Francisco at summer's end, Dixon found times even tougher. Finally, he managed to sell *Navajoland*, a large overmantel painting for fifteen hundred dollars. Dixon also recorded that Lange had started photographing the forgotten man, adding "no paintings of this subject," although he himself had started making sketches as early as 1930.

Lange was still making portraits for people who could afford them. But in 1932, when nearly fourteen million people were without jobs in the United States, she felt an urgency to photograph the unemployed who crowded San Francisco's streets. One day in 1932, she encountered a bread line set up near her studio by a rich woman known only as the "White Angel." Of the twelve exposures she made with her camera that day, one, *White Angel Bread Line*, would be counted among her best-known images. After this first attempt, Lange left her studio at every opportunity to photograph in the streets.

Around this time, a short-lived but powerful influence in American photography emerged in the Bay Area, started by some photographers turning away from academic pictorialism. "Group f/64," they called it, after the aperture at which they set their lenses to achieve maximum depth of field, a sharp image of both foreground and distance. The group included Ansel Adams, Imogen Cunningham, Edward Weston, John Paul Edwards, Henry F. Swift, Sonya Noskowiak, and Willard Van Dyke. Dorothea did not volunteer nor was she asked to join the group, even though she knew all of them. Later she did join one of their shows. Group f/64 had its first exhibit at the M. H. de Young Museum on November 15, 1932. Dixon, who rejected all "orthodoxies" and was infuriated that Lange was excluded, responded to the group's manifesto in a seething letter, "To certain members of group f/64," which he signed "Outsider." Everyone knew who the author was.

> You have now formed a very select professional under the above title. If we outsiders understand it correctly some outsiders are excluded because they do not work according to a formula now in vogue with a certain set of so-called purists.
>
> You have thus, by implication at least, arrogated to yourselves a degree of professional superiority, which in view of the merits of other workers not sanctioned by your cult, is open to serious question. While the writer does not for a moment expect that this letter will cause you to recede from the position you have taken or to fore-go any benefits of prestige or patronage resulting there-from, he wishes to point out that you have not sought to broaden the scope of photography by stressing its variable possibilities as a means of expression (motive of the old Photo—Secession—). To the contrary, you have set up as your criterion of merit a mere slavish conformity to a set of its technical limitations. In so doing you have only advanced one more of those contemptible professional orthodoxies, the outgrowth of narrow-mindedness and intolerance, which have disgraced the practice of the visual arts for the past ten years.
>
> That people of your standing should be guilty of such bigotry would be unbelievable if you had not so proved it. Let me congratulate you, therefore on the

choice of a name which so aptly indicates limited outlook. Your high position in your profession gives you the opportunity to advance the interests of fine photography by stimulating the enthusiasm of its practitioners and wider public interest through demonstrating a more flexible use of the medium which, as self elected masters of the craft, should be yours. You have chosen the opposite.[7]

Rondal Partridge and Roger Sturtevant recalled that Dixon also asked Sturtevant to photograph Maynard's bare rear end and send the picture to the Group f/64 as a statement. Recalled Sturtevant, "[He] wanted to send it to those people to say, this is precision for you, but unfortunately it didn't turn out that technically perfect."[8]

Deciding he needed stimulation from the desert again and to escape the economic pressures, Dixon, accompanied by Lange and the boys, left for southwestern Utah in early June 1933. They stopped for a week in Carson City, then proceeded eastward across Nevada

150. *Nevada*, 1933, crayon on paper, 13½ x 18 inches, collection of Ed Mell

(fig. 150) through Eureka, Austin, Ely, and Pioche, to Cedar City, Utah. From there they traveled south another sixty miles to Zion National Park. The Dixons boarded the boys with a Mormon family in Toquerville and then roamed through Zion's canyons and mesas for two months, camping in the cottonwood groves along the Virgin River or staying with Mormon families in the small towns. Dixon did not think Zion compared to the beauty of Canyon de Chelly, but it seemed grandeur of another sort, "magnificent and awesome by moonlight." He and Lange would pick the boys up on weekends and wander through the quiet towns of Springdale, Rockland, Panguitch, Orderville, and Toquerville, impressed with the kindness of the people and their self-sufficiency, each family an economic unit. "We get pretty ragged but you can't starve us out," they told Maynard.

At the beginning of October, the Dixons left Zion, heading back to San Francisco through Las Vegas, pausing to watch construction at Boulder Dam, and then driving over the Tehachapi Mountains and up the San Joaquin Valley to Refuge, where they stayed a week with the Mordecai family. Dixon painted most of the Utah and Nevada canvases back in his studio, "with results highly unsatisfactory." He exhibited *Men and Mountains* and thirty-six other works, including *Approach to Zion, Moonlight Over Zion,* and *Fields of Toquerville* at Gump's from November 20 to December 11, 1933, and then at Phillip Isley's Gallery at the Ambassador Hotel in Los Angeles. None of the paintings found buyers.

STANDARD OIL
B U L L E T I N

PUBLISHED BY THE STANDARD OIL COMPANY OF CALIFORNIA
MARCH   1933

151. *Standard Oil Bulletin,* March 1933,
California History Section, California State Library

These results forced Dixon to seek sporadic illustration assignments, among them a cover for the *Standard Oil Bulletin* in March 1933, which portrayed an airplane flying over a deep canyon (fig. 151). In this painting, Dixon elaborated upon cubist-realist technique to produce a persuasive image of an insignificant object in a world of rock. He was also asked to illustrate *The Bar Cross Edition of the Works of Eugene Manlove Rhodes,* to be issued in ten volumes by subscription, priced at $50 the set. "It will take $45,000," Rhodes informed Dixon, "to put through the Bar Cross edition, incidental to have one hell of a bunch of work for Maynard Dixon."[9] Rhodes wanted Edward Borein to do half the illustrations and Maynard the other half. But the project failed economically and was abandoned by Rhodes, who struggled with it for nearly a year. This was around the time that Dixon started to seriously document the impact of the Depression, creating small sketches as he encountered labor strife beginning to emerge on the streets of San Francisco (figs. 152–154).

In late October 1933, Dixon answered a knock on his door at the Montgomery Street studio. There stood a young man with a broad smile, who introduced himself as Everett Ruess. Only nineteen years old, Ruess had spent the past three years wandering alone through the Sierra Nevada, along the California coast, and into the desert Southwest, a young mystic seeking inspiration from lonely places. Ruess decided he wanted to meet Dixon after viewing some of his Southwest paintings. Impressed, the older mystic decided to take the boy home to meet Lange. She too, recognized Everett's talent, ambition, and energy, and thought it deserved her time and attention. Perhaps she also felt Ruess could use some motherly support. That night she asked him to go with her and Dixon to attend a lecture by artist Rockwell Kent in Berkeley. In the next several days, the Dixons took Ruess to artists' gatherings and musical events. They also gave him some cooked

meals after discovering he had been living on raw carrots and banana sandwiches for a week. In the next several months, Ruess wandered in and out of the Dixons' lives, often accompanying Lange to the symphony and the opera or watching Dixon work in his studio. Lange even made several photographic portraits of him. Ruess, who had become proficient in both woodblock printmaking and photography, once asked Dixon for advice on composition. In a letter to his mother, he said simply: "The other day I had perhaps the best art lesson I ever had; a lesson in simplicity from Maynard Dixon. That time I really did learn something, I think, and I have been trying to apply what I learned. The main thing Maynard did was to make me see what is meaningless in a picture, and have the strength to eliminate it; and see what is significant, and how to stress it. This he showed me with a little scrap of black and white paper, placed over my drawings."[10] Ruess remained in San Francisco for several months. He explored the city and the dramatic northern California coast, met artists and writers—including Ansel Adams, with whom he traded prints—and attended the opera and symphony. In early March 1934, he finally left for Los Angeles, embarking on a solo trip to northern Arizona and southern Utah. The Dixons never saw him again.

Dixon closed out 1933 with another mural, *The Arrival of Fremont in California*, in three panels, ten by thirty feet, commissioned by the alumni association for the end wall of the study room at the John C. Fremont High School in Los Angeles. The center panel portrayed Fremont and his guide, Kit Carson. It was flanked by panels depicting the first and last periods of Fremont's career. Like many of his murals, they disappeared when the building was remodeled. As 1934 began, the Dixons moved into a two-story house at 2515 Gough Street. As a way to reduce rent expenditures, Lange surrendered her studio, converting some of the second-story space in their house into photography workrooms. Dixon, felled by a severe asthma onslaught, greeted the New Year with his poem "1934":

Horrible—to wake up in the night
and feel time pressing slowly,
    the silent hours sliding through the dark
    as the dumb world turns,
slowly pressing the dim dawn
    inexorably against defenseless window-panes;
    to feel the deep earth shudder
in unimaginable agony,
    slowly, slowly being forced asunder;
    to feel the perfect buildings of our pride,
clean-cut and small, tilted off-balance,
    reel toward darkness;
    and in the torn gap myriads of people,
    puny and helpless,
    struggling like maggots in a wound;
and clear above
a pitiless cold blade of cosmic light—
    ah—horrible![11]

Though Dixon received no benefit from the first of five and sometimes overlapping art projects in Franklin D. Roosevelt's New Deal, he later received many commissions through the federal projects. The short-lived Public Works of Art Project (PWAP) operated between December 1933 and June 1934. The PWAP was followed by the Treasury Department Section of Painting and Sculpture (usually called "The Section") from 1934 to 1943. Section artists were identified and hired on merit rather than financial need. The money came from the construction budgets of federally funded public buildings, primarily post offices. Either direct commissions or competitions were arranged for each building. Regional committees published the prospective mural opportunities and suggested artists for Treasury Department approval on the merit of their sketches. Successful mural artists generally were paid in three installments: after sketches were approved, when the work commenced, and after the mural's installation and final approval by the regional committee. In July 1935, the Section was augmented by the Treasury Relief Art Project (TRAP), which existed until June of 1939. This was the first government art project conceived to offer "relief" to artists. It was funded by the Works Projects (later Progress) Administration (WPA), but of all the New Deal art programs, the one with the greatest impact was the Federal Art Project (FAP), administered by the WPA, which started in 1935 and lasted until 1943. Eventually the Federal Art Project employed over five thousand artists to teach art and produce murals, easel paintings, sculpture, prints, and posters.

The PWAP was organized into sixteen regions, each headed by a local art authority, usually a museum director. San Francisco became District 15, and Dr. Walter Heil, newly arrived from Germany to assume the position of director of the M. H. de Young Museum, was asked to head it. The PWAP sought proven competency and talent first. Relief was a secondary consideration, although E. Holger Cahill, a Federal Art Project director, once remarked that "of all types of American people, the artist needed government aid most." He recalled a cartoon by John Sloan that showed people crowding toward a hole labeled "Depression," only to find an artist at the bottom of the pit who informs them, "This is my home, I've always been here!"[12]

Administrator Edward Bruce selected respected art critic Forbes Watson as technical director for PWAP, and together they insisted that artists should "sell to the American people the idea that art is and should be an integral part of our civilization." Bruce identified two groups he planned to antagonize, using the official patronage of the Federal Government: nostalgia-ridden academic artists supported by the National Academy of Design, and modernists from the Paris schools. He declared that both camps ignored American reality, one by dictation of form, the other by manufacture of irrelevant content. Thus, New Deal art programs officially endorsed American Scene painting, particularly murals that required artists to connect with some visible elements in the local environment in a representational style.

California easel and mural painting during the 1930s became part of the American Scene movement. Complex and contradictory, the movement represented the hope that America had come of age artistically, creating an art expressive of its own traditions and aspirations. The American Scene reflected an increased interest in realistic painting and a growing desire of artists to become effective members of their communities by sharing their experiences with the general public. The public, in turn, enjoyed an art in which their own likenesses and lives were mirrored. Within the American Scene, two groups of artists are identified: regionalists and social realists. Regionalists featured the positive everyday activities of average people and "peopled" landscapes, while social realists portrayed the tensions of modern society. Artists in California and elsewhere in the West had, like Maynard Dixon, long accepted and practiced regionalism, but now they expanded its mandate to encompass the glorification of people, places, and histories in their states. Both groups avoided the extreme elements of European modernist art; the regionalists, in particular, purged their canvases of any nonobjective styles. Pure views of local landscapes faded in importance. The regionalists scorned the flashy decorative brushwork and pale colors of California's impressionists, and instead offered earthier interpretations through careful craftsmanship in oils and bold forceful brushwork in watercolors. A "New Deal" style emerged, characterized by simplified, bulky, sometimes anatomically distorted figures and outlines, and influenced in a general way by the art of primitive cultures and specifically by Mexican muralists Diego Rivera, David Alfaro Siqueiros, and José Clemente Orozco.

The search for a "usable past," most prevalent in mural painting during the 1930s, expanded into other artistic endeavors as well. Artists often looked backward to find themes in their painting that addressed contemporary problems. The themes most often used—people, work, and historical events—constituted the major icons of the Depression-era West, particularly in California. Artists in the 1930s charted and documented the West as never before. They explored urban areas, quiet towns, and rural hamlets, and painted, it seemed, every conceivable subject. Searching for a sense and feeling of place, they scrutinized farm wagons, modern automobiles, railroad yards, revival meetings, political gatherings, old mining towns, small farms, large agricultural complexes, busy streets, and quiet backyards. Most refrained from painting the sadder parts of life in the 1930s, believing their art should inspire the public.

Under the umbrella of this American Scene philosophy, the PWAP began surveying spaces in San Francisco's civic centers, libraries, museums, and public schools, and giving assignments to local painters and sculptors. In the early days of organization, the PWAP approached Dixon, asking him to consider coordinating the projects. He declined, deciding instead to accept the challenge of designing mural decorations for the octagonal rotunda of the Palace of Fine Arts in collaboration with Frank Van Sloun. Dixon painted a set of seven watercolor designs for the project, but when Van Sloun decided to withdraw, Dixon made a new set of mural studies (fig. 155). The PWAP office in San Francisco forwarded their recommendation to Washington, but no decision was made about funding. Dixon determined to enter mural competitions as often as possible. Easel paintings, as he had already discovered, did not sell readily in the Depression economy, while mural and other government art commissions could provide a reasonable income. He continued to seek illustration commissions as well whenever he needed money, which was most of the time. After a thirty-two-year association, *Sunset Magazine* used its last Maynard Dixon image, *In Zion*, on the cover of its November 1934 issue.

In April 1934, Dixon departed for southern Nevada, engaged by the PWAP to document the construction activities that had been underway for three years at Boulder Dam. Dixon stayed in Boulder City for thirty-six days, painting and sketching whatever he wanted: workers and their equipment, the dam rising upward from the turbulent Colorado River, and dramatic landscapes surrounding the construction site. Finding lodging with a workingman's family, he hired a "broken-down fliver" and a young boy to drive him around for a dollar a day, crisscrossing between the Nevada side and Arizona as he sketched and painted the gigantic effort to dam the Colorado River at Black Canyon. The sights overwhelmed him. "It gave me an impression of concealed force—and of ultimate futility."[13] But he started painting immediately. At Boulder he found young Americans, including his brother-in-law, Martin Lange, forced by the Depression into backbreaking manual labor for which they were ill prepared. Four men died during the month Dixon worked at Boulder Dam. Labor unions attempting to organize the workers made little progress because of the labor-town atmosphere: armed guards, stool pigeons,

155. *Mountain Men*, 1934, oil on board, 28 x 24 inches,
photograph courtesy of Coeur d'Alene Art Auction

and company stores. "All these things," an angry Dixon declared, "emerged in a sense of the tragedy of men's labor; the great treadmill of lost endeavor — but in the long run, the desert will have the last laugh."[14]

When not drawing or painting construction activities, Dixon would escape into the barren desert mountains to paint landscapes (fig. 156). Before Dixon returned from Boulder Dam, he exhibited his paintings, watercolors, and drawings in the administration building in Boulder City, then had them forwarded to the M. H. de Young Museum in San Francisco for another exhibition (fig. 157). Dixon returned with twenty-four finished

156. *Hills at Indian Springs,* 1934, oil on canvas board, 16 x 20 inches, private collection, photograph courtesy of Medicine Man Gallery

157. *Okie Camp,* 1934, chalk and pencil on paper, 9 x 13¹/₄ inches, private collection

pieces, but only received $450 from the PWAP for what he considered $3,000 worth of art. Reflecting on his experiences at Boulder Dam, he wrote "Industrial":

Well, somehow I got born,
    all right enough; and grew up somehow;
    got me a girl and got married too,
all right enough,
and that was interesting.
Then we had kids, of course, some six or seven or eight,
and that was interesting. So—then we both worked like hell,
    and got us a home (we thought)
    all right enough,
but soon the bank took that,
and keeping up the insurance
    was some interesting.
Well, the years kept coming and kept coming,
all right enough,
we couldn't stop 'em.
    and then one hungry night we heard
    and that was interesting
we heard God laughing . . . .
    God!—and what a laugh! [15]

After Dixon returned, he painted another cover for the *Standard Oil Bulletin* (fig. 158), then found himself embroiled in the battle between Los Angeles and San Francisco for supremacy as the art center of California. For Los Angeles, San Francisco represented the Bolsheviks in art; to San Francisco, Los Angeles artists seemed inept conservatives. The Los Angeles Art Association staged an All-California Art Exhibition at the Biltmore Salon in the summer of 1934, inviting San Francisco painters to submit a select group of paintings. Dr. Walter Heil (director of the M. H. de Young Museum), E. Spencer Macky (director of the California School of Fine Arts), and artist Charles Stafford Duncan selected what they thought were the fifty best San Francisco paintings. The Los Angeles jury, however, rejected all but six as unworthy. Bitter words flew between the artists' camps, particularly when several of the top prizewinners, among them William F. Ritschel and F. Tolles Chamberlin, seemed to represent a rejection of modernist painting. Dixon received an honorable mention, along with Stanton MacDonald Wright, Conrad Buff, Nicolai Fechin, Phil Dike, and Lee Blair. Still, he jumped into the quarrel, and in a letter to the president of the Los Angeles Art Association, commented,

In view of the . . . pardonable suspicion [that] the aforesaid jury did not truly represent art opinion or appreciation in Los Angeles, the grief manifested by the group of exiled San Franciscans is not well justified—especially as this same group has had things very much their own way here, passing the bouquet back and forth, and has repeatedly and unmercifully slaughtered the Los Angeles content sen[t] to our annual that is, until now few of us protested that: It does not matter whether you like a work or not. Appraise such work by the canons of the school to which it belongs—not by your own personal dogmas.[16]

As the furor raged, Dixon received a letter from May Rhodes, informing him that her husband, Eugene Manlove Rhodes, was dead of a heart attack on June 27, 1934. Rhodes, who had suffered several years from heart problems, had enclosed a prospective epitaph in one of his last letters to Dixon. The complete version appeared in the preface to Rhodes' book *The Proud Sheriff*, published in 1935. "Now hushed at last the murmur of his mirth, \ Here he lies quiet in the quiet earth. \ When the last trumpet sounds on land and sea \ He will arise then, chatting cheerfully, \ And, blandly interrupting Gabriel, \ He will go sauntering down the road to hell. \ He will pause loitering at the infernal gate, \ Advising Satan on affairs of state, \ Complaining loudly that the roads are bad \ And bragging what a jolly grave he had!"[17] Before he could recover from Rhodes' death, and still worried about the labor problems he had witnessed at Boulder Dam, Dixon was shocked by San Francisco's bitter maritime strike, which culminated in violence and rioting along the Embarcadero on July 5, 1934, which came to be known as "Bloody Thursday." Two men were killed and scores more were injured. Lange roamed the waterfront, photographing police, strikers, and the scabs hired to disrupt the strike. Dixon accompanied her with his sketchpad. Unemployed workers, embattled longshoremen, police, California National Guardsmen, vigilantes, and scabs became part of San Francisco's life that year. Brooding over these disturbing scenes, Dixon started to paint the "Forgotten Man and Strike" series, somber, social realist portraits of individuals caught in a "faceless terror."

158. *Standard Oil Bulletin,* January 1934, California History Section, California State Library

During that same fateful summer, Willard Van Dyke gave Lange an exhibit of her documentary photography at his small gallery in Oakland. One of the people who came was Paul Schuster Taylor, an associate professor of economics at the University of California–Berkeley. Taylor specialized in farm labor practices and was investigating the problems of contemporary migrant workers flooding California. He recalled seeing on the gallery walls this striking array of relevant photography by Dorothea Lange, whom he had never heard of. He called and asked Lange if he could have one of the photographs to accompany an article he had written on the maritime strike for the magazine *Survey Graphic*. Later that fall, Lange and Taylor met for the first time at self-help sawmill cooperative near Oroville, California. Taylor had invited Lange, Willard Van Dyke, Imogen Cunningham, Preston Holder, and Mary Jeanette Edwards to document the cooperative's operations. For Lange, it was like a new world—so different from her private photographic enterprise. She remembered the assignment because it not only introduced her to Paul Taylor but also showed her the methods of social science research. They continued their work together with a series of reports for the California Rural Rehabilitation Administration during 1934 and 1935, achieving remarkable results almost immediately and establishing a close working relationship.

Dixon exhibited several "Forgotten Man and Strike" paintings at San Francisco's Artist's Cooperative Gallery during October 1934. The exhibit, *Pictures of Today*, was overlooked by the local art critics but attracted considerable attention from San Francisco newspapers and the public. He also entered three of the paintings in a San Francisco Art Association exhibition, failing again to stir critics' interest. Though the paintings prompted energetic discussion among the people who saw them, no one wanted reminders of the Depression, certainly not for wall decorations. None of the paintings were sold.

Interest in Dixon's social protest paintings continued in the press and periodicals for several years. In February 1937, *Survey Graphic* devoted three pages to "Maynard Dixon Looks at Social Conflict," reproducing *No Place to Go, Forgotten Man, Free Speech, Scab, Law and Disorder*, and *Keep Moving*. And on March 28, 1937, the *St. Louis Post-Dispatch* ran a full-page supplement with four of the paintings reproduced in color. But eventually, he stopped painting labor and depression subjects as his anger subsided and returned to his beloved western landscapes.

Deciding to escape from the tormented San Francisco environment once again, Dixon, Lange, and the two boys journeyed to Carson City, Nevada, in the fall of 1934. They stayed in a small apartment at one end of the old Bliss-Yerington home. LaVerne Bradley remembered that Dixon took over the old family dining room for his large canvas and easel work, while Lange converted the pantry into a darkroom. Lange wandered through Carson City with her camera, looking for vignettes of small town life, while Dixon took to the hills, searching for patterns in the desert. They would have picnics under the trees with sandwiches and cold draft beer from Carson City's old brewery. Lange, in sandals and bright Mexican skirts, would romp with the boys, and Dixon would have one of his sons, either Daniel or John, sit down next to him while he painted at a small easel.

On January 18, 1935, the new San Francisco Museum of Art opened in the War Memorial at the Civic Center, coinciding with the Fifty-fifth Annual Exhibition of the San Francisco Art Association. Four hundred paintings by California and Western artists long held in public esteem and by younger artists just beginning to show were displayed in ten galleries. Dixon had two works included in the exhibition, *Andy Furuseth*, a drawing, and *Scab*, one of his strike paintings. Other artists represented included

Kenneth Adams, Rex Brandt, Rinaldo Cuneo, Phil Dike, William Gaw, Selden Gile, Lorser Feitelson, Barse Miller, Otis Oldfield, George Post, Joseph Raphael, and a young artist, David Park, who would become a force behind the Bay Area Figurative Movement after World War II. At the same time, the Exhibition of Modern French Painting hung in the museum's South Gallery—Paul Cézanne, Edgar Degas, Paul Gauguin, Henri Matisse, Claude Monet, Pierre-Auguste Renoir, and Vincent van Gogh—some of the best works by impressionist and postimpressionist French painters ever assembled in San Francisco. Dixon returned to the South Gallery repeatedly, studying the vitality and vigor of the paintings, particularly van Gogh's works.

Shortly after this important exhibit closed in March 1935, Dixon received disturbing news in a letter from Everett Ruess's mother. Ruess had decided to explore southern Utah's Escalante River region in November 1934, informing his parents he would be gone two months. After three months, they discovered he had not called for his mail at Escalante. Alarmed, they alerted authorities, who formed a search party. To Ruess's mother, Dixon wrote, "This is distressing news. But wanderers like Everett have disappearing habits— and he may yet show up. We wish you luck in your search."[18] Several groups scoured the rugged country until June 1935. They found no trace of Ruess himself, only his burros in Davis Gulch, one of the tributaries to the Escalante River. Dixon may have had Ruess in mind when he wrote "At Last" in May 1935:

At last
>I shall give myself to the desert again,
>that I, in its golden dust
>may be blown from a barren peak
>broadcast over the sun-lands.
>If you should desire some news of me,
>go ask the little horned toad
>whose home is the dust,
>or seek it among the fragrant sage,
>or question the mountain juniper,
>and, by their silence
>will truly inform you.[19]

During February 1935, Paul Taylor and Lange had gone to the pea harvest at Nipomo, California, he to interview migrant workers and she to photograph them. Dixon decided to accompany them. The maps he drew were included in a spiral-bound document (later known as the Taylor-Lange Report) that they prepared, featuring Taylor's narrative and Lange's photographs. Afterwards, Dixon returned to the southern San Joaquin Valley later in 1935 with artist Ray Strong, sketching and painting in the semidesert hills around Shafter and Coalinga.

After returning from the San Joaquin Valley, Dixon helped form the Art Students League as a cooperative art school, assisted by fellow painters Ray Strong, Frank Van Sloun, Herman Struck, and George Post. For eighteen months, Dixon taught drawing and composition at the school without pay, urging his students to produce original independent work based on their own observations. The classes were held in the old Galerie Beaux Arts building on Geary Street. Dixon and the other artists also reopened the Artists Cooperative Gallery that had been allowed to close. He wrote the introductory "Purpose—Not Propaganda" for the Art Students League's announcement:

> A vase of geraniums is a thing of beauty and a joy, no doubt, to the esthete; but a group of linemen stringing electric wires across the sky, the face of a hungry outcast in the rain, steam clouds seen between the timbers of a power hoist—these are realities of our present day work, free for all to behold.
>
> We announce ourselves as part of that widening group of artists whose sense of these realities inclines them strongly to the plain light of day, to vivid, clear facts of line and form and color; who turn away from artificial esthetic problems of the studio, away from theory and imitation, to look in the city streets, the fields, the factories where people are living and working; where something tremendous is happening to humanity today.
>
> A professor of fine art in the University of California recently announced: A true artist is clear about his business, which is to solve certain problems of materials beautifully not to preach politics nor social reforms. [He should] concern himself with the creation of a sort of visual music, with making picture shapes that glow. We disagree with the underlying idea of esthetic detachment here conveyed. We submit that life is more important than cutting out paper dolls or making pretty patterns. We believe that our business as real, as humanly functioning artists is to see the world about us with our own eyes, to solve the problems of our response to its realities in terms of the materials of our art, to find beauty and pathos and power in this world and render them with understanding and integrity.[20]

Busy with his work at the Art Students League, Dixon landed a mural commission near the end of 1935 for a restaurant in San Francisco's theater district, the Kit Carson Café, a popular cocktail and dinner spot (fig. 160). Dixon painted two large canvases in his studio and then installed them on the restaurant's spacious walls. One of the paintings, *Red Butte with Mountain Men* (fig. 159), portrays a light-drenched monolithic red butte with a line of horses and men silhouetted along its base. He also furnished a drawing of Kit Carson for the cover of the restaurant's menu. And, as now seemed customary, he created still another striking cover for the Standard Oil Bulletin that year (fig. 161).

Because of the interest in mural painting prompted by WPA projects, the San Francisco Mural Artists Society had formed in late 1934, meeting weekly in the studios of members, including the young painter Edith Hamlin. By now, Dixon knew his marriage had failed, and he responded to Edith Hamlin's warmth and interest. She had recently secured a divorce from the artist Albert Barrows, who had decided he wanted to marry his best friend's wife. Hamlin described herself and Dixon as "washed up on the same beach," and they began to spend time together. Her studio was at 716 Montgomery, next door to Dixon's. He helped Hamlin with a mural project for San Francisco's Mission High School,

159. *Red Butte with Mountain Men*, 1935,
oil on canvas, 8 x 17 feet, Booth Western Art Museum

advising her about composition details in the preliminary drawings. During 1935, Hamlin and Dixon saw each other frequently, sometimes going on short painting trips. When she moved to a small cottage on Telegraph Hill, Dixon came up there often, referring to it as his part-time home.

Dixon and Lange had accumulated fifteen years of marriage, but it was a marriage now with little emotional foundation. Lange had gone on a field trip to the Imperial Valley with Paul Taylor in the spring of 1935. She realized then that she had fallen in love with him. Shortly afterwards, she called Imogen Cunningham, who had recently divorced Roi Partridge, asking if she, Paul Taylor, and his daughter could come by for dinner. Once there, Lange took Cunningham down into the basement where she confessed she planned to marry Paul Taylor. "But you're married to Maynard," an astonished Cunningham exclaimed. Dorothea replied, "Yes, he's a good man, and strong enough to take it; he helped me come to this decision."[21] In Taylor, Lange had found a solid quiet man who promised the emotional security she felt she needed. Besides, as a university professor, he could provide economic steadiness. Dixon offered neither.

Lange's movement into the irregular life of an independent documentary photographer had complicated their family life. At the same time, Dixon, who had turned sixty, found that his health was deteriorating more rapidly. As a child and throughout his adult life, he had suffered from chronic asthma. Daniel Dixon recalls hearing the sound of his father's heavy, hoarse breathing as he trudged up the street toward their house. By 1935, the asthma had transformed into emphysema. With disciplined work habits and strong will, Dixon struggled against personal tragedy, illness, and depression tides to produce a living for the family. Finally, he wrote these words in his autobiography outline: "tragic interlude; divorce." Saddened and in a reflective mood, he wrote the poem "Sanctuary":

Lonely—lonely and vast . . .
This is the ultimate peak and the outlook:
Here begins the long release and the silence—

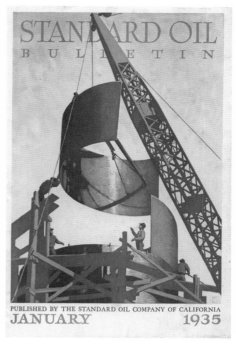

160. *Maynard Dixon Painting
Kit Carson Café Mural,* 1935,
private collection

161. *Standard Oil Bulletin,* January 1935,
California History Section,
California State Library

Here the trail ends.
The good horse is tired now:
Throw the reins down.
Take the bit from his mouth,
Tie up the bridle snug to the saddle-horn.
Let him go free:
He will leisurely find his way
Back to the home corral in the quiet evening.
Here I remain.
Come on then, you hovering buzzards,
From your wide and pitiless circles
And slowly descending glide —
Only a little while yet and you will find me.
Your dark and darkness-confirming wings
To me shall be welcome!
Come on wheeling buzzards, make a clean job:
Tear the old garments away —
The cutworn, ridiculous garments, these, of my life —

Tear them away.
Pick the bones clean —
Let them lie free to the rain and the white cleansing sun.
Leave only my thoughts.
These thoughts that once made me a man
Surely will find their way
Back to the home corral in the quiet evening.[22]

Their son Daniel remembers the day his parents told him about their impending divorce. He went into their bedroom one early morning, and both of them, lying nude on the bed — the way they usually slept — attempted to explain the painful decision. As soon as his parents finished, he ran into the street, screaming at the top of his lungs, "They're getting a divorce!" scandalizing the predominantly Italian neighborhood.[23] Some of Dixon's friends faulted Lange for leaving, partly for breaking up the centerpiece of their social group and partly because she abandoned Dixon for someone younger. "She was desperately hurting someone . . . it was very painful for everyone. . . . Their marriage was an accepted fact of life within the whole group. They were like a picture together. It was like someone slashing a picture in half."[24]

In late summer of 1935, Dixon went to Carson City, Nevada, where he filed for a divorce. Lange did not accompany him, pleading she was too busy with photography assignments. In October 1935, the marriage was dissolved, but Dixon and Lange maintained a respectful friendship, limited only by their respective careers and Lange's marriage to Paul Taylor in December. While in Carson City, Dixon turned again to his poetry for an emotional outlet, writing "The Years":

Now as the years pass more quickly,
And I become better acquainted
With the slowly approaching visage of death —
Seeing more often old friends and relations depart
Beyond the reach of my understanding;
Now that no longer I feel the white fire
Of youthful ambition, nor the blind impetuous urge
Of young passion;
And the great illusion had faded, only to linger
A high and immortal dream — yet I am content.
Ever more do I see that out of the turmoil comes order;
Ever more do I know that to win some happiness here
I must hold myself up, above petty disputes and distinctions,
Keeping some largeness of heart
Alike for those who trust me and for those who distrust me;
To share with them my long held vision of Beauty.
Yes, this is enough. So unhurriedly I will pass
Peacefully, yes, content, under the desert stars.[25]

Dixon stayed once more with the Bradleys at Carson City through the early fall of 1935. He went on short painting trips for a few days out on the desert with only a campfire for companionship. In the evenings he would read poems to friends by the fireplace in the Bradley home (fig. 162). LaVerne Bradley recalled sitting beside him as he painted, watching him fume over the turn of a certain line and listening to his rich, ripe language. Later that fall, Dixon roamed through the southern Nevada and eastern California desert country, sometimes with his old friend Frank Tobin, painting landscapes from Carson City to Las Vegas, a desolate sea of desert with an archipelago of angular mountain ranges—Funeral, Grapevine, Amargosa, Kingston, Paiute, Spotted, Hiko, and Charleston—that march in cadence over the horizon. These were places where a man could be alone with his thoughts and where the hurt could be shared with a million stars blinking in the night.

There has been considerable debate about the art of Maynard Dixon and Dorothea Lange. Who influenced whom? Was there a leader and a follower in their interaction, or were their artistic temperaments and mediums so different as to minimize the effects they had on each other? Lange would never admit to any influence from others on her work, always insisting she had her own vision. There are some connections between the two, though perhaps not measurable by any strict empirical evidence. And there are, of course, differences. Dixon was at the peak of his observational and painting power from 1921 to 1935. His passionate personal interest in the people of the West, his ability

162. *To Good Old Brad,* 1935, oil on canvas board, 10 x 14 inches, private collection, photograph courtesy of Medicine Man Gallery

to record their lives, and his almost pantheistic affection for the land must have had some impact on Lange. Trips to the Southwest, which started in 1922, and her field experiences with Dixon may have prepared Lange to respond the way she did in her Depression photography. Furthermore, between 1931 and 1933, particularly in Taos and in Zion, either camping out or living simply were conditions of their travels, offering Lange opportunities to make photographic images quickly on the spot.

As the Depression began in earnest, Dixon's topics shifted from the romance of the great western landscape to the grim realities of the Depression. He portrayed the down-and-out migrants, hobos, and strikers with the same respect and dignity he afforded Native Americans, cowboys, and others in the West's outback. These Depression-era paintings and drawings are perhaps as close as anything could be to Lange's famous work. Both Dixon and Lange reached for a visual realization of the period; it was a temporary interest for Dixon but a lifelong passion for her. She had inherited an eastern tradition of social reform and a sense of urgency from growing up on the Lower East Side of New York City. Her photography always had a point of view. Although Dixon shared her sense of adventure and emotional intensity, his paintings were rarely didactic. Where Lange reveled in the fact that photography could be embedded in a larger social context, Dixon usually avoided any overt social statement in his work. Both used their art to unite the subject and the context metaphorically, but Lange did so without reservation. For Dixon, the motivating force was the spiritual experience precipitated by western lands; for her, it became the political ignorance or neglect of the people who inhabited that landscape. Not that Dixon avoided social issues; in fact, he was deeply shocked and angered by the tragedy of the early 1930s. His letters then are full of bitterness. But he felt that his art could only stand if it remained neutral, not polarized by this or that viewpoint.

Dixon's personal synthesis—his trademark far horizon, flat planar composition, and total subjugation of detail to larger effects—is seen in Lange's work between 1935 and 1940, according to Therese Thau Heyman. Like Dixon, Lange favored strong compositions, the massing of simple shapes: triangles, columns, and circles. Dixon eventually developed this pattern in his images and rested in it. Lange too was sensitive to what worked in a composition; her photography relied on strong pattern. Of course, shooting pictures with a camera quickly is not the same as standing before an easel in the studio where the composition can be sorted out and rearranged many times. But even with the camera, one can start with a developed vision, an awareness of the low horizontal. One can place figures in silhouette against it, knowing this empowers the image. This was Dixon's consistent approach during most of his career. Perhaps Lange absorbed the technique, as her photography in the late 1930s seems to indicate.

Filmmaker Pare Lorentz, who used Lange for a week along U.S. Highway 99 in California when he was making his film *The Plow That Broke the Plains*, recalled, "You do not find in her portrait gallery the bindle stiffs, the drifters, the tramps, the unfortunate, aimless dregs of the country. Her people stand straight and look you in the eye. They have the simple dignity of people who have leaned against the wind, and worked in the sun and owned their own land."[26] Lange, like Dixon, found her images of people and places outside urban America. Her photographs of migrants, farm workers, and "Okies" are not unlike Dixon's symbolic paintings of the Native American, images that portray the stoic and heroic quality of people standing in a symbiotic relationship to the land.

By the spring of 1936, San Francisco artists clamored for a chance to board the WPA's mural bandwagon. Dixon, rebounding from the breakup of his marriage, pursued the local FAP director, Joseph Danysh, arguing that he wanted a large mural project where he could draw "a big free line." Danysh tentatively assigned him a mural—fifty by four hundred feet—that was projected to cover the south wall of the Salinas, California, rodeo arena. After developing some preliminary large pencil drawings, Dixon waited for the project's allocated funds that had been slowed by the government's nervousness over a bitter strike underway in the Salinas lettuce fields. Meanwhile, the Federal Art Project exhibited Dixon's Salinas rodeo arena drawings at the Shell Oil building in San Francisco during October of 1936, along with other examples of local mural art. Finally, Danysh had to inform him that funds for mural projects were once again depleted.

Dixon, who had desperately wanted the Salinas commission, decided to visit Wyoming's Wind River country and think things over. Daniel, John, and Dixon's friend, Luke Gibney, accompanied him. Gibney, an Irish native from Dublin, had a studio on Montgomery Street, where he painted dark, brooding portraits. Several days after leaving San Francisco, along a desolate stretch of road in Wyoming with Gibney at the wheel, Dixon spotted a little watercourse fringed by willows, an oasis in an otherwise brown landscape. He told Gibney to stop the car. At once, Dixon started to cut and gather willow poles. He inserted their ends into the ground, pulled the tops in, and lashed them together. He asked Gibney and the boys to build a fire, then gather smooth round rocks and place them in it. Meanwhile, Dixon covered the poles with a tarp and willow branches, dug a hole inside the circle, and instructed Gibney to drop hot rocks into the hole. A sweat lodge! Daniel and John never forgot that night: their father chanting Hopi and Navajo ceremonial songs, Gibney singing rousing Irish songs, both fueled by Irish whisky. The boys watched in amazement through the willow fragrant steam as years of embedded soap-impervious dirt surfaced and dripped in long, dark streaks down their arms. Afterwards, they spent a week in the spectacular Wind River Valley, bordered by the wild Wind River Range to the west and the Absaroka Range on the north.

In January 1937, Dixon made preparations for a large exhibition of nearly fifty paintings of Utah, Nevada, and Wyoming subjects to be shown later in the month at the Hotel Ben Lomond Gallery in Ogden, Utah, then at the Art Barn in Salt Lake City during February. At the same time, he commenced work on what he thought would be the largest mural in San Francisco, an ambitious eighteen-by-eighty-five-foot painting for the courtyard wall in the Presidio Junior High School. The mural would portray important events in the Presidio's history, recording the role of wildlife, Native Americans, padres, Spanish soldiers, trappers, and traders. This time, he intended to use a new mural medium, cement color, painting directly on the wall for permanency. Dixon developed full-size working drawings that a crew of workmen could execute. Just before they started work on the mural, Maynard received word from local PWAP administrators that the project had been canceled. In what must have seemed an unsettling pattern, he was told that funding had not materialized.

Soon after, Robert Morey of the Institute of Human Relations at Yale University contacted Maynard about the institute's interest in having him furnish illustrations for a proposed book on the Depression. Dixon replied in a rather characteristic fashion:

Thank you for your compliment. Regarding your idea about illustrations for a book on social and economic inequalities, let me say in the beginning that I have long been out of commercial illustrations and would not feel inclined to go back to it at this late date. Your letter is very interesting and it stirs contradictory impulses. One is to laugh, one is to weep, and the other is to write you a high, wide, and handsome American razz.

Having spent nearly twenty years as an illustrator of books and magazines and six years as a designer of advertising, in addition to having been a painter of the life of the West for twenty-five years, all of which brought me into contact with many kinds of people, brown, yellow and white, you may see that, in my own way, I also have studied the activities of human beings. Therefore, my conclusion is that the only people who might benefit by the kind of books you propose to issue are those who steadfastly refuse to acknowledge the facts you seek to present. If you do not realize by this time that people are already well aware of the tragic inequalities of life under the present set-up and that what they want is not a reiteration of the facts but some definite way to remedy those inequalities, then I should say for scientists such as you, the case is hopeless. You make me think of the bozo who tried to down a jolt of whiskey without letting it touch his tonsils. What most of you profs need is a little more corral dust in your flapjacks.[27]

In the spring of 1937, Herald R. Clark, dean of Brigham Young University's School of Business, a friend and an admirer of Dixon's work, determined to approach him with a proposal that the university acquire representative examples of his art. Clark arrived without notice in San Francisco, hoping to catch Dixon at his studio. Not finding him there, he started searching, finally encountering him on Montgomery Street, where he made the proposition. Dixon agreed but insisted that Clark finalize the transaction with a drink in a nearby bar. Clark concurred but said the drinks had to be milk, and so they were. Dixon let Brigham Young University select and purchase eighty-five paintings, sketches, and drawings, spanning almost his entire career, for thirty-seven hundred dollars. The university exhibited twenty-two of the paintings during August 1937 at their summer school in Provo Canyon. Dixon also showed *Scab* in the 1937 National Academy of Design show in New York, and the Painters and Sculptors of Southern California selected his *Elements of Nevada* for their show.

By August 1937, Dixon and Hamlin determined they were, in her words, "simpatico." They had discussed marriage, but Dixon hesitated because of his health and the age difference. Finally, they agreed that a fond, congenial, even dependent relationship existed between them. So they packed their painting equipment in September of 1937, and went to Carson City, Nevada. There they were married on the big veranda of the Bliss-Yerington House in a brief outdoor ceremony amidst the fall foliage of golden cottonwoods and poplars. Dixon, sixty-two, and Hamlin, thirty-three, thought they could make the marriage work. In their nine years of marriage, Hamlin proved a strong devoted companion. Friends marveled at her love and support for Dixon as his physical strength eroded, and without her, everyone realized Dixon's ability to continue his work would have been severely curtailed. They remained in Carson City for several weeks, content to explore the nearby old mining towns of Virginia City, Gold Hill, and Dayton, quiet echoes of Nevada's turbulent days. Dixon worked on mural drawings but did little painting. In fact, he produced only eleven paintings during all of 1937. Dixon wrote Turbese Lummis, Charles Lummis's daughter, "We plug along here making drawings for Gov't competitions. I am writing some children stories (no painting) and I still struggle with after effects of Expectation, plus asthma, plus a flu cough, plus natural meanness and general debility. And with all that I am married to an angel who asks nothing better than to ease an old grouch over the bumps."[28] Dixon fell seriously ill, however, so they decided to head for Los Angeles, where his doctor would meet him. As they drove down through Nevada and eastern California, Dixon painted several canvases near Indian Springs, Nevada.

When they arrived in Los Angeles, Dixon's doctor discovered he needed an immediate prostate operation, after which Dixon suffered a severe nervous breakdown. While he recovered, they lived with friends in Chatsworth. And during his continuing convalescence during the spring and summer of 1938, they moved into a secluded house at El Cajon in the mountains behind San Diego (fig. 163). "Nice little place," Dixon wrote Joseph Loeb, "mostly chaparral containing rattlers, wood ticks, quail, cottontail, bobcats, sometimes coyotes and deer, a creek, two springs, garden, big studio, no highway, no phone, no radio, no electricity, plenty of dark, rich earth, and we plant corn, melons, beans, etc. Next we build sweat house like Injun."[29] Dixon painted a few small canvases there but most of the time worked on designs for mural competitions. Dixon also managed to design a rather ribald cover for another one of Joseph Coppa's restaurants (fig. 164).

In a national contest for a post office mural in Wyoming, Dixon submitted a seventeen-by-forty-inch painting. The mural design was not accepted; however, he was awarded a contract for a mural in the Martinez, California, Post Office. He started to work on it while at El Cajon but completed it in the San Francisco studio. The mural, *Road to El Dorado*, depicts travelers pausing at Martinez on their way toward California's Mother Lode. He painted it on an eight-by-fifteen-foot canvas that was then glued to the post office wall, where it can still be admired. Figures in the mural—travelers, prospectors, adventurers—are strongly stylized and modeled, portrayed with bold composition and a dramatic use of color. During the 1930s, post office murals often insisted on glorifying westward movement as one of the great generative forces in American life: a journey means progress that always ends in dreams come true. In the Martinez mural, Dixon expressed that version of the nineteenth-century American ideal of hope and promise.

Dixon met mixed success in post office mural competition. Once, for a proposed mural in the Safford, Arizona, Post Office, he painted a small tempera sketch of two Apache Indians waiting in ambush. But this time, Dixon misread the cultural dynamic.

163. *Rock at El Cajon*, 1935,
oil on canvas board, 10 x 14 inches, private collection

His entry was acrimoniously rejected by Safford's inhabitants, who needed no reminder of that brutal part of Arizona's heritage. Artist Seymour Fogel received the award, but only after he modified his design to create a peaceful, symbolic image that celebrated Gila Valley's early pioneers. The Federal Art Project, which sometimes held unsuccessful applicants in reserve for future mural projects, later awarded Dixon a commission for a mural in the Canoga Park Post Office near Los Angeles.

While Dixon recuperated at El Cajon, the San Diego Fine Arts Museum and the Frank C. Orr Gallery organized a joint exhibition of his paintings and drawings. One local art critic remarked that "the feelings and emotions of years shine through these boldly painted canvases of trail and camp life: no melodrama will be found in them; it is the stark reality, the simple beauty and truth of the limitless spaces which inspire this painter."[30] The *San Diego Sun* commented: "It is like a visit from an old friend to find a group of 18 paintings by Maynard Dixon on view at Orr's gallery this week. No one should miss seeing this show, for in it we find the outlook of a rare character, a man who can always dare to be himself and the expression that he puts on canvas is so universal, so simple and timeless that he never can be shelved by the moderns because he is always ahead of them."[31]

Dixon also exhibited several of his "Homeless Man" paintings, along with recent Utah and Nevada landscapes, at the Stendahl Art Galleries in Los Angeles. Reviewing the exhibition, Arthur Millier remarked, "Dixon's country begins where air is dry and earth's bones stick through its skin of mesquite and chaparral. He paints with a temper that matches its ocean like rolling vastness, its severe but subtly articulated forms and surfaces, its clean air and intense blue sky. His painting is a silent rebuke to the phony desert romancers.

164. *Coppa's Restaurant Menu*, 1938,
private collection

He loves the land so well that close analysis of its line, tone and color cannot chill his ardor for it. He can paint it impersonally because he no longer knows where Dixon ends and the West begins."[32]

By the end of 1938, Dixon made a decision to close the Montgomery Street studio and leave San Francisco, something he had thought about after the end of his marriage to Lange. At first, despondent and disillusioned, he wanted to disappear into the Southwest, although not necessarily to abandon painting. He loved San Francisco, but he knew the environment for artists had changed. During the 1920s and early 1930s, a candid relationship existed among the city's artists, but Dixon believed the artists' community had become increasingly concerned with opportunism and self-promotion. In a letter to his daughter, Constance, he made clear his thoughts about the San Francisco scene: "What you don't know is that I worked like the devil to get the Commercial Artists' Guild here to organize on Union lines, without results. They are slave-minded. That I teach at Art Students League without pay because it is co-op. That I have scoffed at the sycophancy of San Francisco artists and their "patrons," thereby getting myself in plenty dutch with the Powers, so that I find myself pretty well ruled out from jobs and sales. On the other hand I have not joined any union nor sought to get mixed up with the rough stuff—I'd be a fool to do so. My natural place seems to be in the middle to throw an occasional jibe this way or that—and apparently I do best that way. I have been trying to develop a technique for puncturing the complacency of my well-to-do friends. Let's add orthodox radicals. This perhaps is not entirely useless."[33] Even more alarming, his health continued to deteriorate, the emphysema aggravated by San Francisco's cool coastal climate and accumulated years of smoking those hand-rolled cigarettes.

As Dixon agonized about the decision to leave San Francisco, the Bureau of Indian Affairs notified him that he had been awarded a major contract through a Treasury Department Section of Painting and Sculpture nationwide competition to paint two murals for the bureau's offices in the new Department of Interior building in Washington, D.C. Murals in federal buildings in the nation's capital required images of universal character. After reflection on the theme, The Indian Yesterday and The Indian Today, Dixon submitted two large drawings that illustrated his feelings about government treatment of Native Americans. In the first drawing, Indian and Soldier (fig. 165), he portrayed a proud undefeated individual, extending the pipe of peace to a soldier and scout. The other, Indian and Teacher (fig. 166), showed the degrading effects of civilization, the subject wears overalls; his back is bent wearily over a hoe and sickly stalks of corn. "I told Maynard it wouldn't be accepted," Hamlin recalled, but he had to get it out of his system."[34] Predictably, the Section rejected the designs. So Dixon moderated his stance and submitted some alternative drawings that were approved. He then started work in the studio on two mural panels, both oil on canvas, measuring eight and a half by thirteen feet. After Dixon completed the murals, the Bureau of Indian Affairs asked him to comment on their theme.

Ever since the founding of Jamestown and Santa Fe our dealings with the Indian tribes had been a long series of wars and broken treaties down to the 1870s and 80s,

165. *Indian and Soldier* (mural study), 1939,
charcoal on paper, 16¹/₈ x 33⁷/₈ inches, private collection

166. *Indian and Teacher* (mural study), 1939,
charcoal on paper, 16¹/₈ x 33⁷/₈ inches, private collection

ending in a sort of carpet bag era during the final settlement of the great Plains and Rocky Mountain regions, 1890–1910, and the breaking up of the great Indian Reservations. Only recently our Government has undertaken a new policy based on a real understanding of Indian character and recognition of Indian rights long denied.

In the former period the Indians dealt mostly with the soldier sent to punish his resistance to the encroachment of settlers. In the present he deals with the teacher (Government Agent) sent to help him make the most of his native resources.

There is a vast amount of material in this subject, but in these two murals I have attempted to summarize it in simple designs. The present tendency in mural painting is to "fill the space"—often ending in complexity and confusion—which does not apply here. There is a starkness of outline in this subject and in the land of its last drama that I have tried to reflect in the paintings. The west is vast, and the forms of men and animals stand clear-cut against great empty spaces. Simplicity of design is also necessary for these walls because they are not large nor architecturally important.

As to subject:

Panel 1—Indian and Soldier: Except for the Apaches (Arizona 1887) our last Indian wars were with Plains tribes; so I have chosen this type, with a cavalry officer of 1865–80. The chief's gesture says: "This is our land. You shall drive us no further." The strip of running buffalo suggests the last of the great herds (1876–82). The half-breed scout carries the old Sharp rifle, the "buffalo gun" of that period.

Panel 2—Indian and Teacher: The Indian says: "The Sun is our father, the Earth is our mother." The white man says: "The ground belongs to us." The Indian says: "We belong to the ground." The white man studies soil chemistry. The Indian prays to the Earth."

The teacher takes a lump of soil from the furrow and tells the Indian boy— the new generation—how to make it produce. The old people look on, somewhat doubtful of new ideas, with some reverence for the old. The large corn plant stands for the generous earth, the young corn for cultivation; the fence for divided lands and the end of freedom. I have always felt something far more tragic in all this— but perhaps here is now also something of hope.[35]

In February 1939, the Golden Gate International Exposition opened at San Francisco's Treasure Island, celebrating the completion of the Golden Gate and Bay bridges. The exposition featured a collection of European contemporary paintings and significant exhibits of work by American and California artists. Not since the 1915 Panama-Pacific International Exposition had art exhibits of equal size and quality been created. The murals, lights, and architecture at the exposition generated praise and enthralled visitors. The massive Pacific Basin outdoor monuments, based on Pan-American, Asian, and Pacific art motifs, drew particular attention. Their centerpiece was a huge statue, Ralph Stackpole's eighty-foot *Pacifica*. The Pacific-style exposition buildings, their clean façades unbroken by windows, lent themselves to outdoor murals. A number of artists were engaged to decorate the buildings. Through the use of some large preliminary designs such as *Cattle Drive* (fig. 167), Dixon created his two largest murals to date, *Grassland* and *Ploughed Land* (fig. 168), which Foster and Kleiser painted directly on the north and south sides of the buildings adjacent to the Court of the Pacifica. The fair's publicity department referred to the murals as *Earth* and *Rain*. Eugen Neuhaus remarked: "In the very nature of things his designs must take a secondary place, but they are no less effective in the special responsibility they assume. On one side is a decorative design, 'Ploughed Land,' on the opposite side 'Grass Land.' Both designs have a charm

that results from a clear and simple use of form and color. Dixon here refrains from any new adventures, and these decorations in their straightforwardness reflect qualities long recognized in his easel paintings. The color scale is conscientiously restricted to the warm earth hues characteristic of the palette of the fresco painter."[36] Both murals were destroyed when the Navy razed the buildings in 1941. Dixon may also have been involved with some other designs for the Golden Gate International Exposition, creating

169. *The Osage;* 1939; charcoal, colored pencil, and conté crayon on paper; 19³/₄ x 16¹/₄ inches; private collection; photograph courtesy of Medicine Man Gallery

portraits of American Indians such as *The Osage* (fig. 169).

For California artists, the exposition provided an opportunity to show their work to an international audience, and for many like Dixon, it marked the peak, if not the end, of their careers. Two separate exhibitions featured important California artists: the Contemporary American Exhibition, held in the Palace of Fine Arts, and the state-sponsored exhibition California Art Today, located at the California State Building in

Sacramento. Several hundred paintings hung in the Contemporary American Exhibition, most selected by Roland McKinney, who had resigned as director of the Baltimore Museum of Art to curate the Treasure Island show. McKinney said he wanted to reveal the full range of contemporary American painting, which represented both established and experimental views. But the collection, once assembled, was weighted toward American Scene paintings. *Art Digest* categorized the paintings hung in the American section as social protest, American Scene, poetic/imaginative, realist, essentialist (bordering on abstract but still retaining recognizable subject matter), and impressionist. Although McKinney assembled a wide range of American art, he considered most of the contemporary American practitioners of social protest in painting to be misguided "messiahs of the brush" who should be engaged in other pursuits. A correspondent for *Art Digest* judged Dixon differently.

> *Hanging in the Palace of Fine Arts is probably the greatest social comment of the last decade, Maynard Dixon's* Destination Unknown, *great because it is simple — a single, lone figure of a beaten, but undefeated man, his few possessions on his shoulder, as he walks the ties of a railroad that extends out into the vast unknown, a future of work and opportunity or a future of repeating misfortune, but never defeat. No shrieking banners proclaim the defect of capitalism; there is only the figure to lift the picture out of the mass of secondary genre painting that will be history's reminder of the Depression and the ineptitude of our social-conscious artists.*[37]

Bypassing McKinney, juries in Los Angeles and San Francisco identified the California paintings that would be represented in the Contemporary American exhibit from a pre-selected group of artists, each one invited to submit three recent works for consideration. In all, the juries chose fifty canvases, thirty-six of them by northern California artists. The San Francisco jury selected Dixon's painting *Destination Unknown* for inclusion in the exhibition. Entries were judged in three stylistic categories — conservative, modern, or liberal — and artists could select the category in which they wanted to enter their work. Most of the California paintings were conservative or liberal; no totally abstract canvas appeared and only minimal traces of cubism. The prevailing style was American Scene. The California State Exhibition included the largest collection of state-sponsored contemporary California paintings ever assembled. Local juries in five geographical regions throughout California selected the entries. As in the Contemporary American exhibit, paintings could be submitted under conservative, modern, or liberal labels. No fully modern works emerged from the jury. Dixon's painting *Earth Knower*, which he entered in the "liberal" category, was included. Again, American Scene painting dominated this exhibit as it did throughout the country during the late 1930s.

A special exhibition had also been assembled for both the Golden Gate International Exposition and the New York World's Fair. Under the leadership of company president Thomas J. Watson, International Business Machines (IBM) purchased examples of con-temporary American art chosen by leading art authorities and museum directors in each of the forty-eight states. The works of two California artists had been selected. William

Wendt's painting *Nature Smiles* was exhibited at the Golden Gate International Exposition. The other canvas, Dixon's *Shorelines of Lahontan,* was included in IBM's exhibit at the New York World's Fair. IBM also offered works by artists such as Georgia O'Keeffe, Grant Wood, and N. C. Wyeth. One critic quibbled with the choices, commenting that Millard Sheets should have been selected to represent California. The Golden Gate International Exposition was the last important art exhibition held on the West Coast before World War II interrupted events in the art world. For Maynard Dixon, the exposition marked the end of the most public period in his art career and the emergence of a quieter, more reflective era.

After they closed the Montgomery Street studio, Dixon and Hamlin decided to take their last painting trip in California—to Death Valley this time. On their way in April 1939, they stopped for several days at Yosemite National Park at the invitation of Ansel and Virginia Adams. Adams remembered that whenever he and Dixon visited, whether in San Francisco or Yosemite and later in Arizona and Utah, Dixon conversed little. "He did not need to," according to Adams, "he was one of these rare and wonderful companions who do not carry with them a request that one engage in constant conversation. The wonderfully warm feeling he radiated—a feeling of recognition, of support, of universal compassion, and of dedication to his art—rendered verbalization unnecessary, even superfluous."[38] Adams recalled Dixon's angry reaction to a painting he saw at the Ahwahnee Hotel during this particular visit. It was an image by a French-inspired artist that depicted Indian basket designs in a stylized contemporary way. Adams found it striking, but Dixon recoiled, viewing the painting as the debasement of one art form in the name of another.

After leaving Adams and his wife, they drove on to Death Valley, renting a primitive cottage at the old mining town of Ryan. However, blooming desert holly exacerbated Dixon's emphysema, so they moved on to Indian Springs, Nevada, north of Las Vegas, where they stayed in a motel run by a friend of Dixon's. His breathing did not improve, so they decided the best location for painting, warmer and more temperate during the winter, would be a place called Desert Camp, six miles below Mecca at the north end of the Salton Sea. Hamlin recalled it was like a gypsy camp. They stayed there until hot weather drove them out in the late spring of 1939. Dixon and Hamlin explored the surrounding desert ranges—the Chuckwalla, Orocopia, and Chocolate mountains—finding colorful formations for painting and drawing subjects. They also visited migrant camps in the Imperial Valley (figs. 170 and 171). Groups of artists would converge for painting sessions in the canyons. Dixon, Jimmy Swinnerton, Clyde Forsythe, Conrad Buff, and Nicolai Fechin often painted together. When not out exploring and sketching, Dixon enjoyed hours soaking in a hot springs adjacent to their tent camp, then sunbathing nude on the warm sand. Jimmy Swinnerton, John Hilton, Clyde Forsythe, and Randall Henderson, publisher of *Desert Magazine,* often lingered at Desert Camp to listen as Dixon read poetry followed by raucous storytelling around an evening campfire. While at Desert Camp, Dixon and Hamlin started to discuss potential places they might live and work. Initially, Dixon thought about Carson City, Nevada, and made a quick trip there, but he concluded that the town had changed too

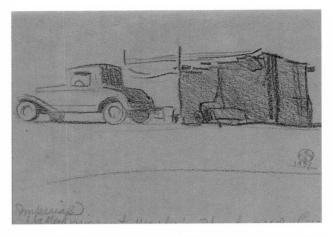

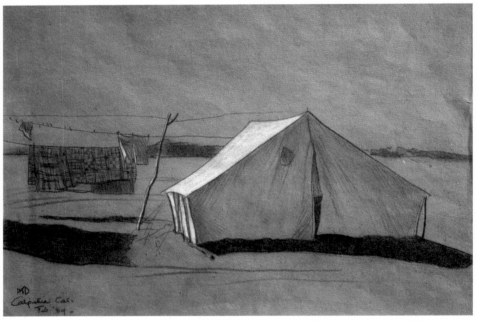

much (fig. 172). Finally, they settled on Tucson and, anxious to confirm their decision, briefly visited the place to explore the possibilities, particularly the art scene, deciding the town would suit their purposes.

In June of 1939, Dixon and Hamlin went to Zion National Park in Utah, camping in two tents located on a small island between the Virgin River and a local irrigation canal. Dixon's sons joined them and had a wonderful time swimming in the river or hiking through the surrounding terrain. Dixon, swamped by worsening emphysema, nonetheless managed to do some painting. Lange and Paul Taylor finally picked the boys up and returned them to San Francisco for school. Hamlin and Dixon stayed on until mid-July, exploring the small valleys around Zion National Park. Delighted with Mount Carmel, they decided this was a place they wanted to locate a summer studio. The town is located in Long Valley, twenty-five miles east of Zion, surrounded by dramatic pale limestone and sandstone cliffs. Nearby, they discovered a little alfalfa field next to a cottonwood grove and an irrigation ditch. The vivid greens in the bottomland, stark cliffs, and clouds boiling up over the mesas made it a visual paradise. The owners sold them one acre including water rights for one hundred dollars. Adjacent property—nineteen acres of hilly pinion and juniper land, including another hollow in the alfalfa field—was purchased for five dollars an acre.

Dixon returned to San Francisco to finish the two Bureau of Indian Affairs murals in his studio and then shipped them to Washington, D.C., for installation in the Department of the Interior building. The bureau invited him to attend the dedication ceremonies scheduled in late July 1939, so he and Hamlin left for the East, first going to New York to see the World's Fair and then visiting Dixon's old friend Harold Von Schmidt at his home in Westport, Connecticut. Hamlin persuaded Dixon to return by ship from New York to New Orleans and to take the train for San Francisco from there. Dixon was dubious, but this was an opportunity to meet historian and folklorist J. Frank Dobie in Austin, Texas, with whom he had been corresponding. Boarding their ship in New York, they heard Ansel Adams shouting at them across the deck. Hamlin recalled that Dixon and Adams kept the weeklong voyage lively with their racy, sometimes sardonic humor and outrageous discussions. This continued for several days while a friend of Hamlin's showed them around New Orleans. When Adams left for San Francisco, Dixon and Hamlin went on to Austin, where they spent several days with Dobie. He had begun the research for his book *The Longhorns* and asked Dixon about using some of his cowboy and range-life illustrations from the early 1900s. After the visit, Dixon and Hamlin returned to Mount Carmel for several months.

Finally, in November 1939, the Dixons drove down to Tucson, renting a little adobe house near Rillito on the northern edge of town. They had met Bill Ronstadt, who ran a Tucson art gallery, and arranged for him to exhibit and sell both Dixon's and Hamlin's work. They met the rest of the clan through him, including Gilbert Ronstadt and his family, who became their next-door neighbors when Dixon and Hamlin purchased two of their twelve acres on Tucson's Prince Road, a strip of land with a clear view of the Santa Catalina Mountains.

En route back to San Francisco from Tucson, Dixon and Hamlin stopped to visit several migrant labor camps populated by Dust Bowl refugees near Casa Grande. When an editorial in the *San Francisco Chronicle* suggested these migrants were not the sort of people that California desired, an angry Dixon responded:

> *Their case seems hopeless, yet in their hearts they are not defeated. After a day in the carrots and peas, they still have the spirit to get out the cracked fiddle or battered guitar and play for you—"The Arkansas Traveler, Oh Susanna, Casey Jones"—the old backwoods tunes that mean America. And what kind of people are*

they? The same kind that carried the long rifle over the Alleghenies and down the Ohio, across the Mississippi and the plains to the Rocky Mountains; the same kind as Sam Houston and Davey Crockett, Kit Carson, Jim Bridger, and California Joe. Most of them come from Missouri, Arkansas, Oklahoma, and West Texas—small farmers, share croppers, farm laborers—driven out of drought, tractor farming, and foreclosure. They have sold their last few holdings, tools, hogs, mules, at pawn shop prices to cross 1500 miles of semi-desert to reach the promised land of sunshine and plenty that our boosters have been advertising for fifty years—golden California— and so they find it golden for those who have gold.[39]

As Dixon and Hamlin made final preparations to leave San Francisco, they announced to the public that Dixon would hold a sale in his Montgomery Street studio, October 12–14, 1939, of paintings, drawings, sketches, Indian artifacts, and cowboy equipment. They hired a saleswoman to oversee the event. Although the sale was planned to last three days, people came for three weeks at all hours, eager to purchase a Maynard Dixon painting or drawing. Dixon sold two or three large canvases, but the majority of purchases were made by housewives, art students, and others able to pay a dollar for a drawing or five dollars for a group of oil sketches. When Dixon discovered how well sales had progressed, he reneged on several things, marking them "sold." One of these was the bleached buffalo skull that had been on his studio wall since 1914, a trophy found not on the Great Plains but in a Connecticut studio in 1912. After the sale, Dixon saw his bank account increased by five thousand dollars. They bought a new station wagon with part of the money and set the rest aside for building their Tucson home.

The San Francisco press lamented Dixon's decision to leave, calling the departure his "swan song." But Dixon replied, "It's a goose honk . . . a shift of base. I'm heading south to Arizona. I'll stay around Tucson and then, if I don't like it, I'll ease over to Texas."[40] Besides his concern with the changes in San Francisco's art environment, Dixon's emphysema had become acute, with a hard cough now constantly shaking his body. Yet, there was still that urge to follow his original ambition of interpreting the West. "I've done all right as far as I've gone, but I'm not done yet. People need more than ever before some realization of this country's pioneer strength—some of its stark simplicity. It's got to carry us through this evil period."[41] Dixon told newspaper reporters he was going to paint the "modern forty-niners, migrants who pause in Arizona enroute to California . . . the strength to catch this new, infinitely tragic flow of humanity, marching from despair to desperation, must spring jointly from the brain, the heart, and the solar plexus. I hope it comes."[42]

Dixon also said he planned to write in Arizona. First would be a book of children's stories, "Skeeter and Tweeter and the Magic Moccasins," for Michael and Ann Adams, children of Ansel and Virginia Adams; next a series of short stories drawn from his numerous travels and experiences in the American West (started when illness curtailed his painting for a year and a half); and finally, his autobiography. He joked that the title of his life story should be "Other Men's Houses," because he had never owned a home of his own. "I am not substituting the pen for the brush," he said, "one will supplement

172. *Cottonwoods of Carson*, 1939, conté crayon on paper, 17 x 14 inches, collection of Drs. Mark and Kathleen Sublette

the other. And later, as my strength grows, I shall try a technique in painting, one that calls for further simplification and emotional intensification."[43] By the late fall of 1939, they had concluded their arrangements to build a pioneer-style log-and-stone house at Mount Carmel, Utah. Local workers dragged large logs through the snow from a canyon higher in the mountains, and Mormon builders "chinked" them by hand with clay in the old style. The house was finally finished in early 1940.

EIGHT

Back to the Home Corral
1940–1946

As Dixon made final preparations to leave San Francisco for Arizona, he assembled a small collection of his early magazine and book illustrations— no originals but mostly proof sheets and clippings—and presented them to J. Frank Dobie, who had requested information on authentic cowboy and range gear. An enthusiastic Dobie wrote back, "How much joy this collection has given me and will give me in times to come. These pictures and many others . . . provoke a response from the bottom of my nature that brings me joy and bright memories."[1] Dobie informed Dixon that he not only wanted to use the material in his book research but also in a course that he planned to teach at the University of Texas. But Dixon cautioned Dobie, "All this belongs to double-dead past. Having slaughtered many people in range wars and bar room brawls on magazine pages over twenty years (I never saw a man shot) I turned away from this evil life in 1921 and since then quieted down and gave my mind to nobler thoughts such as making poetic paintings and selling em to suckers with result that I now have one leg in junk pile and other in shiny new station wagon."[2] Dixon also had sent a letter to Mabel Gillis, State Librarian of California, regarding his early illustrations, which reads in part; "Pawing around amongst the junk of ages I came across 3 portfolios of reproductions of my illustrations for newspapers and magazines (covering the years 1898 to 1922). These will be some day as much a record of their times as (Charles) Nahl's drawings now are of the 1850s. Question: would you consider it valuable enough to accept it . . . and give it a home in your California department?"[3] Gillis quickly accepted Dixon's proposals, and the portfolios, now organized into seven volumes and augmented with additional material, are housed in special collections at the California State Library in Sacramento.

During the winter and early spring of 1940, Dixon and Hamlin resided at Desert Camp while they explored and painted in the surrounding desert and in southern Arizona. At least once they made the trip to the old mining town of Randsburg north

173. *Randsburg*, 1940, oil on canvas board, 12 x 16 inches,
photograph courtesy of Medicine Man Gallery

of Barstow (fig. 173). In May 1940, Dixon exhibited a group of small paintings at the
Biltmore Salon in Los Angeles. Reviewing the exhibit for the *Los Angeles Times*, Arthur
Millier commented,

> *If World War jitters have got you down, drop into the Biltmore Salon between now
> and May 31 and see the great Southwest through the eyes and temperament of
> the desert's foremost pictorial interpreter—Maynard Dixon. Cruising in a station
> wagon this winter the veteran Dixon painted many small pictures. These bring us
> the tang of desert air, the crisp-edged strong shadows, the delicate but pure tones
> of sunlight on red, yellow and gray sand and rock, the long-flowing lines of the
> horizon, the stillness of the beautiful wastelands, touched in with the deftness of a
> great draftsman-painter. Several of his larger canvases of riders and Pueblo Indians
> point up the show. And there is a small room filled with his inimitable drawings of
> desert scenes and people.*
>
> *But these little, recent oils gave me the big thrill. Dixon is so steeped in desert
> forms and color that these little pictures appear to come from his brush like effortless
> lyrics. He knows his subject so well that it would be impossible for him to lie about
> it. He is free to paint, if poetically.*[4]

177. *Last Gleam*, 1941, oil on canvas board, 12 x 16 inches, collection of Bill Schenck

Dixon and Hamlin moved into their house at Mount Carmel in the summer of 1940 and remained there until October. Dixon and Hamlin had agreed that their Tucson home should reflect a Mexican colonial style and, in that spirit, constructed a house of adobe bricks fabricated from the soil on their land. Their architect builder, John Joynt, accepted a large painting as payment for his services. By April 1941, the house stood finished with a living room, a large veranda, two bedrooms, a storeroom, a walled patio, and a studio overlooking the Santa Catalina Mountains. They planted a cottonwood tree in the patio as a celebration, and then erected a sign outside with their address and Dixon's thunderbird emblem.

Tucson was a multicultural mosaic in the 1940s. The Papago Indian Reservation (now the Tohono O'Odham), southwest and west of the city, had native peoples still vested in a desert life, without plumbing or electricity. Yaqui refugees from Sonora, Mexico, practiced ancient traditions at Pascua in southwest Tucson and a smaller community near West Grant Road. The city's large Mexican population celebrated its northwest Mexico origins in and around Barrio Libre. Dixon and Hamlin quickly developed a large circle of friends in Tucson, particularly among the writers and artists, including anthropologist Gwyneth Harrington and her husband, Juan Xavier, a Papago Indian. Harrington and Xavier lived near Mission San Xavier del Bac and often invited Dixon and Hamlin to their home for meals prepared Indian-style. When dinner was finished,

178. *Palomino Ponies—1840*, 1942, 7 x 14 feet, U.S. Post Office, Canoga Park, California

Juan would tell stories and sing Papago songs, and afterwards they would talk about their respective experiences in the Southwest while Dixon quietly sketched.

During 1941, Dixon worked on an important series of seven pen-and-ink drawings that portrayed deserts of the American West. The "Desert Series" illustrates essential landscape forms of the Great Basin, Mojave, Sonoran, and Painted Deserts. Included in the drawings are *Southeast Oregon and Northern Nevada* (fig. 174), *Central Nevada* (fig. 175), and *Southern Arizona* (fig. 176). Through these drawings, Dixon shows his deep knowledge and reverence for desert landscapes. There is enormous diversity in the arid lands of western North America, and these drawings reflect his familiarity with individual characteristics. Frequent painting excursions to Tucson's surrounding area resulted in paintings like *Last Gleam* (fig. 177). At the same time, he started work on his last public mural project destined for the Canoga Park, California, Post Office. Dixon titled the mural *Palomino Ponies—1840* (fig. 178), a theme suggested by the Palomino horses raised on the earliest ranches in the San Fernando Valley. Dixon painted a seven-by-fourteen-foot mural on canvas that represents a herd of six spirited horses in full gallop, matched in speed by a mounted California vaquero. After working on the design for a year, he finally completed the mural in 1942 and then arranged for his friend Harold "Buck" Weaver to install it at the post office.

After America entered the war in December of 1941, Dixon and Hamlin discussed additional ways they could make a living. Who would purchase paintings with a war effort now the major concern? They decided their Mount Carmel house might support itself as a guest ranch. Dixon developed a handsome little announcement with a black-and-white reproduction of one of his Utah paintings on the cover, sending it to all their friends. "Well," Hamlin recalled, "our friends sent their kids, eight teenagers plus Maynard's two sons. We called it the Brat Ranch!"[5] Writing to a friend, Dixon said, "Country is beautiful here now—but our dude ranch seems to be turning into a kid farm. Everybody is scared and wants to unload their brats on us. What's the matter with them out there? No guts left? Too greedy, too rich, too fat. They ought to try asthma a while—then they would not care so much."[6] Somehow they managed to keep the children occupied with horseback rides, camping trips at the North Rim of the Grand Canyon, hayrides, and exploring nearby Zion and Bryce canyons. When Ansel Adams came along on his project to photograph the Southwest's national parks, he used some of their young guests as models. After Dixon and Hamlin tallied expenses, which included the purchase of extra beds, they discovered they had barely broken even, so the guest ranch experiment ended.

During the summer and fall months in the early 1940s, Dixon and Hamlin would schedule frequent painting trips from Mount Carmel to Zion National Park, the Vermilion Cliffs, and Kanab; through the Arizona Strip (that lonely land that lies between the Colorado River and the Utah border); and sometimes to the North Rim of the Grand Canyon. Dixon, less active physically, still worked hard at his painting. His son John Dixon recalls,

Maynard was still able to go on occasional painting sorties and on these occasions we would pack up some "grub," pile into the station wagon and be off in time to catch the late afternoon light, Edie at the wheel. We would bounce off through the sagebrush and junipers to a suitable spot facing the grand line of the white and vermilion cliffs which bounded the eastern edge of the valley in which Mt. Carmel lay. Out would come the camp stools and sketch boxes, Maynard and Edie often working

side by side. I never tired of watching him paint, that thin figure, chest working hard to get enough breath, slender, almost delicate hands, the veins lying in rivers on the backs. On his head the old black Stetson, in his mouth maybe a roll-your-own, with wheat paper. He worked quickly, with great economy of motion, blue eyes squinting, even in the late afternoon light, and the image on the canvas board would begin to take form, like a slow motion Polaroid. He worked at a distance from his canvas, his figure erect, his left hand holding the brush or pencil. When the light would begin to fade, and as they began to clean up and put away, we would begin to collect a heap of juniper firewood, and soon had a bed of coals on which to

179. *Maynard Dixon Self-Portrait*, ca. 1942, pencil on paper, 13 x 11 inches, collection of Drs. Mark and Kathleen Sublette

plop a slab of sirloin steak, one and a half inches thick. A little red wine (mine with
water), corn-on-the-cob, salad and medium rare, well-charred steak. After dinner,
Maynard might roll one of his cigarettes, made fragrant by a mix of George Wash-
ington pipe tobacco and the Indian herb KinniKinnik, which he kept in a tasseled
pouch. We would stare at the fire, shiver a little in the dry, cool air of the high desert,
under brilliant stars. The same mesas that in the afternoon light had been so vivid,
now assumed for me a dark, almost foreboding presence.[7]

The Dixons' Mount Carmel neighbors were an interesting and colorful addition to their life. They gravitated to Dixon, volunteering endless stories about pioneer times in this part of Utah, which he loved to hear. Sometimes, as John Dixon recalls, ambling up the road to the house would be Valentine Tait and Hans Chamberlain. Val Tait, tall, almost gaunt, had first met Dixon in 1933. He had a long, tan head topped by the white forehead of those who wear hats in the sun. Tait herded some sheep, kept a few cows, mowed hay, and had numerous kids and relatives in Mount Carmel. Hans, ruddy, a little stout, owned the general store and movie theater in the nearby town of Orderville. They might have been on their way to or from Fredonia, Arizona, where they could buy liquor. Dixon enjoyed their company, and Val and Hans would always stay until the bottle was finished. When there were no visitors, Dixon spent afternoons in the grape arbor at the back of the house, relaxing in a camp chair, smoking cigarettes, reading, writing lectures, or sketching. Toward evening, he might mix a batch of mint julep from mint picked on the property, using an "old Southern formula" (fig. 179).

Even though Dixon's physical condition continued to deteriorate, he and Hamlin still enjoyed throwing bedrolls in the car and rambling around southern Arizona during the winter months. Their Ford station wagon, with the large red thunderbird on its sides, became a familiar sight from Tucson to Nogales to Sasebe on the Mexican border. They explored the Papago Indian Reservation (now Tohono O'Odham), the cactus and mesquite country around the Baboquivari Mountains, and their other favorite places: the Rincon, Tucson, Santa Catalina, and Tortolita ranges; Patagonia, the old mining town of Bisbee, and Sells, with its colorful annual Papago Indian fair and rodeo. Sometimes they would venture to Nogales, then paint at various locations in the Santa Cruz Valley on their return. These trips produced numerous sketches and small oil paintings. Dixon's Utah and Arizona paintings and drawings were usually exhibited in Tucson at the Temple of Art and Music, Ronstadt Gallery, Studio Strange, Gerry Pierce's Print Room, the Arizona Inn, and at the Arizona State Museum. In Phoenix, the Clay Smith Shop and the Westward Ho Hotel carried his work. During the 1940s, the Biltmore Galleries at the Los Angeles Biltmore Hotel also offered a large stock of his paintings, as did Gumps in San Francisco. Dixon and Hamlin also became involved with members of the University of Arizona art department, which hosted a small informal organization called the Palette and Brush Club.

Dixon's last book illustration occurred in 1942 when George Macy, publisher of the Limited Editions Club, proposed that he furnish illustrations for the club's projected new edition of Francis Parkman's classic book *The Oregon Trail.* The fee was only a thousand dollars, but Dixon wanted to illustrate this long familiar firsthand account of Parkman's

180. *Jim Beckwourth*, 1941, ink on paper,
5 x 3 inches, private collection,
photograph courtesy of
Medicine Man Gallery

181. *Bookplate, R. F. McGraw*,
private collection

adventures among Plains Indians and frontiersmen. "The drawings and samples for Oregon Trail are sent and I hope they land me the job," he wrote to artist Buck Weaver. "I sure need it. On rereading the book in the light of later knowledge I find Parkman not so understanding an observer. If he had not been so sure (so Bostonese) that he was 'civilized' and all the people he met were savages his observations would have been a lot keener."[8] Macy, impressed with the vibrant drawings and watercolors, requested that he undertake the project.

Dixon worked for almost a year on the illustrations, often sending preliminary drawings and watercolors to Macy, making sure they supported the book design. *The Oregon Trail* appeared in 1943, with seventy of his bold pen-and-ink drawings such as *Jim Beckwourth* (fig. 180) and opaque gouache watercolors interspersed throughout the text, with six of them double-page color reproductions. The book appeared in both a trade edition and a limited edition of two thousand copies with leather binding, handsome typography, and a slipcase. He signed all the limited editions at one hundred a day. The Parkman illustrations depleted his strength to the point where he feared permanent loss of his physical vitality. In a letter to Buck Weaver, he said, "I'd about made up my mind to make this summer my last—but Edie came up and persuaded me to go back and make one more try—new treatment—but somehow, though I'll do it for her, I'm doubtful how much an old guy can do on bought blood and borrowed time. All I ask is to be able to work some."[9] A close friend during this period was R. F. McGraw, and Dixon, grateful for his support, designed a bookplate drawn from one of his paintings (fig. 181).

182. *Pattern of Butte and Cloud*, 1942, pencil on paper, 8½ x 10½ inches, collection of Ed Mell

To augment their finances, Hamlin started working at the Consolidated Vultee Aircraft Corporation on the outskirts of Tucson in 1942. Dixon stayed at Mount Carmel that summer, and Hamlin made the long drive up there once or twice a month to visit. In 1943, she contracted Valley Fever and was forced to resign her defense job. Throughout their marriage, Hamlin was homemaker, nurse, and chauffeur. She helped frame and prepare her husband's paintings for exhibitions and carried out his mural designs. These were happy years for them, but Hamlin recalled an undercurrent of sadness, brought by the knowledge that Dixon was slowly dying of emphysema. When he lacked the physical strength to paint, Dixon created numerous drawings, wrote short stories, anecdotes, and reminiscences drawn from forty years' observation in the West (fig. 182). In February 1942, *Arizona Highways* published "Arizona in 1900," his recollections about that memorable first journey into the state when it was a territory. During 1943, he illustrated several articles for *Arizona Highways*, including one about trading posts and another on the early settlement of Phoenix. In his mind, the desert still remained spiritually important when he wrote to a friend: "Here remains the solid mountains and the fluid sky (full of planes) and the sun and stars, and my kin, the wandering desert dust."[10]

183. *Desert Peaks and River Bottom*, 1943, oil on canvas board, 16 x 20 inches, collection of Drs. Mark and Kathleen Sublette

Whenever he was not writing stories or painting, he maintained a vigorous correspondence with friends, particularly about the progress of the war. Ansel Adams, responding to a letter from Dixon in October 1943, let loose his feelings about the war—and about his friend:

> If there ever was a war for things of the spirit, this is it. But through advertising and other forms of baloney, the people are led to believe that we are fighting for colder refrigerators, better electric stoves, faster streamlining, more radiant radio, and more furious fri * * *ng. I happen to be in the minority and believe that the mountains and the clean air, and the long open plains and sea will have their effect on the "postwar" world—and to HELL with the advertisers and the radio boys, and the mavericks of Big Business etc. etc. etc. It will be the same old fight, and the same old compromising—in spite of FM and plastic contraceptives.
>
> It is the truth that people like you—and there are very few of them—have the power of putting forth that certain magical essence of space and earth, with an implied relation to humanity. You people never seem to realize what you are doing—how far you have progressed. Those who have a more obvious approach,

184. *Inyo Mountains*, 1944, oil on canvas board, 16 x 20 inches, private collection

who "fit in" with the mode, who scamper to get ahead of "what is being done" may make a lot of cash, and a lot of superficial friends—well, this sounds like a swell collection of platitudes—but its the truth as far as I am concerned.[11]

Dixon and Hamlin managed an extended painting trip through Utah's Bryce Canyon National Park and Capitol Reef National Monument in 1943 (fig. 183). The higher altitude affected Dixon, but he still managed to paint a series of canvases around Escalante and Boulder and along the northern edge of the Kaiparowits Plateau. But now Dixon found it difficult to paint for extended periods. His lungs screamed for oxygen, and he had to connect himself to an oxygen tank just to keep breathing. Tucson's environment helped keep him going. When illness confined him to his armchair by the great north window of the Tucson studio, he worked on fresh graphic watercolors on western life, many of them representing Tucson's guest ranch and tourist scene. That famous Dixon humor emerged through a series of drawings and watercolors he called "Frontier Pants," in which he poked fun at dudes. "A good way to forget your troubles," he commented. On a more serious note, he portrayed contemporary western ranch life in another group of oils and watercolors. Whenever well enough, he would tackle painting, sometimes drawn from his travels around California and the West (fig. 184).

Dixon spent only three weeks at Mount Carmel during the early fall of 1945 and would never return, since the high altitude made breathing too difficult. His Tucson home then became not only a refuge but also a rendezvous, even a pilgrimage of sorts, for artists like Ansel Adams, Winold Reiss, archaeologist and Indian trader Clay Lockett, nature writer Joseph Wood Krutch, and numerous friends from Tucson, San Francisco, Los Angeles, and elsewhere. Around Dixon, lounging in his long blue Chinese coat and Indian moccasins, gathered those who loved him, his keen talk, his agile humor, and the easy hospitality of his home. One evening, the entire Ronstadt family came by to serenade him with Mexican songs. Sophie Treadwell, who Dixon had not seen for twenty-eight years, visited in late 1945. Hamlin recalled ruefully, "I could construct that passionate romance pretty well through meeting her."[12] To those who saw him then, Dixon appeared a lean, weathered-looking man with drooping mustache and chin beard, a pencil and sketchbook always clutched in one hand. But those who looked closely saw that Dixon's level blue eyes still incessantly searched the glare of the desert horizon (fig. 186).

Along with this steady procession of friends and visitors, he embraced the oxygen bottle day and night. He worked every day in his studio, pouring every shred of remaining energy into his art. Peter Ronstadt, Gilbert Ronstadt's son, recalled that he and Gretchen, his older sister (known as Susie), would come over and play in the studio, where Dixon told them stories about his experiences in the Old West. Often the children trailed after Dixon when he went out to the arroyo behind the house, listening as he patiently identified the Sonora Desert's birds, animals, and plants. Peter remembered that Dixon was "always, always sketching." One of Dixon's last paintings was *Home of Tucson* (fig. 185), Gilbert Ronstadt's home next door.

During September and October of 1945, San Francisco's Gump Galleries presented a major show, Paintings of the West by Maynard Dixon, exhibiting twenty-nine of his recent Arizona and Utah canvases, including *Chollas Against the Mountain, Land of Tilted Mesas,* and *Home of the Desert Rat.* In August 1945, artist Millard Sheets, then teaching art at Scripps College, had contacted Dixon with a proposal that a retrospective exhibit of his work originate at Scripps, then travel to several other museums in California. With Hamlin's assistance, Dixon gathered enough important work to represent his fifty-year career. The show opened in November 1945 at Scripps's Florence Rand Lang Galleries and included early drawings from the turn of the century, original illustrations from the recently completed *Oregon Trail,* mural photos, "cartoons," character study drawings, and a significant group of landscape and figure canvases, along with field sketches and composition layouts.

Dixon, by then too ill to attend the opening, sent a letter to Sheets, who read it to the assembled crowd:

But long ago—about 1915, when "modern art" first "bit the USA"—I had to make a hard decision. Should I go along with the "new movement," adopt a novel and fashionable point of view, get my ideas "imported"—or should I look at my world with more candid eyes, be plainly honest with myself and so achieve something perhaps not startling but at least sincere.

185. *Home of Tucson*, 1945, oil on canvas, 16 x 20 inches,
collection of Drs. Mark and Kathleen Sublette

As often before, I went again into the desert to find an answer—and it was not far to seek. . . . Well—there is the empty desert; there are the arid mountains; they shimmer in the ashen heart of noon, or swim in the far elusive colors of evening—a reality that appears unreal, challenging the imagination. And there the Indian who can withdraw into himself and be silent and unresponsive as a stone. You cannot argue with the silence. It returns your questionings to you, to your own inner silence which becomes aware—a mystical something that is neither reason nor intelligence nor intuition, a recognition of some nameless truth that may not be denied. So my choice was made; I must find in the visible world the forms, the colors, the relationships that for me are most true of it, and find a way to state them clearly so that the painting may pass on something of my vision.

But don't think it was all as dreamy as that. Here I was in the midst of the Real Thing—my western world—and my mind was set to tell the truth of it on paper and on canvas, and that meant work. It meant constant observation and constant drawing.

And to you here who are interested in the arts of painting and design I recommend this first, last and always—to draw, draw, draw. Set about understanding the things that interest you, stating your own observations simply. Accept these facts from Nature for what they are, enrich your store of knowledge by recording them, and experiment with them afterward, if you will. Above all, don't be smart about it. You will succeed only in being smarty, and your product will be only arty.

You will see in this exhibit some sketches, from 1900 on, that show my endeavor to put this idea into practice: to build a solid foundation of factual knowledge of my work. How many such notes I have made, large and small, I have no idea—probably thousands.

But to get rid of the short-cut habits of my illustration days, to emerge from the ways of quick composition and the monotony of black and white into thoughtful planning and true color was not so easy. All this time I was turning out paintings (of a sort)—my vision and my point of view was gradually changing. While I did not tie to any of the current "isms" of modern art, neither did I shun them. They are part of our times. Some painters have accused me of a narrow localism in my work—of refusing to learn from modern art (now 30 years old)—but little they knew how often I have seen some painting of mine hung next to one of the newer school where the contrast sent me to my lair in shame and vowing repentance. From these things, from my own two eyes and the desert silence I learned. So finally I came to the point where the illustrators said I was a pretty good painter, the painters said I was a pretty good writer, and the writers

186. *Maynard Dixon*, ca. 1943, private collection

said I was a pretty good illustrator. Meantime my work grew steadily away from the illustrative, dramatic wild-west ("the mantle of Remington" stuff) and began to take on a more poetic and decorative quality. (Experience in outdoor advertising design and in mural painting had much influence in this.) The next development was into a more structural phase, in which color-shapes and space relations became the dominant factors; and this geometric (though not mathematical) element you may see in most of the later works.

Which brings us up to date and this retrospective show at Scripps, for which again my thanks. I can only hope that somewhere along the line of my endeavor I have expressed to you something of the power and the glory of the painter's worlds that has been revealed to me. Good-bye—and good luck.[13]

187. *White House Ruin, Canyon de Chelly*, 1946, pencil on paper, 8 x 7 inches,
collection of Drs. Mark and Kathleen Sublette

A small pamphlet, *Maynard Dixon: Painter of the West*, printed by Dixon's long-time friend, Edward Dewitt Taylor in San Francisco, with an introduction by Arthur Millier, eight color plates, and numerous black-and-white illustrations, accompanied the exhibit. *Arizona Highways* furnished the color plates from a feature article the magazine had done on Dixon's work in 1945, printing three thousand extra plates for the pamphlet by arrangement with Dixon. Ansel Adams provided a photograph of Dixon as the frontispiece. When the exhibition closed at Scripps, it was sent to the Los Angeles County Museum of Art from February to March 3, 1946. Dixon still made drawings for publications, including *White House Ruin, Canyon de Chelly* (fig. 187), which eventually appeared in a modified form in *Arizona Highways*.

Dixon's last mural commission was for the Santa Fe Railway's new Los Angeles ticket office at Sixth and Hill streets. He decided to select the Grand Canyon, Arizona's greatest icon as the mural's theme in recognition of its prominent role in the state and railroad's history. During his last months, he now used oxygen twenty-four hours a day. This gave his lungs enough fire of life to enable him to get from his bed to his studio chair and then by wheelchair to the shed behind the house where the mural started taking shape. In late August, the design (the most difficult part of the job) was finished and sent to Santa Fe Railway officials for approval. The creation of this massive mural was a formidable task few painters would attempt. The mural, which he titled the *Grand Canyon of the Colorado*, would telescope several views of the canyon into one long, narrow composition, shadows and geometric forces showing the play of sun, light, and the passage of time. By now, too weak to hold a brush steady, he directed Hamlin and his two artist friends, Ray Strong and Buck Weaver, in drawing the mural to scale, then confirming and painting it in full color. The mural was completed, shipped to Los Angeles, and installed at the ticket office on November 8, 1946. Mounted on a curved screen that wrapped around the top of two walls, the mural flooded the building's interior with the Grand Canyon's space, color, and atmosphere. After the office closed, the mural was removed and later presented to the Arizona Veterans Memorial Coliseum in Phoenix.

On the morning of November 13, Hamlin discovered Dixon slumped in his wheelchair, unconscious from a heart attack. Several hours later he died. According to his wishes, he was cremated and his ashes placed in one of the cherished Hopi bowls he had brought back from Walpi in 1923. Hamlin printed an elegant little two-page folder, reproducing his lifelong traveling companion—a thunderbird—on the front (fig. 188). It read, "Announcing the death of Maynard Dixon on November thirteenth, nineteen forty-six, at his home in Tucson, Arizona. He requested no formal services." Inside she inserted his poem "At Last."

Newspaper and wire services throughout the United States from San Francisco to New York carried news of his passing. Telegrams and letters arrived from family members and friends, and from people who had never met Dixon but who had been touched by his vision and passion for the West's landscapes and people. Kem Weber, Porter Garnett, Imogen Cunningham, Roi Partridge, Conrad Buff, Arthur Millier, Frederick Webb Hodge, Sophie Treadwell, and others sent condolence letters to Hamlin. Ansel Adams wrote, "Can't tell you all the emotions that are stirring around within me; perhaps I can some day."[14] Herald Clark at Brigham Young University commented, "It seems to me that his creations were quite like him—they are so genuinely simple, so honest, so frank, and yet so delightfully beautiful. Who ever knew a person who could define simplicity and make it so great as he?"[15] One of Dixon's Mount Carmel neighbors told Hamlin that "Mr. Dixon's request for no formal services and his philosophy of death as expressed in the little poem sounds rather strange to most Mormons, but to me it expresses a spirit of humility before the forces of nature and nature's god that I very much admire."[16]

And Edward DeWitt Taylor, a printer of fine books in San Francisco, wrote, "My friendship with Maynard dates back forty years. It was stimulating experience. He had no patience with sham or fraud or false pretense. And for that . . . I loved him. He lives in his monumental creations, and because of him, the Great West will live, through his eyes forever."[17] In the spring of 1947, Hamlin carried Dixon's ashes up to Mount Carmel, scattered them in and around a small hole on top of the sagebrush- and juniper-dotted ridge behind the house, and then installed a bronze plaque that reads, "Maynard Dixon, 1875–1946."

Nowadays, if you pause if front of 728 Montgomery Street in San Francisco, you will discover that the original building is scheduled to be replaced with upscale condominiums and offices. Only the façade remains. What the 1906 earthquake and fire could not accomplish, development finally would. No physical evidence remains to indicate the importance of the structure's past history.

But once it was a place of magic.

Announcing the death of Maynard Dixon on November thirteenth, nineteen forty-six, at his home in Tucson, Arizona. He requested no formal services.

188. *Announcement of Maynard Dixon's Death, 1946,* private collection

ENDNOTES

Introduction

1. Reed, Walt, *Harold Von Schmidt*, 21.
2. Quoted in Tomananczy, 11.
3. Dixon, Daniel, "The Story Teller," 5–6.
4. Quoted in Hagerty, *Desert Dreams*, xxiv.
5. Adams, "Free Man in a Free Country," 41.

1 Picking Up the Trail, 1875–1893

1. Wallace, *Maynard Dixon*, 22. This is one of the primary sources on Dixon's art and life up until 1936, dictated by him to Gene Hailey, one of his old friends from the early newspaper days.
2. Norris, *The Octopus*, 14.
3. Wallace, *Maynard Dixon*, 27.
4. Dixon, Maynard (ca. 1943, Tucson, Arizona). This is from an unpublished anecdote in the Maynard Dixon Papers, Collection of John Dixon.
5. Wallace, *Maynard Dixon*, 33.
6. Frederic Remington to Maynard Dixon, September 3, 1891, reproduced in Burnside, *Maynard Dixon*, 215. Remington wrote to Dixon again on September 19, 1891, responding to his inquiry about how much he should charge for his work. That letter is also reproduced in Burnside's book.

2 Fin-de-Siecle Illustrator, 1893–1900

1. Wallace, *Maynard Dixon*, 34.
2. Boeringer, "Some San Francisco Illustrators," 71.
3. Wallace, *Maynard Dixon*, 38–39.
4. Dixon, L. Maynard, "Among the People Down the Coast," 300. In this article, Dixon recalls his 1895 trip to the Big Sur, offering vivid impressions of the wild beautiful landscape and encounters with ranchers and vaqueros.
5. *San Francisco Examiner*, "He Draws the Vaquero," November 17, 1895, 11.
6. Unna, *The Coppa Murals*, 45.
7. Lummis, "That Which Is Written," 209.
8. Wallace, *Maynard Dixon*, 33.
9. Ibid., 39.
10. Irwin, "The City That Was," 29.
11. Lummis, "A California Illustrator," 4–11. The article reproduces ten of Dixon's pencil and pen-and-ink sketches.
12. Hagerty, *James Swinnerton*, 9.
13. Jack London to Cloudsley Johns, March 7, 1899, in Labor, et al, *The Letters of Jack London*, 53. Johns was a writer, socialist, poet, and sculptor, perhaps best known as a newspaperman, editor, music, drama, and literary critic for the *San Francisco Post*.
14. Jack London to Elwyn Irving Hoffman, September 5, 1900, in Labor, et al, *The Letters of Jack London*, 203. Hoffman, a San Francisco writer, published his work in California newspapers and magazines. Dixon illustrated his stories in *Overland Monthly* as early as 1895.
15. Maynard Dixon to Charles F. Lummis, May 26, 1900, in Charles F. Lummis Collection.
16. Austin, *The Land of Little Rain*, 3–5.

3 Going East to See the West, 1900–1907

1. Lummis, "In Western Letters," 88. A photograph of Dixon taken by Lummis accompanies the comments.
2. Maynard Dixon to Charles F. Lummis, Needles, California, July 24, 1900, in Charles F. Lummis Collection.
3. Dixon, Maynard, "Arizona in 1900," 17. Although this article focuses on Dixon's first trip to Arizona in 1900, it also includes his 1905 visit and later recollections.
4. Ibid., 17.
5. Maynard Dixon to Charles F. Lummis, Hall's Ranch, Arizona Territory, August 5, 1900, in Charles F. Lummis Collection.
6. Maynard Dixon to Charles F. Lummis, Hall's Ranch, Arizona Territory, 1900, in Charles F. Lummis Collection.
7. Dixon, "Arizona in 1900," 18.
8. Ibid., 19.
9. Maynard Dixon to Charles F. Lummis, Jerome, Arizona Territory, August 15, 1900, in Charles F. Lummis Collection.
10. Maynard Dixon to Charles F. Lummis, Phoenix, Arizona Territory, August 17, 1900, in Charles F. Lummis Collection.
11. Maynard Dixon to Charles F. Lummis, Phoenix, Arizona Territory, August 22, 1900, in Charles F. Lummis Collection.

12. Dixon, "Arizona in 1900," 18.

13. Maynard Dixon to Elwyn Hoffman, Phoenix, Arizona Territory, September 15, 1900, in Maynard Dixon Collection.

14. Maynard Dixon to Charles F. Lummis, San Francisco, California, April 22, 1901, in Charles F. Lummis Collection.

15. Maynard Dixon to Charles F. Lummis, Carson, Nevada, May 17, 1901, in Charles F. Lummis Collection.

16. Wallace, *Maynard Dixon*, 46.

17. Maynard Dixon to Charles F. Lummis, Boise, Idaho, August 17, 1901, in Charles F. Lummis Collection.

18. Quoted in Hagerty, *Desert Dreams*, 31.

19. Ibid.

20. "Manifesto," in *First Exhibition of the California Society of Artists*.

21. Colton and Baxter, *Days in the Painted Desert*, vii.

22. Dixon, Maynard, "Navaho Land," 34.

23. Dixon, Maynard, "Arizona in 1900," 40.

24. Dixon, Maynard, "Navaho Land," 35.

25. Ibid., 34.

26. Quoted in Hagerty, *Desert Dreams*, 35.

27. Ibid., 40.

28. "L. Maynard Dixon's Frontier Studies," 16.

29. Ibid., 22.

30. Unna, *The Coppa Murals*, 54.

31. Ibid., 31.

32. Ibid., 32.

33. Maynard Dixon to Lorenzo Hubbell, quoted in *Querido Patron*, 7.

34. Quoted in Hagerty, *Desert Dreams*, 45.

35. Quoted in *Querido Patron*, 11.

36. Quoted in Hagerty, *Desert Dreams*, 46.

37. Ibid.

38. Ibid.

39. In *Rim-Rock and Sage*, 8–9. This publication features 164 poems written by Maynard Dixon between 1896 and 1937. They offer insight into his thoughts about the art world, personal relationships, the western landscape, and Native American religion. Sometimes lyrical, sometimes dark and sardonic, the poems reveal the intellectual and emotional facets of Dixon's life.

40. Quoted in Hagerty, *Desert Dreams*, 48.

41. Letter From Maynard Dixon to Charles F. Lummis, April 22, 1906, in Charles F. Lummis Collection.

42. Quoted in *Querido Patron*, 15.

4 The New York Years, 1907–1912

1. Maynard Dixon to Lorenzo Hubbell, July 5, 1906, in *Querido Patron*, 15.

2. "In the Wide Awake West," 83. This article mentions that San Francisco's Sequoia Club hosted a rousing party for Dixon prior to his departure for New York.

3. Charles F. Lummis to Maynard Dixon. Los Angeles, September 6, 1907, in Charles F. Lummis Collection.

4. Maynard Dixon to George Rankin, San Francisco, January 15, 1937; copy in the Maynard Dixon Papers, Collection of Donald J. Hagerty.

5. Wallace, *Maynard Dixon*, 38.

6. Ibid., 29.

7. Ibid., 30.

8. Maynard Dixon to Lorenzo Hubbell, Yonkers, New York, July 4, 1910, in *Querido Patron*, 20.

9. Maynard Dixon to Dane Coolidge, Yonkers, New York, May 13, 1911, in Dane Coolidge Collection.

10. Ibid.

11. Maynard Dixon to Dane Coolidge, Yonkers, New York, May 4, 1911, in Dane Coolidge Collection.

12. Quoted in Hagerty, *Desert Dreams*, 62.

13. Maynard Dixon to Dane Coolidge, Winstead, Connecticut, August 25, 1911, in Dane Coolidge Collection.

14. *Rim-Rock and Sage*, 19.

15. Quoted in Hagerty, *Desert Dreams*, 62.

16. Maynard Dixon to Charles F. Lummis, New York, January 29, 1912, in Charles F. Lummis Collection.

17. Quoted in Hagerty, *Desert Dreams*, 64.

18. Maynard Dixon to Charles F. Lummis, New York, January 29, 1912, in Charles F. Lummis Collection.

5 Turn of the Tide, 1912–1920

1. Maynard Dixon to Dane Coolidge, San Francisco, August 20, 1912, in Dane Coolidge Collection.

2. Maynard Dixon to Dane Coolidge, Sulphur Springs Ranch, November 21, 1912, in Dane Coolidge Collection.

3. Wallace, *Maynard Dixon*, 32.

4. Unpublished anecdote by Dixon in the Maynard Dixon Papers, Collection of John Dixon.

5. Quoted in the *Los Angeles Times*, August 2, 1913, 18.

6. Quoted in the *Los Angeles Examiner*, November 9, 1914, 22.

7. Quoted in the *Los Angeles Times*, January 12, 1913, 16.

8. Ibid.

9. In *Rim-Rock and Sage*, 29.

10. Quoted in Hagerty, *Desert Dreams*, 135.

11. Maynard Dixon to Dane Coolidge, San Francisco, October 30, 1913, in Dane Coolidge Collection.

12. Garnett, Porter, from the introduction to *An Exhibition of Original Drawings by Maynard Dixon*.

13. In *Rim-Rock and Sage*, 33.

14. Maynard Dixon to Dane Coolidge, San Francisco, September 22, 1914, in Dane Coolidge Collection.
15. Maynard Dixon to Charles F. Lummis, San Francisco, January 20, 1915, in Charles F. Lummis Collection.
16. In *Querido Patron*, 22.
17. Maynard Dixon to Dane Coolidge, Globe, Arizona, June 19, 1915, in Dane Coolidge Collection.
18. In *Rim-Rock and Sage*, 45.
19. Tolerton, "The Art of Maynard Dixon," xcii.
20. Maynard Dixon to Charles F. Lummis, San Francisco, January 8, 1917, in Charles F. Lummis Collection.
21. Quoted in Hagerty, *Desert Dreams*, 88.
22. Wallace, *Maynard Dixon*, 37.
23. Reed, *Harold Von Schmidt*, 23.
24. Maynard Dixon to Charles F. Lummis, San Francisco, April 21, 1917, in Charles F. Lummis Collection.
25. In *Rim-Rock and Sage*, 52.
26. Charles M. Russell to Maynard Dixon, July 1917; copy in Maynard Dixon Papers, Collection of Donald J. Hagerty.
27. Maynard Dixon to Charles F. Lummis, Glacier National Park, Montana, August 24, 1917, in Charles F. Lummis Collection.
28. Charles M. Russell to Maynard Dixon, Lake McDonald, Montana, August 21, 1917, copy in Maynard Dixon Papers, Collection of Donald J. Hagerty.
29. Maynard Dixon to Dane Coolidge, San Francisco, December 10, 1917, in Dane Coolidge Collection.
30. Quoted in Hagerty, *Desert Dreams*, 92.
31. In *Rim-Rock and Sage*, 75.
32. Charles F. Lummis to Maynard Dixon, Los Angeles, California, June

27, 1918, in Charles F. Lummis Collection.
33. Wallace, *Maynard Dixon*, 74.
34. Quoted in the *San Francisco Examiner*, November 23, 1919, 9.

6 The City and the Desert, 1920–1931

1. In *Rim-Rock and Sage*, 77–79. *Sunset Magazine* reproduced this poem, accompanied by a Dixon drawing, in the January 1922 issue.
2. Reiss, *Dorothea Lange*. Lange discusses her life with Dixon on pages 93–143.
3. Ibid., 95.
4. Ibid., 97.
5. In *Rim-Rock and Sage*, 93.
6. Boynton, "Human Life Minute," 23.
7. In *Rim-Rock and Sage*, 93–95.
8. Wallace, *Maynard Dixon*, 83.
9. Ibid., 84.
10. Reiss, *Dorothea Lange*, 130.
11. Corner, *Taking Measures*, 160.
12. Maynard Dixon to Charles F. Lummis, Polacca, Arizona, November 18, 1923, in Charles F. Lummis Collection.
13. Maynard Dixon to Robert Macbeth, Walpi, Arizona, n.d., in Maynard Dixon Collection, Bancroft Library.
14. Maynard Dixon to Joseph Loeb, San Francisco, California, March 4, 1924, in Maynard Dixon Papers, Collection of John Dixon. Loeb was Dixon's attorney and a close friend.
15. In *Rim-Rock and Sage*, 96.
16. Quoted in Hagerty, *Desert Dreams*, 130.
17. Robert Macbeth to Maynard Dixon, New York, May 15, 1924, in Maynard Dixon Papers, Collection of John Dixon.
18. Maynard Dixon to Robert MacBeth, San Francisco, California, June 27, 1924, in Maynard Dixon Papers,

Collection of John Dixon.
19. Maynard Dixon to Joseph Loeb, San Francisco, California, June 17, 1924, in Maynard Dixon Papers, Collection of John Dixon.
20. Charles F. Lummis to Maynard Dixon. Los Angeles, California, May 19, 1925, in Charles F. Lummis Collection.
21. "Two Painted Hangings," 8–9.
22. Quoted in Hagerty. *Desert Dreams*, 135.
23. Cravens, "Art Notes," 16.
24. Dixon, Maynard. "Toward American Art," 19–20.
25. Quoted in Hagerty. *Desert Dreams*. 154.
26. Millier, "The Art Temperament," 2.
27. McPhee, *Basin and Range*, 45–46.
28. "In San Francisco Galleries," 77.
29. "Letter from Maynard Dixon," 64.
30. Wilson, "The Murals in the State Library," 34.
31. Henry Herbert Knibbs to Maynard Dixon, Los Angeles, California, November 26, 1928, in Charles F. Lummis Collection.
32. Maynard Dixon to Sara Bard Field, San Francisco, February 6, 1929, in Maynard Dixon Papers, Collection of Donald J. Hagerty. Field was a poet and early feminist. She was married to Colonel C. E. S. Wood, who had fought in the Nez Perce War and who became a socialist writer, poet, and reformer. Both were close friends of Maynard Dixon.
33. Kistler, "Maynard Dixon at Galerie Beaux Arts," 20.
34. "Exorcising Ghosts," 6.
35. Wallace, *Maynard Dixon*, 112–13.
36. Ibid., 113.
37. Ibid., 113–14.
38. Ibid., 19.
39. Van Der Zee, *The Gate*, 123.

40. Quoted in Hagerty, *Desert Dreams*, 172.

7 From Chaos to Taos, 1931–1940

1. Maynard Dixon to Mary Austin, Taos, New Mexico, July 12, 1931, in Maynard Dixon Collection, Huntington Library.
2. Wood, *Taos Pueblo*, 6.
3. In *Rim-Rock and Sage*, 105.
4. *San Francisco Chronicle*, "Dixon Paints New Mexico," 14.
5. Quoted in Hagerty. *Desert Dreams*, 187–88.
6. Ibid., 188.
7. Meltzer, *Dorothea Lange*, 73.
8. Ibid., 78.
9. Hutchinson, *A Bar Cross Man*, 335.
10. Rusho, *Everett Ruess*, 118.
11. In *Rim-Rock and Sage*, 112–13.
12. Bermingham, *The New Deal*, 5.
13. *San Francisco Examiner*, "Artist Paints Boulder Scene," 22.
14. Quoted in Hagerty, *Desert Dreams*, 199.
15. Quoted in *Rim-Rock and Sage*, 111–12.
16. Quoted in Hagerty, *Desert Dreams*, 203.
17. Ibid., 203.
18. Ibid.
19. Quoted in *Rim-Rock and Sage*, 124–25.
20. Quoted in Hagerty. *Desert Dreams*, 214.
21. Ibid., 215.
22. Quoted in *Rim-Rock and Sage*, 122.
23. Quoted in Hagerty, *Desert Dreams*, 216.
24. Ibid., 216.
25. Quoted in *Rim-Rock and Sage*, 119.
26. Quoted in Hagerty. *Desert Dreams*, 222.
27. Ibid., 223–24.
28. Maynard Dixon to Turbese Lummis, Carson City, Nevada, September 15, 1937, in Charles F. Lummis Collection.
29. Maynard Dixon to Joseph Loeb, El Cajon, California, March 11, 1938, in Maynard Dixon Papers, Collection of John Dixon.
30. *San Diego Sun*, June 14, 1938, 15.
31. *San Diego Sun*, June 20, 1938, 14.
32. Quoted in Hagerty, *Desert Dreams*, 226.
33. Ibid., *Desert Dreams*, 227.
34. Ibid.
35. Quoted in Hagerty, *Desert Dreams*, 229.
36. Neuhaus, *The Art of Treasure Island*, 112.
37. California Art in Retrospect, 1850–1915, a third exhibit at Treasure Island, was a historical survey of early California art that included Dixon's painting *Migration*, painted in 1923.
38. Quoted in Hagerty. *Desert Dreams*, 231.
39. *San Francisco Chronicle*, "Forced to Choose Health Over S.F.," 20.
40. Ibid.
41. Ibid.
42. Ibid.
43. Ibid.

8 Back to the Home Corral, 1940–1946

1. J. Frank Dobie to Maynard Dixon, Austin, Texas, November 29, 1939, in Maynard Dixon Papers, Collection of John Dixon.
2. Maynard Dixon to J. Frank Dobie, San Francisco, December 10, 1939, in Maynard Dixon Papers, Collection of John Dixon.
3. Hagerty, "Meeting Mr. Hearst's Deadlines," 2.
4. Arthur Millier, "The Art Thrill of the Week," 8.
5. Hagerty, *Edith Hamlin*, 71.
6. Maynard Dixon to Richard F. McGraw, Mount Carmel, Utah, June 11, 1942, in Maynard Dixon Papers, Collection of John Dixon.
7. Quoted in Hagerty, *Desert Dreams*, 237–39.
8. Maynard Dixon to Richard F. McGraw, Mount Carmel, Utah, July 22, 1942, in Maynard Dixon Papers, Collection of John Dixon.
9. Maynard Dixon to Richard F. McGraw, Mount Carmel, Utah, August 20, 1943, in Maynard Dixon Papers, Collection of John Dixon.
10. Maynard Dixon to Joseph Loeb, Tucson, Arizona, October 23, 1943, copy in Maynard Dixon Papers, Collection of Donald J. Hagerty. Tucson had tripled its population after World War II began, and numerous military airfields and aircraft plants were scattered around the outskirts, thus Dixon's reference to planes in the skies.
11. Ansel Adams to Maynard Dixon, Yosemite, California, October 13, 1943, in Maynard Dixon Papers, Collection of John Dixon.
12. Hagerty, *Edith Hamlin*, 76.
13. Quoted in Hagerty, *Desert Dreams*, 251–53.
14. Ansel Adams to Edith Hamlin, San Francisco, California, November 14, 1946; copy in Maynard Dixon Papers, Collection of Donald J. Hagerty.
15. Herald R. Clark to Edith Hamlin, Provo, Utah, November 21, 1946, in Maynard Dixon Papers, Collection of Donald J. Hagerty.
16. Bert Gardner to Edith Hamlin, Mount Carmel, Utah, December 7, 1946, in Maynard Dixon Papers, Collection of Donald J. Hagerty.
17. Edward Dewitt Taylor to Edith Hamlin, November 23, 1946, in Maynard Dixon Papers, Collection of Donald J. Hagerty.

BIBLIOGRAPHY

Books, Periodicals

A

Adams, Ansel. "Free Man in a Free Country." *American West* (November 1969): 41–47.

Ainsworth, Edward. *Painters of the Desert.* Palm Desert: Desert Magazine, 1960.

The American Personality: The Artist-Illustrator of Life in the United States, 1860–1930. Los Angeles: The Grunwald Center for the Graphic Arts, 1976.

"And the Pacific's Supposed to Be Calm." *Art Digest* (June 1, 1934): 6.

Anderson, Timothy J., Eudorah M. Moore, and Robert W. Winter. *California Design, 1910.* Salt Lake City: Gibbs Smith, Publisher, 1974.

The Argus: A Journal of Art Criticism (1927–1929).

"Artist Paints Boulder Scene," *San Francisco Chronicle,* May 18, 1934.

Artists in the American Desert. Reno: Sierra Nevada Museum of Art, 1980.

Artists-Teachers and Pupils: San Francisco Art Association and California School of Design: The First Fifty Years. San Francisco: California Historical Society, 1971.

At Work: The Art of California Labor. Edited by Mark Dean Johnson. Berkeley: Heyday Books, 2003.

Austin, Mary. *The Land of Little Rain.* Boston: Houghton Mifflin and Company, 1903.

———. *Stories from the Country of Lost Borders.* Edited and with an introduction by Marjorie Pryse.

New Brunswick and London: Rutgers University Press, 1987.

B

Baird, Joseph Armstrong, Jr., ed. *From Exposition to Exposition: Progressive and Conservative Painting, 1915–1939.* Sacramento: Crocker Art Museum, 1981.

———. *Theodore Wores and the Beginnings of Internationalism in Northern California Paintings, 1874–1915.* Davis: Library Associates, University of California, 1978.

Berlant, Tony, and Andrew Nagen. "Objects of Integrity." *Artspace* (July/August 1990): 40–45.

Bermingham, Peter. *The New Deal in the Southwest: Arizona and New Mexico.* Tucson: The University of Arizona Museum of Art, 1980.

Bernier, R. L. *Art in California.* San Francisco: P. L. Bernier, 1916.

Bingham, Paul D., and Beverly Bubar Denenberg. "Maynard Dixon as Muralist: Sketches for the Mark Hopkins Hotel Mural." *California History* (1990): 52–59.

Black, Winifred. "Gold of the Burning Desert." *Cosmopolitan* (September 1905): 519–26.

Blue, Martha. *Indian Trader, Life and Times of J. L. Hubbell.* Walnut Creek, California: Kiva Publishing, 2000.

Boas, Nancy. *The Society of Six: California Colorists.* San Francisco: Bedford Arts Publishers, 1988.

Boeringer, Pierre N. "Some San

Francisco Illustrators." *Overland Monthly* 26 (July 1895): 70–90.

Boynton, Ray. "Human Life Minute in Presence of Vastness of Western Wilds Says Maynard Dixon After Trip." *San Francisco Examiner,* August 20, 1922.

Broder, Patricia Janis. *Taos: A Painter's Dream.* Boston: New York Graphic Society, 1980.

———. *The American West: The Modern Vision.* Boston: New York Graphic Society, 1984.

Brown, Milton W. *American Painting from the Armory Show to the Depression.* Princeton: Princeton University Press, 1955.

———. *The Modern Spirit: American Painting 1908–1935.* London: The Arts Council of Great Britain, 1977.

Burnside, Wesley M. *Maynard Dixon: Artist of the West.* Provo, Utah: Brigham Young University Press, 1974.

C

"California Feud." *Art Digest* (July 1, 1934): 19.

California Progressives, 1910–1930. Newport Beach, California: Orange County Museum of Art, 1996.

Clemmer, David. *Serenading the Light: Painters of the Desert Southwest.* Santa Fe: Schenck Southwest Publishing, 2003.

Coke, Van Deren. *Taos and Santa Fe: The Artists Environment, 1882–1942.* Albuquerque: University of New Mexico Press, 1963.

Colton, Harold S., and Fred C. Baxter. *Days in the Painted Desert and the San Francisco*

Mountains. Flagstaff: Museum of Northern Arizona, 1932.

Cooper, Evelyn S. "The Old West Photography of Dane Coolidge." *Arizona Highways* (1988): 16–21.

Corner, James. *Taking Measures across the American Landscape*. New Haven: Yale University Press, 1996.

The Cowboy. San Diego: The San Diego Museum of Art, 1981.

Cravens, Junius. "Art Notes." *The Argonaut* (January 22, 1927): 16.

D

Dickover, Robert M. "Maynard Dixon: Artist of the Bookplate." *California State Library Foundation Bulletin*, 2008, 2–5.

Dixon, Constance. "Montana, 1917." In *Maynard Dixon: Images of the Native American*. San Francisco: California Academy of Sciences, 1981.

Dixon, Daniel. "The Story Teller." In *Maynard Dixon: Images of the Native American*. San Francisco: California Academy of Sciences, 1981.

Dixon, John. "Recapturing the Spirit." In *Maynard Dixon: Images of the Native American*. San Francisco: California Academy of Sciences, 1981.

Dixon, L. Maynard. "Among the People Down the Coast." *Overland Monthly* (October 1897): 300–6.

Dixon, Maynard. "Arizona in 1900." *Arizona Highways* (February 1942): 16–19, 40.

———. "At the Land's End." *Overland Monthly* (August 1898): 181–82.

———. "Navaho Land." *Arizona Highways* (May 1942): 34–37.

———. "Toward American Art." *The Argus: A Journal of Art Criticism* (June 1927).

"Dixon Paints New Mexico," *San Francisco Chronicle*, October 4, 1931.

"Dixon Portrays the Waterfront Strike." *Art Digest* (October 15, 1936): 68.

"Dixon Went Back Home To Do Honest Work." *Art Digest* (May 1, 1938): 12.

Dykes, Jeff. *Fifty Great Western Illustrators: A Bibliographic Checklist*. Flagstaff, Arizona: Northland Press, 1975.

E

"Encyclopedia Britannica Special Number." *Art Digest* (April 2, 1945): 30.

"Exorcising Ghosts." *Art Digest* (August 1930).

F

Ferlinghetti, Lawrence, and Nancy J. Peters. *Literary San Francisco: A Pictorial History from Its Beginnings to the Present Day*. San Francisco: City Lights and Harper and Row, 1980.

Fiske, Turbese Lummis, and Keith Lummis. *Charles F. Lummis: The Man and His West*. Norman: University of Oklahoma Press, 1975.

"Forced to Choose Health Over S.F.," *San Francisco Chronicle*, October 3, 1939.

G

Gelber, Steven M. "Working to Prosperity: California's New Deal Murals." *California History* (1979): 99–127.

Gibbs, Linda Jones. *Escape to Reality: The Western World of Maynard Dixon*. Provo, Utah: Brigham Young University Press, 2000.

Goetzmann, William H., and William N. Goetzmann. *The West of the Imagination*. New York: W. W. Norton and Company, 1986.

Grabhorn, Edwin E. *Recollections of the Grabhorn Press*. Berkeley: University of California, Bancroft Library Regional Oral History Office, 1968.

Griswold, Mary Edith. "A Corner of Bohemia." *Western World* (August 1907): 11–14.

———. "Three Days Adrift."

Sunset Magazine (June/July 1906): 119–22.

H

Hagerty, Donald J. *Canyon de Chelly: 100 Years of Painting and Photography*. Salt Lake City: Gibbs Smith, Publisher, 1996.

———. "The Colorado Plateau: Interpretations by Maynard Dixon and Ed Mell." *Southwest Art* (July 1985): 34–41.

———. *Desert Dreams: The Art and Life of Maynard Dixon*. Salt Lake City: Gibbs Smith, Publisher, 1993; revised edition, 1998.

———. *Edith Hamlin: A California Artist*. Davis: American Studies Program, University of California–Davis, 1981.

———. "Hard Times, New Images: Artists and the Depression Years in California." *Pacific Historian* (1983): 11–19.

———. "History on the Walls: The Maynard Dixon and Frank Van Sloun Murals in the California State Library." *California State Library Foundation Bulletin* (Fall 2000/Winter 2001): 28–32.

———. *James Swinnerton*. Santa Fe: Gerald Peters Gallery, 2001.

———. "Maynard Dixon and a Changing West." *Montana: The Magazine of Western History* (Summer 2001): 36–51.

———. "Maynard Dixon Country." *Arizona Highways* (March 1987): 32–37.

———. "Maynard Dixon, Modernism, and the Desert." In *Kindred Spirits of Bohemia II: On the Road to Modernism*." San Francisco: Bohemian Club, 2008.

———. "Meeting Mr. Hearst's Deadlines: The Newspaper and Magazine Illustrations of Maynard Dixon." *California State Library Foundation Bulletin* (2007): 2–11.

———. "Modernism, The West, and Maynard Dixon." In

Maynard Dixon: Masterpieces from Brigham Young University and Private Collections. Pasadena: Pasadena Museum of California Art, 2007.

———. "The Native American Portrayed." In *Maynard Dixon: Images of the Native American.* San Francisco: California Academy of Sciences, 1981.

———. "Sky and Sandstone: Maynard Dixon and the Arizona Years." In Thomas Brent Smith. *A Place of Refuge: Maynard Dixon's Arizona.* Tucson: Tucson Museum of Art, 2008.

———. "Visions and Images: Maynard Dixon and the American West." In *Maynard Dixon: Images of the Native American.* San Francisco: California Academy of Sciences, 1981.

———. "The West on Walls: Maynard Dixon and the McClaughery Murals." *California State Library Foundation Bulletin* (Summer 1998): 1–6.

Hailey, Gene. "Maynard Dixon's Paintings of the West." *The Wasp* (December 4, 1920): 20.

Hamlin, Edith. "Maynard Dixon: Artist of the West." *California Historical Quarterly* (1974): 361–76.

———. "Maynard Dixon: Painter of the West." *American West* (1982): 50–59.

"He Draws the Vaquero," *San Francisco Chronicle,* November 17, 1895.

Hegemann, Elizabeth Compton. *Navaho Trading Days.* Albuquerque: University of New Mexico Press, 1963.

Heyman, Therese Thau. *Celebrating a Collection: The Work of Dorothea Lange.* Oakland: The Oakland Museum, 1978.

Hjalmarson, Birgetta. *Artful Players: Artist Life in Early San Francisco.* Los Angeles: Balcony Press, 1999.

Hough, Katherine Plake, and Michael Zakian. *Transforming the Western Image in 20th Century American Art.* Palm Springs: Palm Springs Desert Museum, 1992.

Hughes, Edan Milton. *Artists in California: 1786–1940.* 2 Vols. San Francisco: Hughes Publishing Company, 2002.

Huriburt, Laurance P. *The Mexican Muralists in the United States.* Albuquerque: University of New Mexico Press, 1989.

Hutchinson, W. H. *A Bar Cross Man: The Life and Personal Writings of Eugene Manlove Rhodes.* Norman: University of Oklahoma Press, 1956.

———. "New Mexico Incident." *American West* (November/December 1977): 4–7, 59.

I

"I.B.M. Stages Impressive American Art Show at New York Fair." *Art Digest* (June 1, 1940): 8.

"In San Francisco Galleries." *The Argus: A Journal of Art Criticism* (December 1927).

"In the Wide Awake West." *Sunset Magazine* (November 1907).

Irwin, Wallace. "The City That Was." Quoted in Oscar Lewis, *Bay Window Bohemia.* New York: Doubleday and Company, 1956.

J

Jones, Mady. "The San Francisco Art Institute." *San Francisco Magazine* (1980): 50–57.

K

Karlstrom, Paul J. *Kindred Spirits of Bohemia: Paintings of Early California by Artists of the Bohemian Club.* San Francisco: Bohemian Club, 2006.

Kistler, Aline. "An Artist in Search of New Mediums." *Overland Monthly* (February 1927): 48–49.

———. "Maynard Dixon at Galerie Beaux Arts," *San Francisco Chronicle,* November 17, 1929.

Kurutz, Gary F., ed. *California Book Illustrators: A Keepsake in Fourteen Parts for the Members of the Book Club of California.* San Francisco: One Heart Press, 1996.

Kurutz, Gary F. "Maynard Dixon and the State Library: A Symbiotic Relationship Between Artist and Institution." *California State Library Foundation Bulletin* (Summer 1998): 7–10.

L

"L. Maynard Dixon's Frontier Studies." *The Mark Hopkins Institute Review of Art* (1903): 16–22.

Labor, Earle, Robert C. Leitz III, and I. Milo Shepard. *The Letters of Jack London, Volume One: 1896–1905.* Stanford: Stanford University Press, 1988.

Lee, Anthony W. *Painting on the Left: Diego Rivera, Radical Politics and San Francisco's Public Murals.* Berkeley: University of California Press, 1999.

"Letter from Maynard Dixon, A." *The Argus: A Journal of Art Criticism* (November 1927).

Lewis, Oscar. *Bay Window Bohemia.* New York: Doubleday and Company, 1956.

Long, Bob. "Harry St. John Dixon and Constance Maynard Dixon." In *Fresno—Past and Present.* Fresno, California: Fresno City and County Historical Society. 1986.

Lummis, Charles F. "A California Illustrator: L. Maynard Dixon and His Work." *Land of Sunshine* (December 1898): 4–11.

———. "In Western Letters." *Land of Sunshine* (July 1900): 88.

———. "That Which Is Written." *Land of Sunshine* (October 1897): 209.

M

"Manifesto," preamble in *First Exhibition of the California Society of Artists.* April 26–May 3, 1902.

Marling, Karal Ann. *Wall-to-Wall America: A Cultural History of Post Office Murals in the Great Depression.* Minneapolis: University of Minnesota Press, 1982.

Maxwell, Margaret F. *A Passion for Freedom: The Life of Sharlot Hall.* Tucson: The University of Arizona Press, 1982.

Maynard Dixon: Images of the Native American. San Francisco: California Academy of Sciences, 1981.

Maynard Dixon: Painter of the West. Introduction by Arthur Millier. Tucson: Privately Published, 1945.

Maynard Dixon: Portraits of the Southwest. Tucson: The University of Arizona Museum of Art, 1984.

Maynard Dixon Sketch Book. Introduction by Don Perceval; foreword by Lawrence Clark Powell. Flagstaff, Arizona: Northland Press, 1967.

McPhee, John. *Basin and Range.* New York: Farrar Straus Giroux, 1980.

Meltzer, Milton. *Dorothea Lange: A Photographer's Life.* New York: Farrar Straus Giroux, 1978.

Mesas, Mountains and Man: The Western Vision of Maynard Dixon. Tucson: Medicine Man Gallery, 1998.

Millier, Arthur. "The Art Temperament of Northern and Southern California Compared." *The Argus: A Journal of Art Criticism* (August 1927).

———. "The Art Thrill of the Week," *Los Angeles Times,* May 19, 1940.

Minick, Joyce. "Possessions and the Dispossessed: Dorothea Lange's Early Years, 1895–1935." In *Celebrating*

a Collection: The Work of Dorothea Lange. Oakland: Oakland Museum, 1978.

Moure, Nancy Dustin Wall, and Phyllis Moure. *Artists Clubs and Exhibitions in Los Angeles Before 1930.* Los Angeles: Dustin Publications, 1975.

Moure, Nancy Dustin Wall. *Dictionary of Art and Artists in Southern California Before 1930.* Los Angeles: Privately Printed, 1975.

———. *California Art: 450 Years of Painting and Other Media.* Los Angeles: Dustin Publications, 1998.

N

Nash, Steven A., et al. *Facing Eden: 100 Years of Landscape Art in the Bay Area.* San Francisco: Fine Arts Museums of San Francisco and University Press, 1995.

Neff, Emily Ballew. *The Modern West: American Landscapes, 1890–1950.* New Haven: Yale University Press, in Association with the Museum of Fine Arts, Houston, 2006.

Nate, Joseph Cookman. "The History of Sigma Chi: 1855–1930." Unpublished manuscript, ca. 1930.

Neuhaus, Eugen. *The Art of Treasure Island.* Berkeley: University of California Press, 1939.

Norris, Frank. *The Octopus: A Story of California.* New York: Doubleday and Page and Company, 1903.

Norman, Dorothy, ed. *The Selected Writings of John Marin.* New York: Pellegrini and Cudahy, 1949.

O

Orsi, Richard J. *Sunset Limited: The Southern Pacific Railroad and the Development of the American West, 1850–1930.* Berkeley: University of California Press, 2005.

P

Perlman, Bernard B. *Painters of the Ashcan School: The Immortal Eight.* New York: Dover Publications, 1988.

Pielkovo, Ruth. "Dixon, Painter of the West." *International Studio* (1924): 468–72.

Petersen, Larry Len. *The Call of the Mountains: The Artists of Glacier National Park.* Tucson, Arizona: Settlers West Galleries, 2002.

The Popular West: American Illustrators, 1900–1940. Phoenix: Phoenix Art Museum, 1982.

Powell, Lawrence Clark. "Personalities of the West: Maynard Dixon's Painted Desert." *Westways* (1974): 24–29, 86–87.

Q

Querido Patron: Letters from Maynard Dixon to Lorenzo Hubbell. Introduction by Bernard Fontana. Tucson: Friends of the University of Arizona Library, 1987.

R

Rebel in Sentiment: Family Papers of Harry St. John Dixon. Madera, California: The Classroom Chronicles Press, 1994.

Reed, Walt. *Harold Von Schmidt Draws and Paints the Old West.* Flagstaff, Arizona: Northland Press, 1972.

Reed, Walt, and Roger Reed. *The Illustrator in America, 1880–1980: A Century of Illustration.* New York: The Society of Illustrators, 1984.

Reiss, Suzanne B. *Dorothea Lange: The Making of a Documentary Photographer.* Berkeley: University of California, Bancroft Library, Regional Oral History Office, 1968.

Rim-Rock and Sage: The Collected Poems of Maynard Dixon.

Introduction by Kevin Starr. San Francisco: California Historical Society, 1977.

Robertson, Wyndham. *Pocahontas and Her Descendents.* Richmond, Virginia: J. W. Randolph and English, 1887.

Rollin, La Verne Bradley. "Maynard Dixon Remembered." *Nevada Highways and Parks* (1967): 3–8.

Rosenblum, Robert. "The Primal American Scene," In *The National Paradise: Painting in America: 1800–1950.* Edited by Kynaston McShine. New York: The Museum of Modern Art, 1976.

Rusho, W. L. *Everett Ruess: A Vagabond for Beauty.* Salt Lake City: Gibbs Smith, Publisher, 1983.

Ryan, Beatrice Judd. "The Rise of Modern Art in the Bay Area." *California Historical Society Quarterly* (March 1959): 1–5.

S

"San Francisco Presents One Man's Opinion of Living American Art." *Art Digest* (March 15, 1939): 30.

Savage, William W., Jr. *The Cowboy Hero.* Norman: University of Oklahoma Press, 1979.

Schnoebelen, Anne. "Relics of Ephemeral Glory: The Treasure Island Murals of Maynard Dixon." *Art of California* (1992): 53–55.

Schwartz, Ellen Halteman. *Northern California Art Exhibition Catalogues (1878–1915): A Descriptive Checklist and Index.* La Jolla, California: Laurence McGilvery, 1990.

Semple, Elizabeth Anna. "Successful Californians in New York." *Overland Monthly* (August 1912): 104–16.

Smith, Linda Jones. *Escape to Reality: The Western World of Maynard Dixon.* Provo, Utah: Brigham Young University, 2000.

Space, Silence, Spirit: Maynard Dixon's West. Paradise, Arizona: Privately Printed, 2002.

Spangenberg, Helen. *Yesterday's Artists on the Monterey Peninsula.* Monterey, California: Monterey Peninsula Museum of Art, 1976.

Stackpole, Ralph. "Dixon's Spring Valley Mural." *San Francisco Water Department* (October 1923): 5.

Starr, Kevin. *Americans and the California Dream, 1850–1915.* New York: Oxford University Press, 1985.

———. "Painterly Poet, Poetic Painter." *California Historical Quarterly* (Winter 1977/1978): 290–309.

T

The Thunderbird Remembered: Maynard Dixon, the Man and the Artist. Los Angeles: Gene Autry Western Heritage Museum and University of Washington Press, 1994.

Tolerton, Hill. "The Art of Maynard Dixon." *International Studio* (1915).

Tomananczy, Winona. "Remembrances of a Friend," In *Maynard Dixon: Images of the Native American.* San Francisco: California Academy of Sciences, 1981.

Trimble, Stephen. *The Sagebrush Ocean: A Natural History of the Great Basin.* Reno: University of Nevada Press, 1989.

"Two Painted Hangings by Maynard Dixon." *Western Arts* (November 1925).

U

Udall, Sharyn Rohlfsen. *Modernist Painting in New Mexico: 1913–1935.* Albuquerque: University of New Mexico Press, 1984.

Ulph, Owen. "Dane Coolidge: Western Writer and Photographer." *The American West* (November/December 1977): 32–35.

Unna, Warren. *The Coppa Murals.* San Francisco: The Book Club of California, 1952.

V

Van Der Zee, John. *The Gate: The True Story of the Design and Construction of the Golden Gate Bridge.* New York: Simon and Schuster, 1986.

The Visual Arts in Bohemia: 125 Years of Artistic Creativity in the Bohemian Club. San Francisco: Bohemian Club, 1997.

W

Walker, Ben Randall L. *Fresno, 1872–1885: A Municipality in the Making.* Fresno, California: Fresno County Historical Society, 1934.

Walker, Franklin. *A Literary History of Southern California.* Berkeley: University of California Press, 1950.

Wallace, Grant. *Maynard Dixon: Painter and Poet of the Far West.* San Francisco: San Francisco Art Research Project (WPA Project 2874), 1937.

Watkins, T. H., and P. R. Olmstead. *Mirror of the Dream: An Illustrated History of San Francisco.* San Francisco: Scrimshaw Press, 1976.

Westphal, Ruth, ed. *Plein Air Painters of California: The North.* Irvine, California: Westphal Publishing, 1986.

———, and Janet Blake Dominik, eds. *American Scene Painting: California, 1930s and 1940s.* Irvine, California: Westphal Publishing, 1991.

Wild, Peter, ed. *Different Travelers, Different Eyes: Artist's Narratives of the American West.* Abilene: Texas Christian University Press, 2001.

Williams, Michael. "Western Art at the Exposition." *Sunset Magazine* (August 1915): 317–26.

Wilson, Katherine. "The Murals in the State Library."

California Arts and Architecture (November 1929): 33–34, 75.

Wolfe, Bertram, D. *Diego Rivera: His Life and Times*. New York: Alfred A. Knopf, 1943.

Wood, Nancy. *Taos Pueblo*. New York: Alfred A. Knopf, 1989.

Workman, André Marechal. "Modernism and the Desert: Maynard Dixon." *Vanguard* (March 1982): 22–25.

Z

Zega, Michael E., and John E. Gruber. *Travel by Train: The American Railroad Poster, 1870–1950*. Bloomington: Indiana University Press, 2002.

Archival Materials

Charles F. Lummis Collection: Correspondence with Maynard Dixon, Braun Research Library, Southwest Museum, Los Angeles.

Dane Coolidge Collection, The Bancroft Library, University of California–Berkeley.

Maynard Dixon Biographical File, California History Section, California State Library, Sacramento.

Maynard Dixon Collection, The Bancroft Library, University of California–Berkeley.

Maynard Dixon Collection, Huntington Library, San Marino, California.

Maynard Dixon Papers, Collection of John Dixon, Palm Desert, California.

Maynard Dixon Papers, Collection of Donald J. Hagerty, Davis, California.

Maynard Dixon Scrapbook of Illustrations (7 vols.), California State Library, Sacramento.

Exhibition Catalogs (chronological)

"Manifesto," preamble in *First Exhibition of the California Society of Artists*. April 26–May 3, 1902.

The Work of Maynard Dixon. Vickery, Atkins, and Torrey. November 1–15, 1914, 265.

An Exhibition of Original Drawings by Maynard Dixon. Introduction by Porter Garnett. San Francisco: Hill Tolerton, The Print Rooms, November 16–December 1, 1914.

First Exhibition of Painting and Sculpture by California Artists. San Francisco: Golden Gate Park Memorial Museum, 1915.

Official Catalog of the Department of Fine Arts, Panama-Pacific International Exposition. San Francisco: Wahlgreen, 1915.

First Showing: Hammer and Tongs Club. Hill Tolerton, The Print Rooms, June 16–30, 1919.

Maynard Dixon. S & G Gump and Company, November 16–December 11, 1920.

Paintings of the West by Maynard Dixon. Earl Stendahl Galleries, March 5–19, 1921.

Selected Works by Western Painters: First Annual Traveling Exhibition, 1922–23. Foreword by J. Nilsen Laurvik. San Francisco: The Western Association of Art Museum Directors, 1923.

Paintings of the West by Maynard Dixon. The MacBeth Galleries, February 13–March 5, 1923.

Paintings from Tusayan and Other Recent Works by Maynard Dixon. The Biltmore Salon, February 13–27, 1924.

First Exhibition of the Painters of the West. The Biltmore Salon, May 26–June 16, 1924.

Maynard Dixon. University of California Department of Art, March 6–27, 1928, 266.

An Exhibition of Oil Paintings and Drawings by Maynard Dixon. Wichita Art Association, April 15–29, 1928.

Exhibition of the Recent Paintings by Maynard Dixon. Gump Galleries, November 20–December 11, 1933.

Thirteenth Exhibition of Contemporary American Oil Paintings. The Corcoran Gallery of Art, December 4–January 15, 1933.

Academy of Western Painters: First Annual Exhibition. Los Angeles Museum, January 1935.

Fourteenth Biennial Exhibition of Contemporary American Oil Paintings. The Corcoran Gallery of Art, March 24–May 5, 1935.

Art, Official Catalogue, Golden Gate International Exposition. San Francisco: San Francisco Bay Exposition Company, 1940.

Maynard Dixon. Biltmore Art Gallery, June 15–July 4, 1942.

Maynard Dixon. Biltmore Art Gallery, April 2–28, 1945.

Paintings of the West by Maynard Dixon. Gump Galleries, September 6–October 6, 1945.

Maynard Dixon: Painter of the West. Weston Rouge, November 3–23, 1946.

The Indians of California and the Southwest, 1895–1905: The Drawings of Maynard Dixon. Introduction by Donald J. Hagerty. Sacramento: Sacramento Science Center and Junior Museum, 1980.

Interviews (unpublished)

Ansel Adams
Daniel R. Dixon
George Post
Peter Ronstadt
Millard Sheets
Brian Thompson
Winona Tomananczy

Newspapers (period)

Los Angeles Times
Oakland Tribune
Pasadena Herald
Sacramento Bee
Sacramento Union
San Diego Union
San Francisco Call
San Francisco Chronicle
San Francisco Examiner
San Francisco News

A

A Sure Thing Pard, 74, **74** (fig. 44)
Abbey, [Edwin Austin], 62
Abieta, Juan Rey, 58, 59
Académie Julian, 30
Adams, Andy, 94
Adams, Ansel, 138, 188, 217, 219, 220, 227, 231–32, 233, 236, 237
Adams, Jones, 32
Adams, Kenneth, 200
Adams, Michael and Ann, 220
Adams, Virginia, 217, 220
Adobe Walls, Tucson, **91** (fig. 68)
Ahlstrom, Florence, 137
Ainsley Gallery, 169
Aikin, Charles Sedgwick, 71
Aitken, Robert I., 72, 76, 78, 93
Albright, Gertrude Partington, 41, 133, 138
Alford, Bert, 48
All-California Art Exhibition, 197
Alturas, **60** (fig. 33), 61
American Magazine, 89
American Scene, 193, 194, 216
Ancients, The, 145
Anderson, Anthony, 111
Andy Furuseth, 199
Anita Baldwin McClaughry, **107** (fig. 82), 108
Announcement of Maynard Dixon's Death, 237, **238** (fig. 188)
Anoakia, 16, 108, 109
Antonio, 185–86
Apache, The, 15, 88, **90** (fig. 63)
Apache Trail, 17, 160, 163
Apache Trail, The, 163, **163** (fig. 131)
Apache Trail via the Southern Pacific, The, 123, **123** (fig. 96)
Approach to Zion, 189
Archipenko, Alexander 187
Architectural League, 16, 105
Argonaut, 73, 78, 92, 98, 161
Argus, The, 162, 164, 168
Arrival of Fremont in California, The, 18, 192
Arizona Biltmore Hotel, 17, 171, 172
Arizona Highways, 68, 230, 236, **236** (fig. 187), 237
Arizona Inn, Tucson, 228
Arizona Nights, 105

Arizona State Museum, 228
Arizona Veterans Memorial Coliseum, Phoenix, 237
Arroyo Seco, 92
Art Barn, 207
Art Digest, 175, 216
Art Journal, The, 27
Art Students League (NYC), 18, 105
Art Students League (SF), 200–1, 211
Artist's Cooperative Gallery, 199, 201
Artist's Council, 156
Artists of Southern California, 169
Atherton, Gertrude, 43, 71, 89, 179
Atkins, Arthur, 39
Atlantic Monthly, 71
Austin, Charles P., 156
Austin, Mary, 13, 15, 37, 49–50, 71, 77–78, 89, 92, 101, 113, **142** (fig. 114), 143, 155, 157, 181–82
Automobile Club of Southern California, 180

B

Balch, F. H., 71
Baldwin, E. J. "Lucky," 108
Baldwin [McClaughry], Anita, 16, 17, **107** (fig. 82), 108, 110, 143, 146–47, 157, 187
Baltimore Museum of Art, 216
Bandelier, Adolf, 68
Bar-20 Days, 16, 103, **103** (fig. 80)
Bar Cross Edition of the Works of Eugene Manlove Rhodes, 190
Barker Brothers Building, 17, 159, 160
Barrows, Albert, 201
Basin and Range, 167
Beal, Gifford, 116
Bearhead and Constance Dixon, **128** (fig. 102), 129
Beaux, Cecilia, 117
Beery, Noah, 170
Before the Gringo Came, 78
Belli, Melvin, 8
Bellows, George, 95, 96, 98, 116
Ben Blair, 15, 80
Bender, Albert, 138, 187
Benton, Arthur B., 111
Between the Rocks, 81
Bien Venido y Adios, 165, **167** (fig. 136)
Bierce, Ambrose, 31, 48, 72, 73, 98

Biltmore Salon [Galleries], Los Angeles, 17, 157, 168, 197, 223, 228
Bisttram, Emil, 181
Black Mesa at Evening, 145
Black Mesa at Sunset, 146
Black, Winifred, 48, 79–80
Blackfeet Indian Agency, Browning, Montana, **128** (fig. 101), 129
Blair, Lee, 197
Blue Moon, 101
Blumenschein, Ernest L., 15, 94, 105, 181
Bohemian Club, 15, 16, 17, 29, 72, 73, 76, 100, 120, 131, 143, 177
Book Club of California, 157
Borein, Edward, 10, 15, 31, 37, 59, 61, 62, 93, 94, 170
Borg, Carl Oscar, 117, 133, 156, 170
Borglum, John Gutzon, 30, 93
Boulder Dam, 18, 194–95, 198
Bowley, George Hollins and Joan, 142
Boyles, Kate, 102
Boynton, Ray, 164, 178
Bradley, LaVerne, 199, 205
Bradley family/home, 205, **205** (fig. 162)
Brady, Cyrus Townsend, 15, 102
Brandt, Rex, 200
Brangwyn, Frank, 164
Brave Dog Society, 129
Breaking a Hobbled Bronco, 74
Bret Harte Jinks, 72, **72** (fig. 43)
Bremer, Anne M., 117, 133, 175
Breuer, Henry J., 117
Bridge of the Gods, The, 71
Brigham Young University, 18, 208
"Bronco New Year," 14
Bronson, Edgar Beecher, 15, 92, 102
Brooklyn Institute of Arts, 17
Bruce, Edward, 193
Bruce, Patrick, 95
Bryce Canyon National Park, 18, 232
Buck Peters, Ranchman, 103
Buff, Conrad, 17, 50, 173, 197, 217, 237
Bull, W. H., 62, 117
Burbank, Elbridge Ayer, 68, 70
Burchfield, Charles, 180
Bureau of Indian Affairs, 18, 211, 219
Burgess, Gelett, 39, 71, 72, 73, 78, 93
Butler, Frank, 95
Bynner, Witter, 155, 157

C

Cahill, Arthur, 41, 93
Cahill, E. Holger, 193
California Art Today, 215
California Group of Contemporary
  American Artists, The, 16, 133
California Landmarks Club, 36
California, Pais de Sol, 162
California Palace of the
  Legion of Honor, 177
California Rural Rehabilitation
  Administration, 199
California School of Design,
  14, 28, 29, 30
California School of Fine Arts,
  16, 133, 165, 176, 197
California Society of Artists,
  15, 62, 63, 123
California State Exhibition, 216
California State Fair (1928), 17, 170
California State Library, 17, 22,
  31, **164** (fig. 132), 169, 170,
  170–71 (fig. 137), 172, 222
Calipatria, 217, **218** (fig. 171)
Campbell, Blendon, 62
Cannell and Chaffin Gallery, 152
Canoga Park Post Office, 18, 210, 226
Canyon de Chelly, 119,
  119 (fig. 91), 189
Canyon del Muerto, 149, **150** (fig. 124)
Capitol Reef National Monument,
  18, **232** (fig. 183), 232
Carlsen, Emil, 8, 29, 30, 117
Carrillo, Leo, 95
Carroll, Lewis, 78
Carson, Kit, 162, 192, 201, 220
Carson, Nevada, 133, **134** (fig. 106)
Cattle Drive, 213, **214** (fig. 167)
Cattleman, The, 15, 88, **90** (fig. 64)
Cavalier, 93
Cavern of the Dead, The, **40** (fig. 14), 41
Central Nevada, **224** (fig. 175), 226
*Centre of Creation at 122 Degrees in
  the Shade, The*, 52, **52** (fig. 22)
Century Magazine, 13, 92, 93
Cézanne, Paul, 200
Chamberlain, Hans, 228
Chamberlin, F. Tolles, 197
Chase, William Merritt, 100, 116
Chicago Art Gallery, 169
Chicago Art Institute, 145
Chicago Field Museum, 145
Chollas Against the Mountain, 233
Circle of Shimaikuli, 157
City That Was, The, 43
Clapp, William H., 116, 133
Clark, Herald R., 208, 237
Clay Smith Shop, 228
Cleaveland, Agnes Morley, 92
Cloud World, 169, 170
Clouds and Mesa, 147, **147** (fig. 118)

Clouds of Hopi Land, **146** (fig. 117), 147
Club Beaux Arts, 17
Coca-Cola, **122** (fig. 94), 123
Cody, William F. (Buffalo Bill), 95
Cole, George T., 156
Coleman, Oregon, **60** (figs. 34, 35), 61
Collier, John, 157
Collier, John, Jr., 184
Collier's, 13, 71, 93
Colton, Harold, 63
Colusa Sun, 34
Coming of Cassidy, The, 16, 103
Commercial Artists' Guild, 211
Como No (Sophie Treadwell),
  125 (fig. 98), 126
Contemporary American
  Exhibition, 215–16
*Continent's End: An Anthology
  of Contemporary Poets*, 157
Cook Museum, 121
Coolbrith, Ina, 71, 73, 157
Coolidge, Dane, 13, 15, 16, **95**
  (fig. 71), 96, 102, 103, 104,
  105, 107, 113, 115, 117, 127
Coppa, Joseph "Papa," 77, 78, 121, 187
Coppa Restaurant, 84, **85** (fig. 56)
Coppa's restaurant(s), 15, 73, 76, 77, 78,
  82, 84–85, 187, 209, **210** (fig. 164)
Coppa's Restaurant Menu,
  209, **210** (fig. 164)
Coppa, Victor, 187
Cooper, Colin Campbell, 116
Corbin, Alice, 132, 155, 182
Corcoran Gallery of Art, 18, 175
Corner, James, 149
Corner of the Room, The, 43, **44** (fig. 16)
Cornwell, Dean, 164
Corral Dust, 120
Cosmopolitan, 15, 79
Cottonwoods of Carson,
  218, **221** (fig. 172)
Cravens, Junius, 161
Crocker, H. S., 132
Crockett, Davey, 220
Culin, Stewart, 68
Cummings, Byron, 143
Cummings, Earl, 29
Cuneo, Rinaldo, 133, 138, 200
Cunningham, Imogen, 137, 138,
  161, 187, 188, 199, 202, 237
Curly Bear, 129

D

Dane Coolidge, **95** (fig. 71), 96
Daniel Dixon's Birth Announcement,
  159, **159** (fig. 129)
Dante [Alighieri], 78
Danysh, Joseph, 207
Dark Cloud, 95, 121–22
Dasburg, Andrew, 180
Davenport, Homer, 31, 41

Davis, Robert, 145–46
Davis, Stuart, 121
Dawn, Coronado, **27** (fig. 6)
Day, Sam, 68–69, 80
Deer Heaven, 174, 175
Degas, Edgar, 200
Del Monte Art Gallery, 15, 87, 169
Del Mue, Maurice, 117, 123, 133
Delafield Affair, The, 15
Demarest, "Pop," 138
Demas, Don, 38
Demas, Santiago, 38
Demuth, Charles, 121
Denison, Lindsay, 95
Departing Glory, 117
Department of the Interior, 18, 211, 219
Desert Hill, 169
Desert Magazine, 217
Desert Peaks and River Bottom,
  231 (fig. 183), 232
Desert Ranges, Roberts Ranch,
  53 (fig. 23), 54
"Desert Series," 224–26
Desert Shepherdess, 145, 157
Desert Shower, 87
Desert, The, 49
*Design Study of the Golden Gate
  Bridge*, 178, 179 (fig. 146)
Destination Unknown, 216
DeVoto, Bernard, 96
Dike, Phil, 197, 200
Dilley, Perry, 11
Dirks, Rudolph, 144
Dixon, Constance (daughter), 15, 16,
  103, 112, 114, 117, 119, 126–27, **127**
  (fig. 99), **128** (fig. 102), 129, 137,
  138, 139–40, 142, 161, 184, 210
Dixon, Constance (sister). *See*
  Duncan, Constance Dixon
Dixon, Constance Maynard (mother),
  23–25, **24** (fig. 5), 27, 28
Dixon, Daniel Rhodes (son), 10, 17,
  98, 157, 159, **159** (fig. 129), 165,
  173–74, 181, 182, 185, 186, **187** (fig.
  149), 189, 199, 202, 204, 207, 218
Dixon, Harry St. John (brother),
  156, 176
Dixon, Harry St. John (father),
  14, 20–25, **20** (fig. 2), 26, 27
Dixon, Henry St. John (great-
  grandfather), 19
Dixon, John (great-great-grandfather), 19
Dixon, John Eaglefeather (son),
  17, 169, 173–74, 181, 182, 186,
  189, 199, 207, 218, 227–28
Dixon, Julia Phillips (grandmother), 19
Dixon, (Lafayette) Maynard: images of,
  9, **9** (fig. 1); 79, **79** (fig. 49); 88, **89**
  (fig. 61); 92, **93**, (fig. 69), **97** (fig. 73),
  98; life events of, 14–18; describing
  his grandfather, 19–20; ancestry of,

19–21; early life of, 23–28, **24** (fig. 5); artistic beginnings of, 29–50; as an illustrator, 31, 161; and his personal vision, 51, **51 (fig. 21)**; impressions of the Navajo and their environment, 68, 69; and the bohemian lifestyle, 72–78; and Lillian West Tobey, 79–80; in the San Francisco earthquake and fire, 82–85; living back East, 92–106; impression of Charles M. Russell, 94–95; influenced by Eugene Manlove Rhodes, 98; and exaggerated western fiction, 105–6; in his New York studio, 106, **106** (fig. 81); and encouragement of Anita Baldwin, 108; interpreting the old life of the Indian, 110; on painting real nature, 111–12; on taking the family to Arizona, 115; and postimpressionism, 131; natural responses vs. modern art, 134; failed marriage to Tobey, 121–22; moving into the New West, 136; marriage to Lange, 137–18; mystical attachment to the Hopi, 150–52; dogma on painting murals, 156; relying on nature in drawing, 160; and "fancy life," 161; and mural work, **164** (fig. 132), 165; on modern art, 168–69, 177–78, 180; lecturing on mural art, 170; rationale for poetry, 170–71; on *Shapes of Fear*, 176; opinion of Diego Rivera, 176; on Antonio, 186; on Group f/64, 188–89; and PWAP, 192–97; and *Sunset Magazine*, 194; on San Francisco/Los Angeles art styles and philosophies, 197–98; on Everett Ruess, 200; on Art Students League, 201; and his failed marriage to Lange, 202; and Lange influence on art, 205; and Depression-era drawings, 206; his personal synthesis, 206; response to book on Depression, 208; paintings purchased by BYU, 208; marriage to Hamlin, 208–9; nervous breakdown and convalescence of, 209, **210** (fig. 163); on San Francisco art scene, 211; explaining U.S. dealings with Indian tribes, 211–13; on Dust Bowl refugees, 219–220; on his decisions about modern art, 233–35; death of, 237–38
Dixon Family, Northern Arizona, 117, **119** (fig. 90)
Dixon, Maynard, poetry: **42–43**, 75, **81–82**, 84, 89, **104**, **110**, **112–13**, **114**, **119–20**, **126–37**, **130–31**, **140**, **145**, 155, 157, **184**, **192**, **197**, **200**, 237, **202–4**, **204**
Dixon, Rebecca (sister), 78
Dixon, Richard (grandfather),

19–21, 24, 25
Dobie, J. Frank, 219, 222
Doran, George H., 112
Douglas, William B., 143
Doxey, William, 39
Drouth, 55
Dreiss, Hazel, 187
Drury, Wells, 34
du Bois, Guy Pené, 180
DuMond, Frank Vincent, 94, 116
Duncan, Charles Stafford, 133, 180, 197
Duncan, Charles Walter, 123, 178, 179
Duncan, Constance Dixon, 123
Duncan, Isadora, 96
Düsseldorf genre school, 100
Duveneck, Frank, 116

E

Eagle's Roost, 169
Earth (Ploughed Land), 213
Earth Knower, 216
East and West, 86
École de Beaux-Arts, 77
Edge of the Mesa, 81
Edwards, John Paul, 188
Edwards, Mary Jeanette, 199
El Alisal, 37, 50, 79, 97, 134, 170
El Paso and Southwestern Railroad, 79
Elder, Paul, 89, 169
Elements of Nevada, 208
Elkus, Albert, 187
Emerson, Edwin, Colonel, 89
End House of Walpi, The, 156, 157
Envoy of Peace, 109, **109** (fig. 84), 110
Erosion, 140, **141** (fig. 110)
Eugene Manlove Rhodes, 96, **97** (fig. 72)
Everybody's Magazine, 95
Exhibition of Modern French Painting, 200
Eytel, Carl, 50

F

Fairbanks, Douglas, 170
Fall, Albert B., 97
Father Sun, 171, **172** (fig. 139)
Fechin, Nicolai, 197, 217
Federal Art Project (FAP), 193, 207, 210
Feitelson, Lorser, 180, 200
Fewkes, Jesse Walter, 68, 143
Field, Charles K., 85
Field, Sara Bard, 138, 170
Fields of Toquerville, 189
Fire and Earthquake, 83, **83** (fig. 52)
First Annual Horse Show, 115 (fig. 85), 116
Fisher, Bud, 48
Fisher, Harrison, 41, 93
Flathead Indian Reservation, 15, **97** (fig. 73), 98, **99** (fig. 74)
Fogel, Seymour, 210
Foote, Mary Halleck, 31

Forbes, Helen, 138
Forgotten Man, 199
"Forgotten Man and Strike"/ series, 18, 186, 198, 199
Forsyth, Victor Clyde, 50, 156, 217
Fort Miller, California, 21, **21** (fig. 3)
Fortune, E. Charlton, 117
Foster and Kleiser, 16, 122–24, 132, 138, 159, 182, 213
Francisca Reina, 15, 98
Frank Hoffman and Constance Dixon, 127, **127** (fig. 99)
Free Speech, 199
Fremont, John C., 162
Fresno, **22** (fig. 4)
Frieseke, Frederick Carl, 117
Frink, Henry, Reverend, 137
Frontier Ballads, 102
"Frontier Pants" series, 232

G

Galerie Beaux Arts, 17, 168, 169, 172, 175, 176, 178, 182, 201
Ganado, 64, **65** (fig. 38)
Ganado Mucho (Many Cattle), 65, 66
Garber, Daniel, 116
Garland, Hamlin, 68, 71
Garnett, Porter, 39, 72, 76, 77, 78, 85, 132, 237
Garrett, Pat, 62, 97
Gauguin, Paul, 300
Gaw, William, 200
Gay, August, 116
Genius of the West, The, 71, **71** (fig. 42)
Genthe, Arnold, 76, 77, 85, 87, 93, 137
Gerstle, William, 176, 187
Ghost Eagle, 109
Ghost People, 175, 176
Gibney, Luke, 207
Gibson, Charles Dana, 94
Gile, Selden, 116, 200
Gillis, Mabel, 222
Glacier National Park, 16, 126, 130
Glackens, William, 180
Goddess of the Wheat, The, 79, **80** (fig. 51)
Goethe, [Johann Wolfgang von], 78
Goldberg, Rubin (Rube), 41
Golden Age of Illustration, 13, 93
Golden Gate Bridge project, 17, 178, 179, **179** (fig. 146)
Golden Gate International Exposition, 18, 213–15, 216–17
Golden Gate Memorial Museum, 120
Grabhorn, Edwin and Robert, 152, 172–73, 187
Grand Canyon of the Colorado, 18, 237
Grassland (aka *Rain*), 18, 213
Great Basin, 165, **166** (fig. 134), 167, **167** (fig. 135)
Great Depression, 11, 13, 17, 174,

175, 185, 186, 190–99, **191** (figs. 152, 153, 154), 206
Great Northern Railway, 16, 126, 130
Grebs, Emil, 133
Green, Will S., 34
Greene, Charles S., 31
Grey, Zane, 105
Grim Wall, The, 156, 157
Grimsley, Chick, 126
Griswold, Mary Edith, 78, 83, 89
Group f/64, 188
Grove Plays of the Bohemian Club, The, 16, 132
Guaranty Building and Loan Association, 17, 173
Guard of the Cornfield, 145
Gump, S & G, 16, 121, 138, 189, 228

H

Haddock, Arthur, 174
Hall, James, 54–55
Hall, Sharlot, 37, 54–55, 71
Hall, Wilbur, 11
Hamlin, Edith, 18, 201–2, 208–9, 217–20, 225–30, 232, 237–38
Hammer and Tongs Club, 16, 133
Hamptons, 13, 93
Hanna, Forman, 117
Hanna, Phil Townsend, 180
Hansen, Armin C., 8, 117, 133, 152, 157
Hanson, Joseph Mills, 102
Harper's, 27, 28
Harper's Weekly, 15, 55, 62
Harriman, E. H., 83–84, 170
Harrington, Gwyneth, 225–26
Hart, William S., 170
Harte, Bret, 31, 73
Hartley, Marsden, 121
Hassam, Childe, 116
Hazard, Arthur, 156
Hearst, George, 47
Hearst, William Randolph, 14, 47–48, 49, 164
Heil, Walter, Dr., 193, 197
Helgesen's Galleries, 132
Henderson, Randall, 217
Henderson, William Penhallow, 132, 155, 182
Henly, Frank, 88
Henri, Robert, 15. 94, 95, 96, 98
Henry, O., 13, 102
Herriman, George, 144
Herter, Albert, 164
Heyman, Therese Thau, 206
Hidden Water, 15, 96, 102
Higgins, Victor, 181
Hill, Louis W., 130
Hill, Thomas, 44, 72
Hills at Indian Springs, 195, **196** (fig. 156)

Hilton, John, 217
Hittell, John S., 72
Hittell, Theodore, 72
Hobart, Clark, 152
Hodge, Frederick Webb, 237
Hoffman, Elwyn, 48, 57
Hoffman, Frank, 16, 126, 127, **127** (fig. 99), 129, 181
Holder, Preston, 199
Home of the Desert Rat, 233
Home of Tucson, 233, **234** (fig. 185)
"Homeless Man" paintings, 210
Homesteaders, The, 102
Honolulu Academy of Arts, 17, 178
Hopalong Cassidy, 13, 15, 16, 102, **103** (figs. 79, 80), 105
Hopi Ceremonial, **46** (fig. 18), 47
Hopi Girl, 44, **45** (fig. 17)
Hopi Indians, 63, 64, 147–49, 151
Hopi Reservation, 146
Hop Story Teller, 149, **149** (fig. 123)
Hopper, Edward, 95, 180
Hopper, James "Jimmy," 76, 77, 85, 93
Hotel Ben Lomond Gallery, 207
Hotel Bigelow Gallery, 169
Hough, Emerson, 62, 94, 100, 101
Houghton Mifflin, 48
Houston, Sam, 220
Howard, John Langley, 178
Hubbell, John Lorenzo, 15, 17, 64, 65–67, **66** (fig. 39), 70, 78, 80, 83, 86, 88, 100, 103, 117, 119, 149, 180
Hubbell, Lina, 180
Hubbell, Roman, 180
Hubbell's Trading Post, 15, 64, 66, **67** (fig. 40); National Historic Site, 70, 87
Hudson, Grace, 41
Hunter, Leslie, 62

I

Iesaka Waken, 145, 157
Illustrated Letter to Emerson Hough, 101, **101** (fig. 77)
Imperial Valley, 217, **218** (fig. 170)
In Miners Mirage Land, 49
In Navajo Land, 81
In Old Tucson, 88, **91** (fig. 65)
In the Dust, 117, **119** (fig. 89)
In Zion, 194
Indian and Soldier, 211, **212** (fig. 165), 213
Indian and Teacher, 211, **212** (fig. 166), 213
Indian Defense Association, 157
Indian Hall, Anoakia, 16, **108** (fig. 83), 109, **109** (fig. 84), 110–12, 114
Indian on Horseback, 74, **75** (fig. 45)
Indian Sign, **31** (fig. 8), 33
Indian Today, The, 18, 211
Indian Yesterday, The, 18, 211

Injun Babies, 17, 152
International Business Machines (IBM), 18, 216–17
International Studio, 16, 120
Inyo Mountains, 232, **232** (fig. 184)
Irrigation, 15, 88
Irwin, Wallace, 93
Irwin, Will, 43, 72, 93, 132
Isleta, New Mexico, 57, **57** (fig. 30)
Isleta Pueblo, 58, 71, 149
Isley Gallery, 189

J

Jackass Meadows, **32** (fig. 9), 33
Jackling, D. C., 121
James, George Wharton, 49
Jeffers, Robinson, 157
Jim Beckwourth, 229, **229** (fig. 180)
Jinks Room, Anoakia, 16, 108, 112, 114
John C. Fremont High School, 18, 192
Johns, Cloudesley, 48
Johnson, Frank Tenny, 156
Johnson, Willard "Spud," 155
Joullin, Amedee, 8
Joy of the Chinese New Year, 47, **47** (fig. 19)
Joynt, John, 225
Jugend, 49, 81
Jury of Awards, Bohemian Club Dinner, 116, **116** (fig. 86)

K

Kahlo, Frida, 177
Kahn, Irving and Beatrice, Bookplate, 152, **154** (fig. 127)
Kant, [Immanuel], 78
Kayenta, Arizona, 143, **143** (fig. 115)
Keep Moving, 199
Keith, William, 44, 72, 85, 87, 116
Kelly, Florence, 15
Kennedy, Norman, 164
Kent, Rockwell, 95, 98, 190
Kibbey, John, 160
Kilpatrick, Aaron, 156
Kipling, Rudyard, 43
Kistler, Aline, 172
Kit Carson Café, 18, 201, **202** (fig. 159), **203** (fig. 160)
Knibbs, Henry Herbert, 157, 170
Kopta, Emry, 149
Krutch, Joseph Wood, 233
Kuhn, Walt, 121
Kuniyoshi, Yasuo, 180
Kyne, Peter B., 16, 107, 109, 112

L

Labaudt, Lucien, 138, 177
Labor Despair, 190, **191** (fig. 152)
Labor Progress, 190, **191** (fig. 153)
Lafler, Harry, 78, 85

Laguna Pueblo, 71
Lake McDonald, Montana, 16
Lake Tahoe, Tallac Lodge,
  142 (fig. 113), 143
Land of Little Rain, The, 49–50
Land of Poco Tiempo, The, 36
Land of Purple Shadows, The, 15, 102
Land of Sunshine, 14, 35, 37, 41, 45,
  51, 54, 92, 97; *see also* Out West
Land of Titled Mesas, 233
Lang Galleries, Florence Rand, 233
Lange, Dorothea, 11, 13, 16, 17, 18,
  137–40, 142–44, 145–47, 152, 157,
  159, 161, 165, 173–74, 177, 180–81,
  182, 184, 186, 187, 188–89, 192, 198–
  99, 200, 202, 204, 206–7, 211, 218
Lange, Martin, 142, 194
Lark, The, 14, 39, 41, 73
Last Gleam, **225** (fig. 177), 226
Laughing Horse, 155
Laurvik, J. Nilsen, 133
Law and Disorder, 199
Lawrence, D. H., 155
Lawson, Ernest, 116
Lazy Boy, 129
Leaves of Grass, 17, 172–73
LeConte, Joseph, 72
Lee, Don, 152
Ledge of Sunland, 145
*Legend of Earth and Son,
  The*, 17, 171, **172**
Leigh, William R., 144
Lentala of the South Seas, 98
Les Jeunes, 39, 77
Life, 13, 93
Lillibridge, Will, 80
Lillie, Gordon (Pawnee Bill), Major, 95
Limited Editions Club, 18, 228
Little Knight of the "X Bar B," The, 102
Little Sister, 81
Little Sister, 130, **130** (fig. 105)
Lo-To-Kah, 14, 41
Lockett, Clay, 233
Loeb, Joseph, 152, 157, 209
Loeb, Margaret Loeb, Bookplate,
  152, **153** (fig. 126)
Logan, Maurice, 116, 133
Loma Himna, 147–49, **148** (fig. 119)
London, Jack, 13, 14, 48, 71, 72, 73, 89
Lone Hopi Priest, **148** (fig. 121), 149
Lone Pine, **173** (figs. 141, 142),
  174, back endsheet
Lone Trail, The, 106
Longhorns, The, 219
Loom of the Desert, The, 15, 89, 94
Lorentz, Pare, 206
*Lorenzo Hubbell's Trading Post,
  Ganado*, 66, 67 (fig. 40)
Los Angeles Art Association, 197
Los Angeles County Museum

of Art, 18, 236
Los Angeles Daily Times, 86
Los Angeles Examiner, 110
Los Angeles Public Library, 17, 164
Los Angeles Times, 36, 110,
  111, 164, 185
Lost Borders, 113
Louis, Parley, 73–74
Luhan, Mabel Dodge, 155, 182
Luks, George, 180
Lummis, Charles F., 14, 15, 17, 35–37,
  35 (fig. 12), 41, 42, 44–46, 49, 50,
  51, 54–55, 56, 57–58, 59, 62, 63,
  68, 69, 71, 79, 85, 92, 97, 106, 110,
  112, 115, 117, 121, 126, 132, 134,
  149, 157, 159, 170, 171, 209
Lummis, Turbese, 209
Luncheon Club, San Francisco
  Stock Exchange, 176
Lundborg, Florence, 39, 117

M

M. H. de Young Museum,
  120, 188, 193, 195, 197
Macbeth Gallery, 17, 98, 145, 156
Macbeth, Robert, 145, 150, 156
MacDonald–Wright, Stanton, 180
Mack Popular Prize, Harold L., 17, 175
Macky, Constance, 178
Macky, E. Spencer, 133, 197
Macy, George, 228–29
"Malamute Kid," 14, 48
Man with a Hoe . . . , 48
Manyhorses, 180
Marin, John, 121
Mark Hopkins Hotel, 17, 160, 163, 169
Mark Hopkins Institute of Art,
  14, 15, 29, 30, 74, 85
Mark Hopkins Review of Art, 74
Markham, Edwin, 48, 62
Martinez, California, Post Office, 209
Martinez, Xavier, 8, 15, 29, 30,
  37, 44, 62, 73, 76–77, 78–79,
  83, **83** (fig. 53), 85, 87, 133
Mary Austin Lecture Announcement,
  142 (fig. 114), 143
Matarango Peak, Inyo, 145
Mathews, Lucia K., 117, 133
Matoaka, 19
Mathews, Arthur F., 8, 30,
  44, 62, 87, 116, 133
Matisse, Henri, 121, 200
Maule, Mary K., 102
Maynard Dixon, 9, **9** (fig. 1), 92, **93**
  (fig. 69), 233, **235** (fig. 186)
*Maynard Dixon and Daniel
  Dixon*, 185, **187** (fig. 149)
*Maynard Dixon in His New York
  Studio*, 106, **106** (fig. 81)
Maynard Dixon, Montana,

97 (fig. 73), 98
Maynard Dixon, Painter of the West, 236
*Maynard Dixon Painting Kit Carson
  Café Mural*, 201, **203** (fig. 160)
*Maynard Dixon Painting Tucson
  Murals in His Studio*, front
  jacket, 88, **89** (fig. 61)
Maynard Dixon Self-Portrait,
  2, **227** (fig. 179), 228
*Maynard Dixon, Tehachapi
  Mountains*, 174, **175** (fig. 144)
*Maynard Dixon Working on
  The Pageant of Tradition*,
  164 (fig. 132), 169
*Maynard Dixon, Xavier Martinez,
  and Friends*, 79, **79** (fig. 49)
Maynard Dixon's Easel,
  128 (fig. 103), 129
McArthur, Arthur Chase, 171
McClaughry, Anita Baldwin. *See*
  Baldwin [McClaughry], Anita
McClure's, 13, 71, 93
McClurg, A. C., 15, 80, 102–3
McComas, Francis, 116
McEwan, Arthur, 48
McGee, W. J., 62
McGraw, R. F., 229, **229** (fig. 181)
*McGraw, R. F. McGraw,
  Bookplate*, 229, **229** (fig. 181)
McKinney, Roland, 216
McPhee, John, 167
McTeague, 48
Medicine Owl, 129
Melchers, Gari, 116
Men and Mountains, 182, 189
Metcalf, Willard L., 117
Merging of Spring and Winter, 175, 178
Migrant worker project, 18
Miles, Nelson, General, 68
Miller, Barse, 200
Miller, Joaquin, 71, 72, 73
Millier, Arthur, 164–65, 185,
  210–11, 223, 237
Mills College, 172
Mills, William R., 126
Moeur, Benjamin B., 117
Mohave Desert, 169
Monet, Claude, 200
Monson, Frederick I., 63
Montana, 15, 16
Monterey, California, 15
Moody, Charles Stuart, Dr., 98
Moon Over the Desert, 169
Moonlight Over Zion, 189
Montezuma's Castle, 55, **55** (fig. 25)
Moqui, 81
Moqui Priest of Oraibi, 74
Mordecai: George Washington,
  26, 32, 189; Julia, 26
Morey, Robert, 208

Morrow, Irving Foster, 178
Morrow, William C., 98
Mountain and Meadow,
   129 (fig. 104), 130
Mountain Men, 194, **195** (fig. 155)
Moving, 83, **83** (fig. 52)
Mrs. Black, 174, **174** (fig. 143)
Muir, John, 13, 71, 72
Mulford, Clarence E., 13, 15, 16, 102–3
Mulford, Prentice, 72, 73
Murrieta's Gold, 59, **59** (fig. 32)
Mystery Stone, 145, 157

N

Nahl, Charles, 222
Nahl, Perham, 117
Namoki, 147–48, **148** (fig. 119)
Nampeyo, 66
Nappenbach, Henry, 41
Nash, Willard, 155, 180
National Academy of Design,
   New York, 16, 17, 18, 100, 105,
   106, 145, 186–87, 193, 208
National Museum of American
   Art, Washington, D.C., 187
Nature Smiles, 216–17
Navajo Country, 105
Navajo Indian from Life, 15, 73, 117
Navajo Indians, 64–70, 73, 80, 180
Navajo Journey, 106, **106** (fig. 81)
Navajo Reservation, 143
Navajo Woman, 74–75, 81
Navajo Women, 115, 121
Navajoland, 188
Navajos, The, 143
Navajos Traveling, 121
Navajos, Tuba Arizona,
   144, **144** (fig. 116)
Neilson, Charles P., 62, 63
Nelson, Bruce, 117, 152
Nepperham, New York, 15
Neuhaus, Eugen, 30, 87, 116, 213–14
Nevada, **189** (fig. 150)
New Deal, 192–94
New Mexico Juniper, 182, **183** (fig. 148)
*New San Francisco Emergency
   Edition,* 83, **84** (fig. 54)
New York Society of Illustrators, 16, 105
New York World's Fair, 18, 216–17, 219
Newberry, Perry, 78
Newspaper Artists League, 15, 75
Nez Perce Indians, 98
Nietzsche, [Friedrich], 78
No Place to Go, 199
Noguchi, Yone, 39
Norris, Kathleen, 71
Norris, Charles G., 71
Norris, Frank, 48, 72, 73
Noskowiak, Sonya, 188

O

O'Connell, Daniel, 72
O'Keeffe, Georgia, 146, 217
Oakley, Annie, 95
Oakland, Antioch, and
   Eastern Railroad, 123
Oakland Art League, 17, 169
Oakland Technical High
   School, 17, 162
Octopus, The, 48
Okie Camp, 195, **196** (fig. 157)
Old Adobe by Moonlight, **91,** (fig. 66)
Old Adobe, Monterey, **99** (fig. 76), 100
*Old Barracks, Santa Fe, New
   Mexico,* **58** (fig. 31)
Old Beaver Woman, 129
Old Lady White Calf, 129
Old Stingy, 129
Older, Fremont, 138
Oldfield, Otis, 10, 138, 176, 200
On the Corral Fence, 74
On the Plains, **127** (fig. 100), 129
Oregon, Cowboy, 61, **61** (fig. 36)
Oregon Trail, The, 18, 228–29, 233
Orozco, José Clemente, 194
Orr Gallery, Frank C., 138, 210
Osage, The, 215, **215** (fig. 169)
Otis, Harrison Gray, 36
Out West, 71, 92
Outdoor Life, **93**
Outing, 71
Over the Border, 124
Overland Monthly, 13, 14, 31, 32, 33, **33**
   (figs. 10, 11), 34, 36, 39, 41, 43, 48, 98
Owen Heavy Breast, 129

P

Pack Train, 134, **135** (fig. 107)
Pacific Monthly, 71, 86
Pacific Mail Steamship, 16, 17, 140
Pacific Southwest Exposition, 17, 169
Pacifica, 213
Pageant of Tradition, 17, **164** (fig.
   132), 169, 170, **170–71** (fig. 137)
Pages, Jules, 116
Painters and Sculptors of
   Southern California, 208
Painters of the West, 17, 156–57
Paintings of the West by Maynard
   Dixon, Gump Galleries, 233
Palette and Brush Club, 228
Palomino Mare, The, 115, 121
Palomino Ponies, 18, 226, **226** (fig. 178)
Panama-Pacific International
   Exposition, 16, 29, 115, 121, 213
Park, David, 200
Parker, Forrest, 81
Parker, Lawton S., 117
Parkman, Francis, 228–29
Parrish, Maxfield, 94

Parshall, DeWitt, 157
Parshall, Douglas, 157
Parsons, A. W., 164
Partington, Gertrude. See Albright,
   Gertrude Partington
Partridge, Roi, 123, 137, 138,
   161, 187, 202, 237
Partridge, Rondal, 161, 189
Pate, Juan, 38
Patigian, Haig, 74, 177, 179
Pattern of Butte and Cloud,
   230, **230** (fig. 182)
Payne, Edgar, 156
Pearson's, 13, 93
Peixotto, Ernest, 39, 41
Penelo, 85
Pennsylvania Academy of Arts, 17
Peters, Charles Rollo, 72, 87
Pflueger, Timothy, 176
Phillips, Bert, 68
Phoenix, **56** (fig. 26), 57
Phoenix, Arizona Territory,
   56 (fig. 27), 57
Piazzoni, Gottardo F. P., 8, 10, 29, 30,
   31, 62, 76, 77, 87, 133, 138, 152
Picasso, Pablo, 121
Pickel, Mart, 95
Pictures of Today, 199
Pierce Arrow, 123, **123** (fig. 95)
Pierce's Print Room, Gerry, 228
Pima Village, 57, **57** (fig. 29)
Pine Street Studio, 43, **44** (fig. 15)
Pioneers, The, 112
Piute Indian, **31** (fig. 7), 32
Ploughed Land (aka *Earth*),
   18, 213, **214** (fig. 168)
Plow That Broke the Plains, The, 206–7
Poems and Seven Drawings, 17, 152
Poetry, 132
Pogany, William, 164
Polk, Willis, 39, 109, 156
Pony Boy, 157
Pool, The, 109
Poole, Nelson, 178
Poor, Henry Varnum, 133
Porter, Bruce, 39
Post, George, 200
Prairie Shower, 146
Presidio Junior High School, 207
Press Club, 15
Prisoners, The, 124, **124** (fig. 97)
Prospector, The, 15, 88, **90** (fig. 62)
Prospectors, **95** (fig. 70), 96
Proud Sheriff, The, 198
Pueblo Indians, 159
Public Works of Art Project (PWAP),
   18, 192, 193, 194, 207
Putnam, Arthur, 62, 72
Putnam, G. P., 152
Pyle, Howard, 94

R

Rain (Grassland), 213
Rain in "Dobe Town," 117, **118** (fig. 88)
Rain Wind, 133
Rainbow Ridge, Nevada,
  165, **167** (fig. 135)
Raleigh, Harry, 93
Ranch House on the Plains,
  140, **141** (fig. 111)
Ranchero, Guadalajara, 79, **80** (fig. 50)
Ranchero of Old California,
  76, **76** (fig. 48)
Randolph, Lee, 133
Randsburg, 222, **223** (fig. 173)
Ranger, Henry Ward, 17, 187
Raphael, Joseph, 29, 117, 133, 200
Recuerdo de Guadalajara, 81
Red-Blooded Heroes of the
  Frontier, The, 15, 102
Red Butte with Mountain Men,
  201, **202** (fig. 159)
Red Paint Restaurant, 121, **121** (fig. 92)
Redfield, E. W., 116
Redmond, Granville, 29
Reed, Verner Z., 14, 41
Refuge, 16, 21, 32, 140, 142, 189
Reiss, Winold, 233
Remington, Frederic, 14,
  28, 34, 113, 234
Reminiscences of a Ranchman, 102
Renoir, Pierre-Auguste, 200
Rhodes: Eugene Manlove, 13,
  15, 18, 37, 92, 94, 96–98, **97**
  (fig. 72), 105, 190; May, 198
Richardson, Mary Curtis, 117
Riders of the Purple Sage, 105
Riding Herd, 120
Ridgeway's, 86
Rinehart, Mary Roberts, 68
Ritschel, William F., 117, 197
Rivera, Diego, 176–77, 180, 194
Riverside Hotel, 168
Road to El Dorado, The, 18, 209
Roberts, John, 54
Roberts Ranch, **53** (fig. 23, fig.
  24), 54, front endsheet
Robinson, Charles Dormon, 8
Rock at El Cajon, 209, **210** (fig. 163)
Rogers, Will, 95
Ronstadt, Bill, 219
Ronstadt family, Gilbert, and home,
  219, 233, 233, **234** (fig. 185)
Ronstadt Gallery, Tucson, 228
Ronstadt, Gretchen (Susie), 233
Ronstadt, Peter, 233
Room of the Dons murals, 17, 160–61
Roosevelt, Franklin D., 192
Ross, Gordon, 41
Ruef, Abe, 88
Ruess, Everett, 18, 190–91, 200

Russell, Charles M., 10, 15, 16,
  94–95, 126, 127, 129, 136
Ryan, Beatrice Judd, 160, 176, 178, 187

S

Sacred Rock, The, 149, **149** (fig. 122)
Safford, Arizona, Post Office, 209–10
Sage and Rabbit Brush,
  165, **166** (fig. 134)
Salmagundi Club, 16, 105
San Diego Fine Arts Museum, 210
San Diego Sun, 210
San Francisco Art Association, 15, 17,
  29, 30, 48, 49, 62, 76, 85, 131, 133,
  143, 169, 175, 176, 177, 180, 199
San Francisco Artists Society, 81
San Francisco Bulletin, 47
San Francisco Chronicle, 13, 15, 34,
  47, 62, 76, 78, 79, **80** (fig. 51),
  85–86, **86** (fig. 57), 87, 172
San Francisco earthquake and
  fire, 15, 71, 77, 82–85, **83**
  (fig. 52, 53), 97, 115, 138
San Francisco Examiner, 13, 14, 34,
  39, 47–48, **47** (fig. 19), 49, 51, 59,
  62, 79, 86, 88, **89** (fig. 60), 134, 182
San Francisco Labor Council, 176
San Francisco maritime strike, 198
San Francisco Men, **70** (fig. 41), 71
San Francisco Mission High
  School, 201–2
San Francisco [Morning] Call, 13,
  14, 34, 37, 43, 44, 47, 59, 62
San Francisco Mural Artists Society, 201
San Francisco Museum of Art, 199
San Francisco Press Club, 48, 76
Sandona, Matteo, 62
Santa Barbara Art League, 169
Santa Fe Museum of Fine
  Arts, 16, 17, 132, 182
Santa Fe Railway, 18, 63, 237
Sargent, John Singer, 62, 100, 116
Saturday Evening Post, 93, 97, 187
Savage Tires, 122, **123** (fig. 93)
Scab, 199, 208
Schmitz, Eugene E., Mayor, 88
Schnier, Jacques, 178
Schofield, Walter Elmer, 117
Schultz, James Willard, 110
Scott, Hugh L., General, 68
Scribner's, 13, 27, 71, 93
Scripps College, 18, 233, 235–36
"Section, The," 192, 211
Seltzer, Olaf, 95
September Moonlight, 146
Sequoia League, 36
Service, Robert, 102
Shakespeare, [William], 78
Shapes of Fear, 17, 175–76, 180, 186–87
Sheeler, Charles, 121

Sheets, Millard, 180, 233
Shephard, A. D., 87
Shinn, Charles Howard, 41
Shorelines of Lahontan, 217
Short Stories, 13, 93
Shuster, Will, 155
Siegrist, Louis, 116
Sierra Nevada, 140, **141** (figs. 110, 111)
Silver State, 16
Simplicissimus, 49, 81
Sinel, Joseph, 182
Siqueiros, David Alfaro, 194
Skies of New Mexico, 182
Skinner, "Dad," 133
Skinner, William, 133
Sloan, John, 98, 193
Smith, Jack Wilkinson, 157
Society of Six, 116
Son of the Wolf, 48
Southeast Oregon and Northern
  Nevada, **224** (fig. 174), 226
Southern Arizona, **162** (fig. 130), 164
Southern Arizona, **224** (fig. 176),
  226, inside back endsheet
Southern Pacific Railroad, 15, 17, 71,
  78–79, 83, 88, **89** (fig. 61), 92, 108,
  123, **123** (fig. 96), 133, 160, 163, **162**
  (fig. 130), **163** (fig. 131), 164, 171
Southwest Museum, 36, 112, 143
Southwest Museum of the
  American Indian, 112
Spanish-American War, 43, 48
Spanish Pioneers, The, 36
Sparks, Will, 87
Spear, Ben, 52, 54
Spinner's Book of Fiction, The, 89
Spirit of India, 17, 169
Spirit of the City, The, 83,
  84 (figs. 54, 55)
Spirit of the Grape, The, 86, **86** (fig. 57)
Spirit Trail, The, 102
Springtime on Bear Mountain, 175
St. Ignatius, Montana, 98, **99** (fig. 74)
St. Louis Post-Dispatch, 199
Stackpole, Ralph, 8, 10, 29,
  133, 138, 176–77, 213
Standard Oil Bulletin, 123, 134,
  135 (fig. 107), 138, **139** (fig. 108),
  157, **158** (fig. 128), 172, **173** (fig.
  140), 190, **190** (fig. 151), 197, **198**
  (fig. 158), 201, **203** (fig. 161)
Standing Cowboy, **99** (fig. 75), 100
Starr, Kevin, 36
Steffens, Lincoln, 88
Stendahl Art Galleries, 138, 210
Sterling, George, 71, 72, 73, 76,
  77, 78, 85, 132, 138, 157
Stevenson, Fanny Osbourne, 109
Stevenson, Robert Louis, 109
Stieglitz, Alfred, 146

Stoddard, Charles Warren, 71, 72
Stokes, Frederick A., 98
Strand, Paul, 184
Strauss, Joseph, 178, 179
"Strike" series, 18
Strobridge, Idah Meacham,
  15, 49, 89, 92, 102
Strong, Ray, 200, 237
Struck, Herman G., 117, 200
Struggle Upward, 190, **191** (fig. 154)
Studio Strange, Tucson, 228
Study for Shapes of Fear,
  175, **175** (fig. 145)
Sturtevant, Roger, 189
*Sue—California Ranch
  Girl*, 76, **76** (fig. 47)
Summer Storm, 182, **183** (fig. 147)
Sunol Water Temple, The, 17, 156
Sunset Magazine, 13, 15, 16, 18, 71,
  73, 74, **75** (fig. 46), 76, 81, 83, 84,
  84 (figs. 54, 55), 86, 87, **87** (fig.
  58), 88, **89** (fig. 59), 92, 101–2,
  107, 109, 117, 124, 157. 175, 194
Survey Graphic, 199
Survivors, The, 157
Sweeney, Dan, 41
Swift, Henry F., 188
Swinnerton, James G. "Jimmy," 31,
  41, 48, 50, 94, 144, 177, 217
Swinnerton, Louise, 144
Sycamores, El Alisal, 20, **20** (fig. 20)
Sycamores, The, 20

T

Tack, Augustus Vincent, 164
Tah-a-Mont ("Dark Cloud"), 95
Tait, Valentine, 228
Tales of the Sun-Land, 14, 41
Tallac, **142** (fig. 113), 143
Taos Pueblo, 182
Taos Society of Artists, 105
Tarbell, Edmund C., 116
Tavernier, Jules, 8
Taylor-Lange Report, 200
Taylor, Edward Dewitt, 236, 238
Taylor, Paul Schuster, 18,
  198–99, 200, 202, 204, 218
Tehachapi Mountains, 17, 174,
  175, **175** (figs. 144, 145)
Tempe, Arizona, **56** (fig. 28), 57
Tempe Butte, 117, **118** (fig. 87)
Temple of Art and Music, Tucson, 228
Texican, The, 16, 96, 102, **102** (fig. 78)
Three Godfathers, The, 16, 112
Thunderbird totem/icon, 8, 41,
  54, 225, 237, **238** (fig. 188)
Tiffany, Louis C., 116
Tilden, Douglas, 72
To Good Old Brad, 205, **205** (fig. 162)
Tobey, Lillian West, 15, 16, 75,

79–80, 82–83, 88, 92, 98, 100,
  103, 104, 105, 106, 107, 112, 114,
  117, 119, 120, 121, 126, 139
Tobin, Frank, 165
Tobin's Camp, 165, **166** (fig. 133)
Todhunter, Francis, 133
Tohono O'Odham, 225, 228
Tolerton, Hill, 16, 114, 120, 137
Tomananczy: Winona,
  179, 187; Paul, 187
Touring Topics, 17, 180
Toward Kaibito, 145
Town Crier, The, 81
Town Talk, 76
Tradition, 169
Tragic Mood, 169
Trail in Oregon, The, 115, 117, 121
Trail of Ninety-Eight, The, 102
Tramp Across the Continent, A, 36
Treadwell, Sophie, 15, 86, 105,
  125 (fig. 98), 126, 233, 237
Treasury Department Section of
  Painting and Sculpture, 192, 211
Treasury Relief Art Project, 192–93
Truesdell, Amelia Woodward, 98
Tsay-yih, 81
Tucson murals, 18, 88, **91**
  (figs. 65–68), 108
Tucson Barrio, **91** (fig. 67)
Twachtman, John, 116
Twain, Mark, 73, 107
Two Guns White Calf, 129

U

Ufer, Walter, 181
Union Pacific Railroad, 83
University of California–Berkeley,
  17, 29, 169, 172, 187, 198
Uplands of Pei-ki-hat-tsoh, 81

V

Vals de Monterey Viejo, **38** (fig. 13), 41
Van Dyke, John Charles, 49
Van Dyke, Willard, 188, 198, 199
van Gogh, Vincent, 200
Van Sloun, Frank, 17, 117, 152,
  160–61, 176, 178, 194, 200
Victory Song, **108** (fig. 83), 109
Vierra, Carlos, 68
Virginian, The, 105
von Eichman, Bernard, 116
Von Schmidt, Harold, 9, 10,
  123, 124, 133, 187, 219

W

Walker, John M., 107–8
Wallace, Lew, General, 68
Walpi, 148, **148** (fig. 120)
Watson, Forbes, 193
Watson, Thomas J., 216

Weaver, Harold, "Buck," 226, 229, 237
Weber, Kem, 123, 159, 187, 237
Weber, Max, 121
Weeks, Charles Peter, 160, 169
Wells, Carolyn, 39
Wendt, William 165, 170, 217
West Wind, The, 15, 102
Western Arts, 159
Western World, 15, 89
Weston, Edward, 188
Westward Ho Hotel, Phoenix, 228
Wetherill: John, 17, 143–44; Louisa, 143
When a Great Sequoia Falls,
  88, **89** (fig. 60)
Whistler, James McNeill, 62, 116, 155
Whitaker, Herman, 124
White Angel Bread Line, 188
White, Clarence, 137
*White House Ruin, Canyon de
  Chelly*, 235 (fig. 187), 237
White, Stewart Edward, 13, 71, 102, 105
Whitewing, George, 110
Whitman, Walt, 17, 172–73
Whitney Studio, 98
Wichita Art Association, 17, 169
Wiezorek, Max, 157
Wickson, Guest, 178
Wild Horses of Nevada, 169
Wilde, Oscar, 30, 82
Wildman, Rounseville, 31
Williams, Virgil, 72
Winship, George Parker, 41
Wise Men, The, 169
Wister, Owen, 105
Witch of Sikyatki, The, **151**
  (fig. 125), 152, 157
Wittick, Ben, 69
Women of Oraibi, 64, **64** (fig. 37)
Wonders of the Colorado Desert, The, 49
Wood, Charles Erskine Scott, 138
Wood, Grant, 217
Wood, Nancy, 182
Wores, Theodore, 8, 29
Works Projects (Progress) Administration
  (WPA), 174, 193, 201, 207
Wright, Frank Lloyd, 171
Wright, Stanton MacDonald, 197
Wyeth, N. C., 94, 116, 217

X

Xavier, Juan, 225–26

Y

Yelland, Raymond D., 31
Yosemite National Park, 14, 32–33,
  142, **142** (fig. 112), 217

Z

Zeitlin, Jake, 169
Zion National Park, 18, 189, 218–19

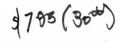

A.D.
Lone Pine, Calif.